Mu-ga:
The Ritual Songs
of the Korean Mudangs

Mu-ga
The Ritual Songs
of the Korean Mudangs

Compiled and Edited by
Im Sŏk-jae

Translated, Annotated, and
with an Introduction by
Alan C. Heyman

ASIAN HUMANITIES PRESS
(An Imprint of Jain Publishing Company)
Fremont, California

ASIAN HUMANITIES PRESS

Asian Humanities Press offers to the specialist and the general reader alike the best in new translations of major works and significant original contributions to enhance our understanding of Asian literature, religions, cultures and thought.

ASIAN HUMANITIES PRESS
[An imprint of Jain Publishing Company]
Web Site – www.jainpub.com

Acknowledgement is made to Korea Literature Translation Institute (LTI Korea) for financial assistance in the production of this book.

Cover: Kim Kŭm-hwa, a *Mudang* from Hwanghae Province who has been designated a "Human Cultural Treasure" by the Korean government, invites the gods to descend to the ritual area during a performance of the *Ch'ŏlmuri Kut* ("The Great Ritual of Good Fortune"). (photo: Kim Su-nam)

Library of Congress Cataloging-in-Publication Data

Mu-ga : the ritual songs of the Korean mudangs / Compiled and edited by Im Sŏk-jae; translated, annotated, and with an introduction by Alan C. Heyman.
      p. cm.
Includes bibliographical references.
  ISBN 0-89581-829-9 (alk. paper)
  1. Folk poetry, Korean–History and criticism. 2. Folk songs, Korean.–History and criticism. 3. Folk songs, Korean–Translations into English–Texts. 4. Incantations, Shamanist–Korea (South) I. Im, Sŏk-jae. II. Heyman, Alan C.

PL960.25.M84 2003
398.2'09519–dc22

                                                              2003021510

Dedication

To Im Sŏk-jae,

without whom this work would never have been possible,

And in commemoration of the
100th Anniversary of the
Founding of the
Korea Branch of the
Royal Asiatic Society,
For its great contribution to
Korean Culture

Contents

APPENDICES

ILLUSTRATIONS

Preface

This work is mainly comprised of a translation into English of four complete large-scale Korean Shaman ritual songs transcribed from tape recordings, which, until the present time, have remained either entirely untranslated, or, if otherwise, are only quoted in the form of brief excerpts in a few short articles. The song contents cover a broad regional spectrum (P'yŏng-an, Chŏlla, and Cheju Provinces) which contain invaluable materials related to Korean folklore, mythology, literature, history, and religion, and offer deep insight into a facet of Korean culture that has remained largely overlooked and unexplored.

Acknowledgements

I wish to express my gratitude to my daughter, Hae Laam, and to my student, Hong Ye-eun, for the great deal of time and effort spent in typing the manuscript, and to my dear friend, David Mason, for both spiritual and material support.

Alan C. Heyman
Seoul, Korea
April 14, 2000

About the Songs

The written materials that go to make up this publication were recorded and compiled, for the most part, between the years 1970-80, and the work in its embryonic form began to take shape from the latter part of 1980. The authors are indebted to the Asian Literature Program of the Asia Society and to the Korean Branch of the Asia Foundation for grants made in part in the years 1970 and 1972, respectively, and to the Foundation for the Translation of Korean Literature for grants made in part in the years 1999 and 2000.

Section I

1. Introduction

Korean folk art has been passed on down through the centuries largely unrecorded, thus making it difficult—almost impossible in some instances—to find primary source material relating to it. However, its living form can be found embodied in the folk religion of Korea called *Musok* which is believed to be the oldest form of religion extant in Korea today. It is generally—and more conveniently—referred to these days as Shamanism; however, even though it may, in some instances, appear to approach a form of Shamanism, the similarities, in the strict sense of the word, are only superficial, and, as will be pointed out later, differences between the two are many.

Though regional differences exist, the professional practitioners of folk religion are called *Mudang* or *Mu-in,* and the songs they sing during a ritual are called *Mu-ga.* The contents of the Mu-ga deal largely with folk epics and legends telling of the origin of the gods for whom the ritual is being held. In this respect, they represent a great storehouse of folk literature which often brings to mind the mighty epics of Greek and Nordic mythology. This treasury of Korean folk literature has for too long been overlooked, and it is for this reason that the very arduous task of translating into English the four large-scale songs and several smaller ones contained in this work was undertaken.

The *Mu-ga is* a song whose words and music have been handed down from antiquity. It is not composed by any one individual or improvised, but is learned by the Mudang during the apprenticeship period to an elder or senior Mudang.

The text of the Mu-ga is sung to the accompaniment of music in time with the rhythm and is interspersed with dance. However, the song texts, musical or dance scores were traditionally nonexistent,[1] but were learned wholly by rote, practice, and observation. This being the case, one might readily assume that modifications are frequent in occurrence; but, actually there is very little modification, and they have been handed down in near-perfect form.

3

Such can be proven when we compare songs recorded some sixty years ago[2] and those which have been collected recently. The only changes that may have occurred are due primarily to memory slips on the part of the Mudang, which may, in turn, be related to her mood or mental condition, a factor that may be the cause of omissions, reversions, or rearrangement of the standard order. However, the basic form, the most common and important usages, the vocabulary, etc., are maintained per se. In the aforementioned transcription of sixty years ago, it was found that tedious parts of the song and straight or brand narration were omitted, and only quaint and novel parts were retained (for audience attraction)—and even of these, only the outline was sung. This was due primarily to the fact that, at that time, the recording of the text was done by hand and the Mudang was stopped after each stanza, thus breaking the continuity. Modern tape recordings, however, have eliminated that problem; therefore, the texts and music are complete.

Korea has traditionally been an agricultural society and everyday activities have been associated with the agricultural cycle. With the developing complexity of the society, certain rituals evolved which were related to various aspects of life. Probably some of the first ceremonies were for spirits of heaven and earth, the mountain, rain and the household. The ancient Chinese chronicle, the *Hu-Han-Sŏ-Wi-Sŏ* ("The Writings of the Later Han and Wei Dynasties"), compiled sometime between the 6th and 7th century A.D., tells us that in the 13th century B.C. many barbaric tribes were roaming the northern and central parts of the Korean peninsula. One of these tribes, the Puyŏ, who occupied the area that is now Manchuria, held a festival during the 10th month of the lunar calendar (November-December in the solar calendar) called *yŏng-go,* which they celebrated with songs and dances. The *Ye* people in the northeast held a festival called *much'ŏn* in or around the month of October, and this also included songs and dances. It is believed that invocatory group dances characterized these sacrificial ceremonies. In the three Han kingdoms (*Mahan, Chinhan, Pyŏnhan*) in the south, thanksgiving festivals were held twice annually, after rice transplantation and after harvest. The *Munhŏn Tonggo,* an ancient Korean literary work, describes these dances: they were ". . . performed by a dozen dancers who lined up in a single file and followed the leader, raising their hands up and down stamping on the ground to the accompaniment of music . . . the ceremonies were presided over by the leader who might well have been a Mudang, who was, at the same time, lyricist, composer-musician, and dancer . . ."[3]

However, the earliest known Chinese reference on these types of ritual festivities, if we may call them such, is found in the *San-Kuo-Chi,* or *Sam Guk-Ji,* as it is pronounced in Korean ("The History of the Three Kingdoms"), compiled in 287 A.D., in the section dealing with the Eastern People (the inhabitants of the Korean peninsula), telling of the ritual practices held by various tribes up until the 3rd century A.D.: "In the fifth month (lunar calendar), they sacrifice to spirits; all day and night, without rest, they sing, dance and drink wine."[4]

Some scholars claim these references in the ancient chronicles of China and Korea to be rather vague and ambiguous, and that they might be construed as being simply descriptions of farmers' festival music and dance, known today as *Nong-Ak* (literally, "Agricultural Music"), or merely songs and dances performed solely for entertainment devoid of any religions connotation whatever. Though there might be some element of truth in these interpretations, there is more reason than not to believe that there were early beliefs surrounding these festivities, and that to fully understand folk art, it is essential that they be duly considered. It might be relevant to add here that Nong-Ak, which is considered by many to be the oldest form of dance extant in Korea today, still maintains a close kinship with Musok practices, in the rural areas primarily, as do the mask dance-dramas, which also boast a long history dating back over a thousand years, being often employed to exorcise evil spirits or to supplicate the beneficence of the gods.

In the *Sam-Guk Yu-Sa* ("The Reminiscences of the Three Kingdoms"), written in the 13th century A.D., it is recorded that the third king of the Shilla Dynasty was called *Mu,* but whether he was the same as the present-day Mudang is unknown.[5] The rituals and their accompanying songs practiced during the Shilla period (c. 37 B.C.-935 A.D.) are also unknown because there in no precise record. *Ku-Ji Ga*[6] is believed by some to be a type of Mu-ga. It was sung by the people when a king was sent to them from heaven, inside a box tied with a rope. The box contained an egg from which a child emerged, who was then later enthroned as the first king. Therefore, it might be assumed that Ku-Ji Ga is a spell or oracle for the coronation of a king rather than a Mu-ga per se. If it were a Mu-ga, it would have survived, even partially, in the ritual song repertoire; but, until now, not a trace or even a suggestion of it can be found.

In the 12th century A.D., Yi, Kyubo, a famous scholar of the Koryŏ period (935-1392 A.D.), wrote a Chinese-style poem, *No Mu P'yŏn* ("The Old Mudang"), which contains material about the Mudang ritual, the properties used, and the audience of the time; however, there is no record of song or text, it being stated only that the Mudang sings a chant. As Yi, Kyu-bo's description was in poetic style, he therefore described only the most impressive things in a vague manner, thus omitting details. Through his description, though, we can guess that period's Mudang ritual was akin to that of present-day Seoul and its environs. From this material, then, we can reason that the Seoul-style ritual of today began from that period at least. When the Mu-ga of other regions began we know not, there being no record in existence; but it may be a pretty safe guess to say that they were being sung long before Koryŏ, perhaps even as far back as the Three Han kingdoms, some 2,000 years ago.[7]

With the exception of the Shrine Ritual Songs of Cheju Island, the texts of the Mu-ga contain many Buddhist, Taoist and Confucian idioms and usages; thereby do some reason that the Mu culture was established after the introduction of the aforementioned from China during the Shilla period. Such reasoning is rather shortsighted and hasty, based solely on conjecture in light of the absence of facts and records. Though the introduction of foreign creeds at first took hold only among the upper classes of the society, it gradually influenced the beliefs and daily life of the commoners, and thereby were the religious practices, customs and idioms adopted and eventually permeated into the fabric of the song texts themselves—though only on a very superficial basis, as we shall observe. Buddhist, Taoist and Confucian idioms were utilized as piecemeal ornamentations, so to speak, but the basic discipline and thought were never adopted, and neither did the Mudang act to propagate nor interpret them to everyday life; thereby was the basic underlying concept of Mu not destroyed by the inclusion of adopted foreign religious expressions.[8]

In the song texts, for example, there is no conquest of the agony of real life nor salvation; neither is there any afterlife, such as Paradise and Hell, though the Buddhist usage is applied again only superficially, as in the Ritual Song of the Bridge, included in this work. In the actual Mu concept, there is no upward Heaven or downward Hell; they are both in the same place—*Chŏ Sŏng*[9]—beneath the ground where man is buried. Also *Pul-Shim*, the "Buddhist mind" or "spirit," the transfiguration or transmigration of the soul, and the concept of the body as the prison of the soul, i.e., the disregard and the destruction of the body so that the soul may be released to Paradise, all these are absent from the Mu-ga, which dwells on the ever-present and the delight of "this frame."[10]

The "Five Elements" of Taoism, the *Eŭm-Yang* (Chinese, *Yin-Yang*) concept and fortunetelling are sometimes used in the Mu-ga (see, again, the Ritual Song of the Bridge), but there is no preaching of the Taoist doctrines of *Pul-lo* ("Everlasting Youth"), *Chang-Saeng* ("Long Life") and *Shin-Sŏn-Hwa* ("To become an immortal"). The foreign religions then are merely borrowed usage employed to "catch the current," so to speak, and are perhaps utilized in absence of their own (Mu) doctrine, which deals with reality and that which is desired—this being principally the "Five Fortunes" (Wealth, High Rank or Status, Health, Long Life and many Sons) undisturbed by misfortune, damage, suffering, anxiety or trouble whereby life is passed in peace and safety. Unlike Taoism, which recognizes only eternal youth and life and not death, the Mu, though desiring long life, accept the eventual destiny of man, with the hope and prayer that the end may be peaceful and nonviolent, and not accidental or unnatural. In this respect, the Mu doctrine can be said to be realistic.

Like the Mu doctrine itself, the song texts deal basically with realism. Though fantasy and symbolism do sometimes exist (see the "Ritual Song of the God *Chesŏk*), they are weak by comparison. The description of myth in most cultures is generally thought to be comprised of fantasy and romance, but in the Korean Mu-ga, it is strong realism that prevails. Also, the words used to summon the gods, the prayer words for the god's blessing and the song text of the banquet for the god's entertainment are all connected with realism. Realism also dominates the nature of the Korean people as a whole, and these factors, taken together, may serve to explain why a religion such as Buddhism or Christianity, although eventually absorbed to a large extent after a period of time, could probably never have originated in a country such as Korea.

In *Musok* practice, there is no such thing as a temple or church for assembly or preaching, only the place where the god descends, or has descended, such as a shrine. Also, the Mudang wears no ecclesiastic robes in everyday life, but only in the ritual proper; neither does she, like a Buddhist monk or Taoist priest, live in a special type of dwelling. The Mudang practice no meditation, asceticism, or celibacy (a husband is, in fact, highly essential in that he provides the musical accompaniment—or vice versa in cases where the Mudang is male). They preach no doctrine, thought or philosophy, and so there is no communication between them and the congregation, if we may refer to it as such, except shortly before (in the case of the persons holding the ceremony) and during the ritual. There is no special intercourse between the *Mudang* and the populace when all is well and safe and no trouble occurs. When a ritual is needed for illness, misfortune, and the like, only then is the Mudang summoned. From these factors we can thereby ascertain, to some extent, that the Mudang, in all probability, had firmly established a unique religious system long before the introduction of foreign beliefs, and even after they were introduced into the country, the Mudang never abandoned their original type of religious system. Where outside influences exist, they do so, as has been pointed out, only for the sake of embellishment or as an accessory, but the actual core itself has been truly affected.

Since the *Mu-ga* are sung in a religious ceremony, one would expect their texts to be primarily sacred in content; however, this is not necessarily true in every case. In fact, the majority of them are made up largely of legendary material—tales in which the origin of the god, to whom the ritual is dedicated, is unfolded in song and recitative. For example, in the "Song for Summoning the Gods," only the blessing for summoning the gods is sung, i.e., "The Grace of the Gods," "Supplication for the God's Assistance," and "Divine Protection." There is no praising the greatness of the gods, nor is there any detailing of the god's miracle, the god's will, or the god's revelation. There is no intercourse with the gods, nor is there any ecstasy or deeply moved affection. There is no song containing the method of devotion to cleanse the mind and body of sinfulness ("God is God and I am I"), as in the Christian will to emulate Jesus, the desire for purification; nor is there any song to directly foster or call up a moral and religious mind or spirit (in the "Ritual Song of the Bridge" the *Mudang* only sings to suggest such, and then it is asserted, again, only superficially). Also, in the Mu-ga, the devotee's own personal supplication is not voiced, but only the objective one by the Mudang. There is no prayer spell of profound belief, as, for example, one finds in the Tibetan lame spell, nor is there extensive detail, as in the biblical writing concerning the miracles and thought of Jesus.[11]

As the *Mu-ga is* a song form, it is sung in lyric poetry, as one might expect, but it is without rhyme and in free-style.[12] Sometimes the recitative is interspersed (see the "Ritual Song of the God Chesŏk"); this is done either in a monologue or in a dialogue with the musicians or audience. The recitative serves as a pause for the Mudang after long and arduous singing and also as a relief from the strict poetical form. The style of the *Mu-ga* is generally an uninterrupted epic-narrative-dramatic song, but not always (see Part I of the "Ritual Song of the Bridge").[13] Though the Mudang are uneducated and illiterate, a vulgar or distasteful word never appears in the lyrics, which contain only courteous, euphonious, solemn and noble phrases (the only exception to be found in the songs included in this work is in Part III of the "Ritual Song of the Bridge," but here the Mudang is indirectly quoting the wrath vented by the Ten Kings of Hell on the evil soul standing in judgement before them). In order to make the lyrics appear more elegant, as was mentioned previously, they sometimes use Buddhist and Chinese words and expressions which have been revered down through the ages. To gain more respect from the audience, they also use ancient and obsolete language and vocabulary not commonly found in everyday life. However, because they do not always understand the meaning, many words arc mispronounced or the meaning twisted, or yet another word of similar sound is mistakenly used (a thorn to the translator). For example, in one Mu-ga (not included in this work), there suddenly appears the *wŏn-ang-sae* ("mandarin duck"), followed by the names of other birds. But after long and tiring research, the word is actually found to be *wŏn-wang-saeng,* which means "I will go to Paradise for eternal life by the force of Buddha." So the Mudang, who is largely ignorant of Buddhist meanings, misinterprets these words because of the similarity in sound. Also, in some other Mu-ga, we find the expression "the fishhook comes out of the river." But, in actuality, it is the "miracle of *Ha-To Nak-Sŏ.*"[14] Miracles are frequently mentioned in the *Mu-ga,* and the expression "the fishhook comes out of the river," could, in itself, very well be a miracle, but the original meaning is quite different. However, even though the use of the alien language (Chinese) is twisted, it served the Mudang a useful purpose; even though the language contains ancient and dead words, borrowed Chinese, Buddhist and Taoist letters and expressions, the meaning of which is very difficult to fathom, the Mudang uses them quite freely and functorily, purely for the sake of euphony and to give the impression of their being the mystical words of the gods. The common people do not strive to understand the meaning, nor do they make any attempt at rationalization; nevertheless, upon hearing these words, an aura of majesty and sanctification is created.

As was mentioned previously, there is no Mu-ga text in existence, with the exception of that which has been recorded by anthropologists, ethnologists and other scholarly researchers. The fact is that even if there were, it would be of no practical use anyway since the *Mudang* are illiterate and sing entirely by rote. However, even though the Mudang have a very excellent memory, there are always bound to be some errors and memory slips. Therefore, when the researcher wishes to make a complete and accurate recording for academic purposes, it must be repeated many times and large-scale editing undertaken. It is here that the use of the tape recorder affords a great advantage in that the tape can be replayed after the ritual proper in the presence of the Mudang, whereupon she can be consulted on passages of ambiguous or diverse meanings, or where the sound becomes indistinct or difficult to detect (this occurs frequently when, for example, she moves away from the microphone, or when her voice is drowned out by loud drums and/or gongs that often make up part of the rhythmic accompaniment). However, sometimes the Mudang herself is either uncertain or confused about the meaning of the words, and herein lies one of the greatest problems in the transcription and translation of the *Mu-ga.*

The type of *Mu-ga,* the melodies that are sung, and the rhythmic accompaniment that are played are many and various in number, owing primarily to the existence of various types of Mudang practices and functions for the particular occasion. The length of the Mu-ga also varies, some requiring up to three or four hours to sing, some only thirty minutes.

The contents of the songs also differ, again according to the various types that are sung; it is somewhat difficult, therefore, to make a succinct selection of the most common components to be found. Some of the more prevalent ones, however, may be outlined as follows:

1. The place and surname of the ceremony-holder or person employing the Mudang to supplicate the gods. This is always announced at the start of the ritual (see the "Ritual Song of the God *Son-Nim*").

2. The ceremony-holder displays his loyalty and sincerity in summoning forth the god.

3. The description of the offering (e.g., steamed rice cakes, meat, flowers, etc.), prepared with the utmost care and sincerity.

4. The prayer of supplication, sung by the Mudang. In some instances, two or three songs are sung; but sometimes it is omitted entirely or only partially sung, in which case the following are either substituted or added:

5. The myth telling the origin of the god summoned (see the "Ritual Song of the God *Chesŏk*").

6. The limitation of the blessing, e.g., for good fortune (see the "Ritual Song of the God *Chesŏk*"); for safe guidance of the soul to Paradise (see the "Ritual Song of the Bridge").

7. The song used to appease or entertain the summoned god.

8. The Banquet song. The song for entertaining the god.

9. In some regions, the Mudang sings a preliminary-type song, termed by the author *Chŏn-ga* ("Before Song" or "Prelude"), and a *Hu-ga* ("After Song" or "Postlude").

10. The oracle (*kong-su*), recited between the ritual songs proper; it is practiced largely in the central and northern provinces.

11. The *chŏm* ("fortunetelling")—practiced largely in the central and northern provinces.

Thus, when we examine the contents of the present-day Mu-ga gathered from many different regions, we can find the eleven components mentioned above; however, there is no one song in existence today that actually contains all eleven components.[15]

In respect to the size and type of ritual performed, the songs may be classified into four categories, ranging from those of a very short duration to those requiring more than several hours to perform.[16]

The most simple ritual is called the *Pi-Son*. It can be held at anytime when an unexpected phenomenon or accident occurs, or whenever felt to be necessary. There is no appointed day or time, no taboo, and it is usually held in the devotee's own home or back-yard, but also occasionally in the isolation of a deep mountain. In this type of ceremony, the only thing to be found on the sacrificial table is a bowl of clean water. The Mudang sits before the table rubbing her palms together and recites an impromptu chant, there being no rhythmic or melodic accompaniment and no lyric verse—only prayer words. As this ceremony is so very simple, even a common housewife can perform it without the presence of the Mudang—as is often the case. Though the concept of the Pi-Son is akin to that of a ritual in the strict sense, no verbal acknowledge-ment of it as such is to be found.

More elaborate than the Pi-Son is the *P'u-Tak Kŏri*, used for curing diseases of a long duration, insanity, and continual ill-fortune. For this ritual, an appropriate day must be selected and the house must be cleansed very thoroughly. In this instance, the ceremony-holder keeps some taboos, e.g., only members of the immediate family may come and go; others are not permitted entrance to the house. This is made known by hanging a string with strips of white paper dangling from it in front of the gate, and lining the pathway leading to it on both sides with small mounds of clay, it being the road the god will supposedly enter through. Special foods for the sacrifice are prepared, and a Mudang is employed who sings both the Mu-ga proper and prayer chants as well.[17] However, the only accompanying musical instruments are the percussion type, e.g., drums and gongs.

A bit larger in scale is that which is termed *Kosa,* but is actually not always very much more elaborate than the aforementioned ritual; however, the Kosa is held only to supplicate for good for-tune, e.g., when opening a new business, fishing, mining, etc. The Kosa is also held at lunar new year festivities, in spring (for good crops) and in autumn (for thanksgiving), in which case it is held annually at about the same time. But in cases where it is held for such purposes as the long life and prosperity of a family, a safe journey, the completion of a new house (a "housewarming," so to speak), a favorable election result, etc., it is then held, of course, in accordance with expediency. The preparation and taboos for the Kosa are similar to that of the P'u-Tak Kŏri.

The *K'ŭn Kut*[18] ("Great Ritual")[19] is the largest of all rituals in scale, and comprises four categories: (a) Supplication for the soul's safe and peaceful passage to Paradise (see "The Ritual Song of the Bridge"); (b) Supplication for good fortune (see "The Ritual Song of the God *Chesŏk*"); (c) Supplication for the curing of a disease (see "The Ritual Song of the God *Son-Nim*"); (d) Supplication for the well-being of the village (see "The Ritual Song of the Tutelary God Shrine of Sŏ-Gwi-P'o").[20] In the *K'ŭn Kut*, many Mudang and musicians are employed, and the sacrificial foods and objects used are very elaborate,[21] therefore the cost is very high. Various costumes and properties are also used, along with all the Mudang's wisdom and arts exercised to the fullest extent. The shortest duration of the ritual is three days, the longest one week, continuously throughout the day and night.[22] The function and object of the K'ŭn Kut is the same everywhere in Korea; only the names differ, e.g., the ritual for the soul's passage to Paradise in Seoul, the capital city of Korea, is called *Chin-Ogwi*, in P'yŏngyang, the capital city of P'yŏng-Ahn Province in North Korea, it is called *Shi-Wang Kut* (the "Ritual of the Ten Kings") or *Tari Kut* (the "Ritual of the Bridge"), in Cholla Province it is called *Shik-Kim Kut*, in Kyŏngsang Province it is called *Ogu Kut*, and in Hamgyŏng Province in North Korea it is known as *Mang-Mu Kut*.[23] The order of the songs, the melody and rhythm also differ according to the regions; it is rather interesting to note, in this respect, that the melody and rhythm resemble the folk music of the particular area where the songs originate.

In the K'ŭn Kut, there are approximately twelve types of songs common to all regions. A song is call kŏri (Seoul and P'yŏngyang) or sŏk (Chŏlla Province). The songs contained in this work include those for the departed soul, good fortune, disease exorcism, and the village guardian deity and are representative examples of each category from different regions. Because there are twelve songs contained in this largest of all rituals (a total of 48 in all four categories), the duration of performance is quite lengthy. For the *K'ŭn Kut*, the day, time and place is appointed and the site made clean. In this case, however, the ceremony is open to all who wish to come, friend and stranger alike. Outwardly, it displays religious significance, but it is, in fact, more like a festival. In the ritual for the departed soul, to cite one instance, the proceedings should ordinarily be solemn and sorrowful throughout; however, from the middle part to the end, many joyful melodies, dances and comic interludes filled with nonsensical humor are found to be included in the ceremony proper, thereby creating a most convivial atmosphere. Thus does the ritual become a kind of entertainment. Other similar examples may be found in the ritual of the village guardian deity and that for good fortune, where a carnival-like atmosphere prevails from the very outset through to the end. During the proceedings, the guests partake of the wine and food used in the ceremony, and so, together with the music, dance and comic interludes, they naturally fall into a festive mood. In this way also does the *K'ŭn Kut* present an opportunity for the host to display this wealth and generosity, and thereby enhance his own prestige. The entertainment provided also serves as a banquet for the gods, the singing, dance, drama and sound of the musical instruments enticing them to assemble at the place and be thus more favorably inclined toward the supplications of the devotees, the belief being that the nature of the gods is akin to that of man himself.

In the *K'ŭn Kut,* the twelve songs that are sung cover practically all phenomena in human existence, thereby paying homage to a great number of gods who, in turn, will be favorably inclined toward the supplicator. This is evidenced by the clause found in every Mu-ga beseeching many gods to assemble, and, with the sameness of mind, grant blessings. An example of this can be found in the "Ritual Song of the God *Son-Nim*," where the Measles God, the Cholera God, the Typhus God, etc., are summoned and supplicated to.

In Korean Musok, there are no good or evil gods per se. Therefore, even if the *Son-Nim* God, the god of illness, is treated well, he will bestow good fortune rather than disease. In other words, any god that is treated well will return the favor; if neglected, or treated badly, he will punish the individual with misfortune.

Though the number of gods in the Musok pantheon is practically immeasurable, there is no hierarchy among them. There are no greater or lesser gods, as, for example, in the instance of the Greek gods Zeus and Mercury. They never command or obey each other, nor do they consult each other on any matter. Among the gods of the house, for example, there is the Kitchen God, the Gate

God, the Toilet God, the Yard God, etc. They too, like the other gods, never obey or consult each other; each has his own equal ability and responsibility, totally independent of the other. A pantheon such as this is unlikely to be found elsewhere and has never been subjected to theological research, according to the best knowledge of the author. Might then we not for such a pantheon coin the term "parallel theism?"

Some inconsistencies do exist, however, in regard to categories of gods; in some instances there is only one, e.g., *Yŏm-Na*,[24] the God (or "King") of Hell, and Ch'il-Sŏng,[25] the God of Life; however, in some categories there are many gods, e.g., Sŏngju, the God of the House, and *San-Shin*, the God of the Mountain, depending on whose house and which mountain they dwell in. So, for example, we find Mr. Kim's Sŏngju, Mr. Lee's Sŏngju, etc., and Sŏrak-san (the name of a mountain) San-Shin, Halla-san San-Shin, etc.[26]

In Korean *Musok*, the god is not revered for his own sake, but for that of the supplicator in a strictly utilitarian sense. Therefore, the purpose of the ritual is not, in actuality, to pay homage to the god himself, but to make offerings to him and gain his favor so that the devotee's wishes may be granted. This is done, as mentioned previously, by means of music, dance, comic interludes, and the various offerings. Korean Musok may be regarded, therefore, not as religion in the strict sense of the word, but only a method to gain the god's favor and utilize his power in controlling the phenomena of everyday life.

Since quite some time ago, Korean *Musok* has been branded simply as "Shamanism"; however, upon thorough examination, one finds that the two are, in actuality, quite different. The use of the word itself was begun, in fact, by American Christian missionaries at the turn of the century. Their observations were largely based however on some of the ritual practices performed by Mudangs of the northern, northwestern and north-central areas, which, to the nonprofessional eye, bear some similarity to those of the Siberian Shaman and practitioners of various other primitive religions found throughout parts of the world. Their studies and observations were, however, lacking in ethnographical methodology, and thereby did they apply the convenient label of "Shamanism," to any and all forms of Musok that existed throughout Korea.[27] Thereafter did Korean intellectuals and the educated classes, in general, too readily and without careful research into the matter, adopt the

missionaries' casual labeling of *Musok* as "Shamanism" in a euphonious sense in preference to the vernacular, due, for the most part, to
the base connotation of the word "Musok" and the very low station
of the Mudang in the society, whom the Shilla and Koryŏ Buddhist
clergy, the Yi Dynasty Confucian elite, and the 19th and 20th
century Christians looked down upon with perpetual disdain.[28]

The word "Shaman" originated from the polar Siberian tribal
religious system, whose religious practitioners fall into a kind of
"ecstasy," their bodies shaking and spontaneously emitting shouts
while jumping up and down. To become a Shaman, they must enter
into this abnormal "Ecstasy" state, the so-called "Shaman Disease,"
or what is more commonly referred to as "possession." The Shaman
acts as prophet, fortuneteller, practitioner of magic, etc.; in other
words, a person who is possessed with extraordinary powers.[29] The
Korean Mudang does not ordinarily act this way; that is to say, it is
not a standard part of the ritual—though it is outwardly sometimes
taken to be such. The use of magic is found more often in Seoul,
P'yŏngyang and Hamgyŏng Province (central and north Korea),
but generally not in the south. Also, in Korea, there are those who
become afflicted with the "Shaman Disease" and are regarded as
Mudang, but only in the superficial sense. Such individuals are,
again, more often found in the central and northern provinces;
particularly in the south the Mudang are primarily such by lineal
descendency.[30] However, during the ritual proper, some Mudangs
fall into a state of what appears to be "ecstasy," but when they come
to an important part or to the Mu-ga, they awake immediately from
the trance, indicating that the "ecstasy" may, in some instances at
least, be only a pretension.

The Mudang does not ordinarily, like a Shaman, play the role
of a medium, except in Seoul and P'yŏngyang—never in Chŏlla
Province. The Mudang bears only the responsibility of pleasing the
gods and thereby exorcising any prevailing evil or misfortune;
therefore, from this point of view, the Shaman and Mudang represent two totally different religious systems. In the same respect,
though Shamanist elements can be found in Buddhism and Christianity, the structure is wholly different from Shamanism; thereby,
would no one attempt to apply the label of "Shamanism" as a whole,
nor would he claim that they originated from such. The same can
be said of the Korean Mu. It appears, in short then, that the term
"Shamanism" has become synonymous with "folk religion," a sort of

catchall, be as it may, for any type of the ritual practice that does not fall within the realm of the so-called "established religions," i.e., Buddhism, Taoism, Confucianism, Hinduism, Islam, Christianity, etc. By the same token then, might it not also be referred to as "sorcery," "witchcraft," "black magic" or "voodooism," and its practitioners (as has often been done) as "sorcerers," "witches," and the like? The time is obviously long overdue to cease referring to Musok in these terms ". . . for lack of a better terminology." Until the day when we can find a better terminology for it in English, might we not just simply refer to it as "folk religion?"[31]

On the basis of what the practitioner is called, how they become such, structure of song, order of ritual, and the relationship between Mudang and suppliant, we may generally, with some modifications, make three classifications: (a) Cheju Island (located off the southern tip of the mainland), (b) south of the Han River in Seoul (includes all land areas from Seoul southward to the southernmost coastal areas), and (c) north of the Han River (includes all land areas northward to the Manchurian border).[32]

In Cheju, the practitioner is called Shinbang ("God's Room" or "God's House").[33] There are both male and female practitioners who are accorded equal status. There are hereditary Mudang and those who come from other families, both of whom are also given the same status. The Cheju ritual is not divided into twelve songs as on the mainland; rather, it comprises one continuous song throughout. The Shinbang serves as a bridge between the gods and the supplicants; and, even though they occasionally engage in the practice of fortunetelling, their purpose is only to know the god's will and not to display their supernatural powers (in Seoul, it is sometimes the other way around).

In Cheju, every village has its tutelary god, or guardian deity, and the myth telling the origin of the deity is sung in the Mu-ga, (see the "Ritual Song of the Tutelary God Shrine of Sŏ-Gwi-P'ŏ"). The myth is unique in that similar contents cannot be found in myths on the mainland, and, as mentioned previously, the songs themselves are, in general, remarkably free of the Buddhist and Taoist usages that otherwise are found employed throughout the Mu-ga sung on the mainland. This may be attributed to the fact that Buddhist influence was hardly felt on the island, even during its zenith when it supposedly replaced Musok as the national religion in the Unified Shilla and Koryŏ periods (c. 668-1392 A.D.).

Periodically, throughout the year, the people of Cheju hold special public rituals for the deity. Rituals are also held when misfortunes occur, but in this case some parts are similar to the mainland, as are some of the mythical elements.

In North and South Chŏlla, Ch'ung-Ch'ŏng, and Kyŏngsang Province, what is commonly referred to as the South Han region, though minor differences are to be found, the ritual songs are generally of the same type. In this area, the Mudang is also called *Tan'gol* Mudang, or just *Tan'gol*.[34] The Tan'gol are all hereditary, and they do not accept practitioners from outside their clan. Though the practice is restricted solely to females, the Mudang lineage is always paternal, and they can marry only into another Mudang family. Therefore, a Mudang's daughter can never become a Mudang in her own house, but only in that of her husband's, i.e., it is only the Mudang's daughter-in-law that can succeed her in the profession. The male members of the family are never concerned with religious matters, but only provide the musical accompaniment.[35]

Generally, only one Mudang dwells in a village and is responsible for all rituals and other related religious matters. Though her social status, as elsewhere, is of the very lowest rank, she, in all probability, regards herself, mentally speaking, as queen of the village, as the inhabitants would never think of disobeying her word, especially during the ritual proper.

The K'ŭn kut contains the full complement of twelve songs. The song contents of the different provinces in the south are basically the same, but the melody and rhythm differ, particularly those of Chŏlla and Kyŏngsang Provinces. The song is interspersed with recitative (called *aniri*) telling of the god's deeds (see the "Ritual Song of the God Chesŏk"). This is not to be found in Seoul or P'yŏngyang, where its counterpart lies in the oracle instead. In this and other respects as well, the songs of the South Han region attain a higher level of sophistication than those of the North Han. The melody and instrumental technique are believed to have laid the foundation for much of Korean folk music as we know it today,[36] and the songs that are of the *p'an-sori*, the narrative-epic-dramatic song that was later to be transmitted into a permanent part of folk music culture by wandering minstrels.[37] The dance is performed to a slow rippling tempo and is calm in nature,[38] whereas that of the North Han region is rapid and at times attains an almost violent nature, the Mudang jumping up and down and waving about in what appears to be a state of frenzy.

In the southern regions there do from time to time appear women who also become afflicted with the "Shaman Disease," or ecstasy. They are rather derogatorily referred to as *Sŏn Mudang* ("Unripened Mudang") or *Tol-P'ari* ("Selling around") and are looked down upon by the hereditary Mudang for their self-made rituals. During the ritual they become possessed and unintelligible words babble forth incessantly from their mouths; when the ritual is over, they cannot recollect anything said or done. It is perhaps for this type of individual that we can more accurately apply the term "Shaman." They are common women, usually past middle age, and their mysterious disease, or state of mind, is incurable. They claim to be possessed by some gods and are directed by them. They are able to relate the past history of persons they do not know, and also occasionally issue statements concerning the future. As their prophecies sometimes prove to be true, many ignorant persons are prone to follow and revere them. These so-called "pseudo-Mudang" usually erect a shrine in their house and place paintings and various implements of the gods on the wall, and it is here that they hold their rituals at anytime when called upon to do so. There is no periodic ritual. Outwardly, the ritual resembles an ordinary Mudang rite, but the song, melody and lyrics are purely improvisational and self-contrived. They have no successor and engage in fortunetelling by use of a variety of implements; occasionally, they issue forth oracles. Therefore can they with all justification be tagged "pseudo." Though everyone in Korea is familiar with the word Mudang, many are not cognizant of the true nature of such; thereby do the "pseudo-Mudang" survive. Small wonder it is, then, that foreigners are often misled in their conception of the Mudang.

The North Han region generally includes the city of Seoul (north of the Han River) and P'yŏng-An, Hamgyŏng, Kangwŏn, Hwanghae and Kyŏnggi Provinces,[39] and comprises another type of Musok. Here the Mudang is also called *Man-Shin* and *Pak-Su*. The terms Mudang and Man-Shin apply only to female practitioners, and Pak-Su only to males.[40] The females make up the bulk of the profession; males are few in number by comparison, except in North Hamgyŏng Province where the practice was restricted solely to males.[41] In the North Han region we find both hereditary

Mudang and otherwise (those afflicted with "Shaman Disease") co-existing. Here, however, the nonhereditary Mudang outnumber the former; in fact, possession is a required characteristic of all Mudang in this area, hereditary or not. Women who become possessed are sent to a hereditary Mudang and become apprenticed to her, whereby they enter into a mother-daughter relationship. When the "mother" Mudang dies, her clothes and properties are bequeathed to the "daughter."[42]

The rituals of this area make use of various kinds of magic, fortunetelling and oracles. The dance, as mentioned previously, is fast in tempo and quick in movement. Each province's ritual song melodically resembles that particular area's folksong,[43] the only exception being that of Hamgyŏng Province, whose Mu-ga sometimes resemble Buddhist sacred songs. The Hamgyŏng songs contain many myths, but in Seoul there is only one and in P'yŏng-An two. In Seoul and P'yŏng-An, the Mudang concentrate on the showier aspects of the ritual, employing many brightly colored costumes[44] and making more frequent use of the dance.[45] In P'yŏng-An, they rely heavily on the comic interlude, in which it is not altogether uncommon for one to hear some rather bawdy puns thrown in as well. The music is very noisy, cymbals and gongs playing continuously fortissimo throughout—this in contrast to the ritual of Chŏlla Province in the south where the instruments are played softly and the cymbals are absent (the song is also more gentle in nature and solemn in tone).[46] The devotees themselves often participate in the dance while the Mudang accompanies them on one of the percussion instruments (drum, gong or cymbals), but this is not done in Hamgyŏng Province.[47]

The Korean Musok system dominated the country for a long period of history; its music and song and dance form became the fountainhead of Korean folk art, and was handed down by the hereditary Mudangs for countless generations.[48] The intellectual elite and upper classes of the society, however, from the advent of Buddhism down to the present, have had little else but contempt for the Mudang, and statesmen have continually persecuted, suppressed and attempted to drive them to extinction, particularly in the Confucianist-dominated Yi Dynasty (1392-1910 A.D.), when they were designated as one of the eight lowest classes of the society and their religious practices regarded as little else but primitive superstition, thereby denying them power, education and civil rights.[49]

Such a rigid social atmosphere created by the edicts laid down in both the Confucian and subsequent Neo-Confucian doctrines was quite antithetical to the freedom of expression that existed in Musok. And so it was that, in the years to follow, folk religion and arts were to suffer a repression heretofore unknown in their long history and were relegated to the lowest strata of the society, considered fit only for uneducated commoners, a position they never really recovered from until recently when the government of the Republic of Korea began to hear the pleas of concerned scholars of ethnology and folklore to save the remnants of folk arts and religion—the little that was left after the bulldozing effects of annexation, war, westernization and modernization—from complete and virtual extinction, and to elevate their position in the eyes of the society as "Intangible Cultural Properties," or "Assets," or "Treasures," as they have officially been so designated, to be protected and preserved for posterity, and to awaken modern society to the existence of their own cultural heritage.[50]

The contemptuous regard of Musok by the society in general has also been carried over into the Mu-ga. If any thought were given to them at all, they were regarded as little more than mere accompaniment or one of the many props upon which the Mudang depended for their execution of the ritual. The songs as works of art in themselves, as valuable transmitters of oral literature, folk myths, legends, folk songs, and folk tales have—with the exception of brief excepts that will pop up in a publication or two every now and then—never been given serious consideration, nor have they, until now, ever been translated in their entirety.

Yet, despite all adversities, the Mudang, like the phoenix, have persevered and never died out entirely, preserving and maintaining their way of life. And, thereby, has Musok miraculously managed to survive—though only in rather threadbare remnants for the most part—throughout the many social and political upheavals that have taken place down through the ages. However, with the sweeping changes that have occurred in modern Korean society, the introduction of democratic thought and the overthrow of the class system, the old distinctions of high and low status have been replaced largely by purely economic factors. Owing to this trend, the Mudang, who suffered maltreatment for so long at the hands of society, are now, ironically and at long last, abandoning their ancient profession and taking up new occupations in the very society that once rejected them. Consequently, the younger generations of the *Mudang* families are, by and large, no longer learning the ritual practices or songs; therefore, nowadays, when we seek a genuine Mudang, we are compelled to find one who is a least fifty years of age or over, but even they are becoming increasingly more difficult to locate. To record and transcribe a Musok ritual completely and accurately in its entirety today has, indeed, become an increasingly difficult task for the researcher and translator.

Notes

1. However, some songs which are claimed by several scholars to be Mu-ga are found recorded in the *Shiyong Hyang'akpo* ("Scores of Contemporary Korean Music"), presumed to have been published prior to the Japanese Hideyoshi Invasion of 1592, which contains eleven songs, written in a form of mensural notation, that are purported to have been sung in the Musok ritual during the early part of the Choson period. None of the songs, however, exist in the Musok repertoire of today. In addition, the terms *Shinbang-gok* and Shimbang-gok ("Song of the God's Room") mentioned in Sŏng Hyŏn's (1439-1504) *Yongjae Ch'onghwa* ("Assorted Writings of Yongjae," published during the reign of King Sejo of the Choson period) and in various other works are also said to refer to Mu-ga. It is also interesting to note here that the Mudang of Cheju Island still refer to themselves as *Shinbang*.

2. Akamatsu Chijo and Akiba Tokashi, *Chosen Fuzoku no Kenkyu* ("A Study of Korean Shaman Practices"), Keijo (Seoul): Osaka Yago Shoten, 1938.

3. Sŏng Kyŏng-rin, "Korean Classic Dance," *Korea Journal*, Vol. III, No. 2, Seoul, 1963, p. 6.

4. Ibid., p. 6.

5. "It is commonplace in studies of ancient Korean culture that the founding rulers of the Shilla Dynasty (which was established in the early years of the present era and united the Korean peninsula in 668 A.D.) were chief shamans in whom were combined both political and religious functions. An early Shilla word used to designate the 'king,' *ch'ach'aung*, is said to have meant 'shaman.' The eighth-century Shillan scholar Kim Tae-mun is quoted in the *Sam-guk Sagi* ("History of the Three Kingdoms"), written in

1145 A.D., as having defined this title in the following way: 'This means shaman. The shaman waits upon the spirits and gods and conducts religious services. Therefore, the people respect him with awe. Accordingly, they called their chief a shaman.' See Kim Chong-gwon, tr., *Samguk Sagi* written by Kim Pu-shik (Seoul: Sonjin Munhwa Sa, 1960), pp. 4, 18." Quoted by Marshall R. Pihl in "Korea in the Bardic Tradition: *P'ansori* as an Oral Art," *Korean Studies Forum,* No. 2, Spring-Summer, Seoul, 1977.

6. A song of the Karak (or Kaya) kingdom (c. 42-562 A.D.) recorded in the *Samguk Yusa* ("Reminiscences of the Three Kingdoms") written by the Buddhist monk Ilyŏn in the late 13th century; it was sung at Ku-Ji Mountain where a tortoise is said to have appeared.

7. A photo of a bronze rattle with eight tiny bells dating from the Late Bronze or Early Iron Age (3rd-2nd century B.C.) may be found in Alan C. Heyman's article "Mu-ga: The Shaman Song of Korea," *Korean Culture,* Vol. 1, No. 1, New York, 1980, p. 10. It is believed that objects such as these served some ceremonial function, being somewhat similar in form to the cluster of small bells suspended from a metal rod that is used by present-day Mudangs to invoke the spirit. A similar instrument was unearthed on December 4, 1980 from a Kaya period tumulus in Pusan, which is believed to have been built in the early fifth century, and is believed to be strongly indicative of Musok rituals in the fourth to early fifth century Kaya (Karak) Kingdom.

Halla Pai Huhm, in her work entitled *Kut: Korean Shamanist Rituals* (Seoul: Hollym Int'l. Corp., 1980), in a description of the *Chesŏk Kori* (the Ritual of the God *Chesŏk*), states (on p. 80) that ". . . *Chesuk Kori* . . . originated in the days of *Koguryŏ* . . ." (dating back some 1500 years or more), but no references are cited to substantiate this.

8. Pihl (op. cit., pp. 8-9) makes some highly interesting comments on the matter in this regard:

> Whereas in his earliest incarnation, it is known that the priest-poet performs a sacred function among his people, who vest in him the highest social authority, we might theorize that he loses this place of honor with the passing of time: upon the introduction of new cultural institutions, the priest-poet of the indigenous culture would be displaced in his social function and his literary arts differentiated from those of the new formal culture. The distinction between the two would be exacerbated in cases where the native literary tradition is oral and the imposed literature written, particularly where the new conventions are expressed in a different dialect or language. The divorce would be complete when the philosophy of the imposed

institution condemns the ideas that invest the narrative tradition. Such a process would be possible whether the imposed institution is alien or autochthonous.

To which is further added:

> . . . Chinese Buddhism and Confucianism pushed aside Shamanistic traditions at home and also in peripheral areas, such as Korea.
> While some . . . appear to have believed in the new religion . . . others, less convinced, simply adapted their material to suit their patron and please the authorities.

Huhm (op. cit., p. 66) also makes a noteworthy commentary on this point in a description of the rite known as the *Pulsa Kori*:

> One may be tempted to think that the *pulsa* god in *pulsa kori* is a Buddhist god. It is one of the celestial gods invoked in *kut* along with the highest of the heavenly gods of Taoism, gods of the sun, the moon, and stars, gods of the seven stars of the Big Dipper, shaman god. Yi Chi-san (a famous Mudang) theorizes that *pulsa kori* later became known as such because there was a time when shamans propagated Buddhism. He goes on to point out that although in *pulsa kori* the shaman brings a message from the dead there are no Buddhist terms used in it. Yet the t'aryong (a type of Shaman-ritual song) performed following *pulsa kori* mentions well-known Buddhist temples in Korea and glorifies Buddhism.

9. Chŏ Seŏng means "that place": so the good man goes to the "good place" and the bad man to the "bad place."

10. For a discussion on some differing viewpoints of the soul in Musok see Kim, T'ae-gon, "The Idea of Soul in Korean Shamanism," and Kim, Yol-Kyu, "Concepts of the Soul in Korean Myths," in *The Idea of Soul in Asia*, Seoul: Association of Asian Folklore, 1979.

11. In the "Ritual Song of the God Chesŏk," for example, though the leading character of the myth that is sung is a Buddhist monk, only his actions are recorded, never his religious practices. What is more, in the finale, he renounces his celibacy and returns to the "human world."

12. In Chinese-letter poetry there is rhyme, but not in Korean.

13. Some parts of the Mu-ga are sung in atrophic form with a refrain that the Mudang sometimes sings together with the assistant Mudang and accompanying musicians or, according to regional differences, in alternation with them.

14. *Ha-Do* is an idiom of Chinese origin. Legend says that in ancient China, in the age of *Pok-Hi-Shi,* there appeared a miracle from the Yellow River, which is told thusly: From the "Dragon Horse's" (tortoise) back there sprouted curly hair in a form that appeared quite mystical, from which the Chinese made the "Eight Trigrams," used in Chinese philosophy and divination. Nak-Sŏ is also an idiom of Chinese origin. In ancient China, during the reign of Emperor Tang-yao (B.C. 2357-2258), there fell a continuous nine-year rain. Wu controlled the flood, and eventually became king. At that time, a mystical tortoise appeared from the waters of the Nak River. On its back there appeared some letters from which the Chinese made the *Hong Pŏm Ku Ju,* the so-called "Magna Carta of China."

15. Huhm (op. cit., p. 14), in quoting Yim Sok-chae (Im, Sŏkjae) in her article entitled *"Han 'guk musok yŏn 'gu sosŏl"* ("Introduction to Korean Shamanism") in *Asea Yŏsŏng Yŏngu,* Vol. X (1971), n.p., lists the components as follows:

1. Report of the name and rank of the suppliant.
2. Narrative of the material and spiritual devotion of the suppliant to the performance of the rituals.
3. Narration of the process in which the offerings were made and prayer for the god's acceptance of the feast.
4. Narration of prayer for blessings and elimination of all misfortunes in the forthcoming year.
5. Narration of the mythology of the god being invoked.
6. Narration via *t'aryong* (a ballad), dance, jugglery, and talent show designed to please the invoked god.
7. Narration of jubilation for having achieved aspirations by the grace of the invoked god.
8. Narration of offering food to assorted demons, accompanied by the following in some regions
9. Opening song for a lesser *kut*
10. Concluding song for a lesser *kut*
11. Words of the invoked gods to human beings
12. Narration of the god's will by divination
13. Narration of sending back the invoked god.

16. "Folk religious rites, apart from Confucian and Buddhist rites have many forms, depending upon the inclination of the master of the rite, the occasion of the rite, and the scale of the rite. The master of a folk rite could either be a *Mudang,* or Shaman, performing song and dance in a

large-scale ritual or could be a professional chanter chanting scripture, as in Taoism or Buddhism, or a fortuneteller, or a court sorcerer. In each case, the forte of the ritual varies, but, in general, each entails nature-oriented religious rites accompanied by song and dance."—Huhm, ibid., p. 9.

17. Huhm (ibid., p. 15) states that this rite may also be performed by a fortuneteller, and that the duration of the ritual is from three to four hours.

18. "Since long before the advent of Confucianism and Buddhism, religious rites oriented in nature have been performed in Korea. These rituals are known as Kut in Korean, a word widely used, according to scholars of Korean folklore, in the Yakut language. In Korean, the word denotes not only religious rituals oriented in nature but frequently refers to the music, dance and drama integrated into those rituals, and many theatricals have stemmed from the music, dance and drama of religious rituals."— Huhm, ibid., p. 9.

19. Huhm (ibid., p. 10) refers to the *K'ŭn Kut* as the "greater *kut*," and to the other rituals as "lesser Kut" (p. 14).

20. To these four categories Huhm (ibid., p. 12) adds ". . . The *shin kut* for the spirits worshipped by the Shamans . . . and the *yongwang kut* for the dragon god."

21. " The offerings in a greater kut consist of rice cakes; cooked rice; seasoned vegetables; grilled food such as fish, meat, and bean curd; apples; pears; persimmons; dates; chestnuts; many kinds of pastry mixed with oil and honey; beef broiled on a skewer; boiled bovine hooves; boiled whole pig; and dried Alaskan pollack.

"Offerings vary according to the god invoked. The number of ceremonial tables varies according to region and in a greater kut according to the kind of kut to be performed, ranging usually from three to ten tables. In a lesser kut, different sets of tables are sometimes prepared, sometimes not."—Huhm, ibid., p. 15. For a more detailed discussion of ritual offerings, see pp. 33-39.

22. Huhm (ibid., p. 12) places the duration at ". . . From one to several days."

23. Huhm (ibid, p. 12) records this as *Mang-mugi kut*. In addition, for the P'yŏng-An and Hwanghae Provinces, she lists *Kilmi kut*, and for Cheju Island, the *Siwang maji kut*.

24. SK: *Yama*; Chinese: *Yien Lo* (see the "Ritual Song of the Bridge").

25. Ch'il-Sŏng means "Seven Stars"; therefore is the god also referred to as the "God of the Big Dipper" (see the "Ritual Song of the Bridge"). There is some dissension among scholars here as to whether this is an adaptation from Taoism, some maintaining that the god existed in the Musok pantheon before the introduction of Taoism, but under a different name.

26. For an in-depth study of the God of the Mountain, see Canda, Edw. R., "The Korean Mountain Spirit," *Korea Journal*, Vol. 20, No. 9, Seoul, 1980, pp. 11-16, and Mason, David A., "A Study of Korea's Mountain Spirit (San-sin) and It's Relationship with Korean Buddhism," Yonsei University, M.A. Thesis, Seoul, 1997.

27. For a detailed account of a Christian missionary's views and observations on Korean Musok practices, see Clark, Charles Allen, *Religions of Old Korea*, written in 1930.

28. Huhm (op. cit., p. 102), in the conclusion of her work, makes this commentary:

> One thing to keep in mind when studying Shamanistic practices is that there exists a sort of dualism, a contradiction, in the Korean consciousness. Western Christianity has exerted a powerful and lasting influence on the Korean people, it is true. Yet among many Koreans there persists a strange attachment to the beliefs of Shamanism, a deep inner feeling permeating much of the contemporary Korean culture.

29. "Shamanism is not an organized religion with a systematic canon of belief. It rests upon the assumption that all things, animate or inanimate, are possessed of a spirit. It is the function of the shaman to mediate between his people and these spirits, since they themselves are not capable of doing so. This is done by the shaman while in a state of disassociation, be it ecstasy or trance. Only the shaman has the inspired eloquence to summon forth spirits, benevolent or malevolent, and cope with them in the name of those who have asked his services. The magical power of words is his stock in trade, and, for this reason, the professional, and more especially the intellectual life, of the people is almost wholly vested in their shamans (Chadwick and Chadwick, *Growth*, III, 195). Since the profession is largely inherited and each shaman prepared for his task by rigorous training, the words he utters are far from haphazard but, rather, represent an ancient tradition of formulas, themes, and dramatic structures. While

everything expressed is invested with religious significance, the forms of
his utterances range over hymns, prayers, blessings, precepts, and dramatic
monologues (ibid., pp. 198-210). Therefore, the shaman is at one the re-
pository and the creative source of the oral literature of his culture. A close
study of the shaman institution would probably throw light on the sacred
function of the shadowy priests of ancient Europe. Chadwick and
Chadwick, *Growth*, III, 192; Victor Zhirmunsky, "Epic Songs and Singers in
Central Asia," in Nora K. Chadwick and Victor Zhirmunsky, *Oral Epics of
Central* Asia (London: Cambridge University Press, 1969), p. 292." Quoted
by Marshall R. Pihl, op. cit., p. 94.

30. Lee, Jung-young, in his article entitled "Korean Shamanism and
Sexual Repression," (*Asian & Pacific Quarterly,* Vol. XII, No. 1, Seoul, 1980,
p. 31), states the following:

> There are commonly two types of shamans: priestly shamans who are
> primarily prevalent in the southern or Honam (Chulla) provinces
> and charismatic shamans who live primarily in the northern or
> middle provinces. Since Seoul belongs to the northern portion of
> South Korea, the shamans there in general are charismatic and
> more authentic than the priestly shamans of the Honam area.

Here, Dr. Lee's point is interesting but highly controversial, unless
of course by use of the word "authentic" he is comparing the "charismatic"
Shamans of Seoul with the polar Siberian Shamans. Also, Dr. Lee's use of
the word "priestly" in regard to the Mudangs of the south is a poor choice
indeed. They are far from being "priestly" in any sense of the word; a
far better and more accurate descriptive would have been the word
"hereditary."

31. Huhm (op. cit., p. 9) also makes a reference to this point:

> Although the Korean word *mudang* is often translated as "shaman,"
> some Korean scholars claim that the Korean *mudang* has many char-
> acteristics that differ from those of the Siberian shaman. Therefore,
> they maintain, the word should not be translated as "shaman," nor
> should Korean *kut* be described as shamanistic rites.

32. Huhm (ibid, p. 10) prefers to use the classification of South
Korean, North Korean and Eastern Seaboard:

> The South Korean type covers the Cholla provinces, Ch'ungch'ong
> provinces, Kyonggi province south of the Han River, the southwest-
> ern part of the Kyŏngsang provinces and Cheju Island: the North
> Korean type covers the P'yŏngan provinces, Hwanghae province, the
> Hamgyong provinces, Kyonggii province north of the Han River;

and the Eastern Seaboard type covers the eastern coastal area of Kangwŏn province and the Kyŏngsang provinces.

She further subdivides the rituals of the Seoul area (p. 19) into ". . . three separate and distinct forms, i.e., the western form, the eastern form, and the southern form."

33. Huhm (ibid., p. 10) uses the term *shimbang* here.

34. Huhm (ibid., p. 10) uses the term *talgollae*. Whether this is accurate or not, however, is open to question.

35. "The shamans of the south intermarry within their class with a *mubu,* who is also called a *chaein, kongin,* or *hwarang* . . . He assists the shaman in the invocation of spirits mainly by providing the musical accompaniment. He is an artist specializing in music; and the association of such musically-skilled *mubu* is called a *mubu-gye.* Akamatsu and Akiba, II, 31, 33, 209, 234, 281 (II, 131)." Quoted by Marshall R. Pihl, ibid., p. 104.

"In the terminology of Korean shamanism, as described by Akamatsu and Akiba, a *ch'angbu* is the musician-husband of a shaman who serves as her accompanist on the drum and can also perform as a singer in his own right (II, 31, 33, 209, 234, 281). The *Ch'angbu* section of the ch'onsin kut consists of three parts. The first is an invocation addressed to the spirit of a dead *ch'angbu,* and the second is a first-person promise of protection by the spirit who sings through the medium of the shaman. The third part is an account by the shaman (again in the third person) of Creation and ancestral beginnings, followed by a narration of the journeys of *ch'angbu* to the capital where they meet the new licentiates and accompany them back home to perform the *toktam,* 'chant of fortune' (I, 107-115)." Quoted by Marshall R. Pihl, op. cit., p. 103.

Huhm (ibid., pp. 10.21) states the following:

Women who play the *changgu* (hourglass-shaped drum) (as well as the gongs and cymbals)[47] and assist in the singing of shaman songs at rituals are known as *kidae* in the Seoul area. They are persons well-versed in rituals but in whom the spirits have not appeared (and so they are classified as assistant shamans). They are . . . in most cases female, but occasionally there are males among them. Any woman who has mastered the (percussion) instruments and the songs can became a *kidae.* The musicians (all male) who play the music accompanying shamanistic songs and dances at the kut hall are known as *chonak* or *aksu chaebi* and in most cases are related to shamanistic families.

36. Two examples of folk music forms whose origins may be traced to the accompanying music of the South Han ritual are the *Sanjo* (improvisational music for solo instrument, usually strings) and *Shinawi* (improvisational music for instrumental ensemble).

37. A very excellent treatment of the *P'an-sori* has been done by Marshall R. Pihl, op. cit. Also see Heyman, Alan C., *"P'an-sori*: The Dramatic-Epic-Narrative Song of Korea," *Essays in Asian Music and Theatre*, New York: Pratt Institute Press, 1972.

38. Commonly called *Sal-P'uri* ("Exorcise the Devil"), it has also become a permanent part of the folk dance music repertoire.

39. Kyŏnggi Province is the border line between the North and South Han regions; therefore, the area north of Seoul belongs to the North Han region and that south of Seoul to the South Han region.

40. Here, Huhm (op. cit., p. 10) adds the term *mugyŏk* for the male Mudang, and, further, "In the Hamgyŏng provinces, a female shaman is referred to as *osimi* and a *mugyok* as a *t'osaebi.*"

41. The author uses the past tense here because since the end of World War II, Hamgyŏng, P'yŏng-An, Hwanghae and the northern parts of Kangwŏn and Kyŏnggi Provinces have been under the communist totalitarian rule of North Korea. It is doubtful, therefore, whether the practice of Musok is still in existence there. It should be noted here, however, though Musok may no longer exist in North Korea, several Mudangs from the northern provinces fled to the south before the outbreak of the Korean War in June of 1950, where some of them still continue to hold their ritual practices.

42. "In the northern part of Korea, most shamans become professional when the spirits appear in them, regardless of sex or age. In most cases, this happens between the ages of ten and thirty. When the spirits dwell, the recipient suffers from an indeterminable ailment, behaves oddly, and divines things at the prompting of the spirits. With the performing of a ceremony, the recipient, by now recovered from the illness, becomes a shaman.

"The person in whom the spirits have appeared goes to visit a recognized shaman/enters into a foster parent-child relationship, and studies the *kut* craft. The foster parent is called the 'spiritual mother' and the apprentice the 'spiritual daughter.' The apprentice, having mastered the *kut* craft, builds an altar, usually in one of the rooms of her home, installs an image of the spirits, places the *kut* tools, and offers supplications and prayer morning and evening."—Huhm, op. cit, pp. 10-11.

43. "Many Shamanist songs were similar in melody to folk songs but some Shamanist songs had a rhythm that could not be found in folk music."—Yi, Po-hyong, "Performing Style of Korean Traditional Music," *Korea Journal,* Vol. 20, No. 11, Seoul, 1980, p. 30. Also see Huhm, ibid., p. 16.

44. "The costumes of the shaman vary according to the kind of *kut* to be performed and according to the region. In the central region, including the Seoul area, a large variety of costumes is in use. In the Seoul area, the shaman uses a different traditional costume according to the god to be invoked, for example, a martial costume for a heavenly god. In the southern region, costumes are limited to everyday clothes or a few different kinds of shaman costumes. Regardless of the region, the common ceremonial dress of a shaman consists of a deep blue *ch'ima* (skirt) and a white *chogori* (jacket). This is essentially the woman's ceremonial dress in the Korean family, and it is used in most family rites and lessor *kut*."—Huhm, ibid., pp. 15-16.

45. For a detailed study of three Shaman dances in the Seoul area of Kyŏnggi Province, see Huhm, ibid., pp. 15-16.

46. The musical instruments employed in the rituals of the south include the *taegŭm,* or *ch'ottae,* (transverse bamboo flute), *p'iri* (bamboo oboe), *changgo* (hourglass-shaped drum) and large gong (*ching*). The ritual ensemble of Chindo Island also includes a *kayagum* (twelve-stringed instrument) and an *ajaeng* (seven-stringed bowed instrument), but these are felt to be rather recent innovations. The ritual ensembles of the north add the *haegeum* (two-stringed fiddle), a pair of small cymbals (*chegeum*) or large cymbals (*para*), and occasionally a round barrel drum (*puk*). Conical oboes (*t'ae-p'yŏng-so, hojok,* or *saenap*) are employed as auxiliary instruments in some rituals, but are restricted largely to processionals and preliminary sections. For a fuller discussion of the music used in the Musok ritual, see Yi, Po-hyong, op. cit., pp. 29-30, No. 6.

47. This practice sometimes serves as a kind of catharsis for curing psychosis. For a further discussion of the subject, see Kendall, Laurel: "*Mugam*: The Dance in Shaman's Clothing," *Korea Journal,* Vol. 17, No. 12, Seoul, 1977, pp. 38-44.

48. Huhm (op. cit., p. vii), in the preface to her work, substantiates this in saying "Korean Shamanism . . . is a source of Korean cultural arts

with hundreds of years of tradition behind it. Dances in the rituals of Korean shamanism, considered as dances of a lowly class, . . . have long been treated with contempt . . . But in recent years the outstanding artistry of shamanistic dances are considered indispensable in the research of folk arts. Shamanistic dances in Korea were branded as the vocation of one of the lowly classes of people under the Yi dynasty. But . . . It is believed that shamanistic dances are the parent body of Korean dances originating in religious rituals."

49. Yet, in spite of public inhibition and condemnation, when natural disasters, wars or social mishaps occurred, even the royal palace was known to have summoned them forth to hold a ritual when all else failed.

In this respect, Keith Pratt, in his article entitled "Politics and Culture Within the Sinic Zone: Chinese Influences on Medieval Korea," (*Korea Journal*, Vol. 20, No. 6, Seoul, 1980, p. 24) makes a further observation on the matter:

> Despite the Confucian-inspired interest professed by the early Koryŏ kings in their subjects' welfare, it is unlikely that the latter had any interest in Confucianism. Buddhism affected their lives more, as it did the lives of the Chinese lower classes. Truly popular religion in Korea however was shamanistic. In Hsu Ching's opinion, it is their habit to make excessive sacrifices to the spirits. At times the court and even the kings were unwilling to dispense with the shaman's services. The shamanistic *p'al-gwanhoe* ceremony became an annual rite. Originating in the old Koguryo village sacrificial rite *tongmaeng*, banned in 981 as uncanonical and too noisy, it was reintroduced in 1010 and frequently attended by kings. After attending one such occasion in the 11th moon of 1115 King Yejong stayed outside the Hammun Gate, ordering his players to sing and dance until the third drum. He was rebuked by the Chief Censor.

50. In concluding his article, Lee, Jung-young (op. cit., p. 30) makes a very pertinent statement in this regard:

> My final remark is that it is going to be a sad commentary on our times if shamanism is to be eliminated for the sake of modernization. Modernization is neither Westernization or technocracy. Modernization ought to be seen in its full context, which should not exclude tradition and culture. If we love and preserve museum pieces because they have traditional value, then we ought to appreciate the living tradition, shamanism, which is a custodian of Korean culture and tradition. Modernization must not aim at uniformity but must allow divergent elements like shamanism to coexist and meet the needs of modern man. What we need is not the elimination of shamanism but to reform it from a technique of instant and projec-

tive solutions of problems to a process of inner experience and transformation of life. That is precisely to return to the essence of shamanism from its superficial manifestations. This is a most delicate and sensitive task that requires extreme care and thought so that shamanism can reform itself without losing its significance as a custodian of rich traditions of the past. This kind of task demands a unified approach of various disciplines and a great deal of research.

To this, Yoon, Soon-young ("Magic, Science and Religion on Cheju Island," *Korea Journal*, March, 1976, p. 10) adds some significant views from the ethnomedical-anthropological standpoint:

—shamanism has a justifiable role to play. The roots of its strength are not ideological but socioeconomic, and shamanism will not be destroyed by New Village Movement propaganda or, at times, force. Indeed, modern medicine can learn from shamanism, which is not as we tend to see it, a religion, but pre-science. In this case, Korean Westernized science contemplates itself and the very basis of Korean culture. Perhaps that is too great a challenge for a country that has developed a consciousness of "underdevelopment" to a point that anything "unscientific" is a cultural embarrassment. Shamanism will rise and fall in the natural organic process of peasant transformations.

Shamanism depends on the economic and social structure of a family-based agricultural society for its legitimacy and survival. That is its strength and its weakness. Shamanism is a religion with no temple, no bible, and no fixed priesthood. When the agricultural structure of society changes, shamanism will decline. It will retreat into the dark alleys of fortunetellers, and ritual myths now used for healing will become children's fairy tales.

Yi Ch'un-ok, a *Mudang* from P'yŏng-an Province (center), dressed in Buddhist ceremonial garb, to the accompaniment of a drum and gong, sings an invocation supplicating for the peaceful passage of the departed soul to Paradise during a performance of the *Tari Kut* ("The Ritual of the Bridge"). (photo: Kim Su-nam)

2. *Tari kut*:
The Ritual Song of the Bridge[1]
(also known as the *Su-Wang Kut* or
Shi-Wang Kut: The Ritual Song of the Ten Kings)[2]

Introduction

The Mudang begins by playing the cymbals while her assistants play the drum and gong. After this, she begins to sing while the assistants continue the instrumental accompaniment and, at the same time, intone the sacred Buddhist words *Namu Amit'a-bul* as a refrain after each line of verse. This is repeated throughout the entire ritual except during the Boating Song at the end. It is said that the words Amit'a-bul should be repeated three thousand times in order to gain entrance into Paradise (Nirvana) because the Buddhist paradise is composed of the "Three-Thousand Worlds." In repeating these words the Buddhist devotee calls upon Amit'a,[3] the "Buddha of Infinite Light and Boundless Life," the ruler of the "Western Paradise," the "Pure Land," for salvation. Amit'a was a king who left his throne to seek Buddhahood. He vowed never to accept his reward (Nirvana) until all beings had arrived in his paradise, which they may do by calling upon him for salvation. The souls of the faithful are transported by boat[4] to their reward.

Prologue

> Na-mu Amit'a-bul,
> (repeated three times).
>
> Let us go and see,
> Let us go and see!
>
> Na-mu Ami-t'a-bul,

The way to Paradise.

Na-mu Amit'a-bul,

Let us go and see,
The soul-bearing chariot.

Na-mu Amit'a-bul!

Let us go and see,
The way to Paradise.

What is Paradise?

Paradise is the place
Where there's no pain of any sort,

And where one can make his home
On the Lotus Blossom Peak.[5]

Where one can make a fence
Of the everlasting thicket!

Where the Eight Angels
Are seated round!

Where the Place of Reincarnation is,
Where the Amitabba Master reigns;

Where all the soul's ancestors
Wait in welcome.

So let us go to Paradise
This very day;

Let us go,
Let us go!

To Paradise,
This very day.

I.

The contents of this portion of the ceremony are based on the "Yin Yang," Five Elements cosmology, in which the Mudang prays for the ascension of all souls into Paradise. The Five Elements referred to specifically here are those of metal (or gold, or iron), wood, water, fire and earth (or soil, or field), after which the "Five Stars" are named: Gold Star (Venus), Wood Star (Jupiter), Water Star (Mercury), Fire Star (Mars) and Earth Star (Saturn). They were recognized by ancient astronomers of the East only after formation of the lunar calendar, which was based on observations of the sun and moon. Profoundly impressed by the seemingly patternless movements of these five stars, Chinese astronomers, in about 400 B.C., attributed them to divine will. The assumption was soon developed into an accepted conclusion that, being based on divine will, the movements of the five stars were indicative of fortunes, not only of man himself, but also of the universe as a whole, and that all changes in the universe were caused by changes in the five elements. Since the five stars were believed to have been created with masses of each respective element, their movements are indicative of events which happen in the universe. It is significant to note also that the days of the week derived their names from the sun, moon and five elements. And so, in Korea, we have:

> Sunday—the day of the sun
> Monday—the day of the moon
> Tuesday—the day of fire
> Wednesday—the day of water
> Thursday—the day of wood
> Friday—the day of gold
> Saturday—the day of earth

Therefore, it is even more interesting to note the striking analogy that exists in the West where the Sun and Moon are similarly associated with Sunday and Monday, Mars with Tuesday, Mercury with Wednesday, and Saturn with Saturday.[6]

This theory is also not without its counterpart in other Asian cultures. In the Hindu scripture known as the *Bhagavad Gita* (the third verse of the seventh chapter) for example, it is stated: "My nature is of the Eight Orders—Earth, Water, Fire . . ." Another

example may be found in the Songs from Bengal,[7] where Radha
sings her praises of love for Krishna:

Let the earth of my body be mixed with the earth my beloved walks on.
Let the fire of my body be the brightness in the mirror that reflects his face.
Let the water of my body join the water of the lotus pool he bathes in.

The Yin-Yang philosophic concept is employed in the Ritual
Song of the Bridge in its "male-female" connotation to the extent
that all things, whether they be human beings or stars, are believed
to be composed of the male-female (Yin-Yang) element. And so the
Mudang sings:

> *The man and woman*
> *Who are the Gold in the Sea . . .*

> *The man and woman*
> *Who are the Star of Gold . . .*

And again later in Part II:

> *The man of this earth . . .*
> *From father's bone*

> *And mother's flesh . . .*
> *. . . was created.*

In Korea, the naming of the year is based on an ancient Chinese system which designates ten Chinese characters to represent
"Heaven" (the trunk) and twelve for "Earth" (the branch), one symbol from each of the two worlds being joined together in successive
pairs to form a total of sixty different combinations in all, those of
the celestial group always preceding those of the world below.
Therefore, in Korea, one is said to have completed the full life
cycle[8] upon reaching his sixtieth birthday.[9]
The ten symbols of "Heaven" are:

1	2	3	4	5	6	7	8	9	10
Kap	Ŭl	Pyŏng	Chŏng	Mu	Ki	Kyŏng	Shin	Im	Kye

The twelve symbols of "Earth," which also make up the Far Eastern zodiac, are as follows:

1	2	3	4	5
Cha (Rat)	Ch'uk (Cow)	In (Tiger)	Myo (Rabbit)	Chin (Dragon)

6	7	8	9	10
Sa (Snake)	O (Horse)	Mi (Sheep)	Shin (Monkey)	Yu (Chicken)

11	12
Sul (Dog)	Hae (pig)

And so, the year 1986 (in the Western calendar), for example, was Mu-Shin (5-9), commonly referred to as "The Year of the Monkey."[10]

It is customary in Korea for both the prospective bride and bridegroom to consult a fortuneteller to determine whether their marriage can be successful. The fortuneteller's prophecy, known as *Kung-Hap* ("Conjugal Compatibility"), is based largely on the above philosophy and is determined primarily on the exact date and time of birth of the man and woman according to the lunar calendar.

> 1. The man and woman
>   Who are the Gold in the Sea,
>
>   Were born in the year of
>   Kap-Chaŭl-Ch'uk;
>
>   The man and woman
>   Who are the Star of Gold
>
>   Were wedded one to another
>   And appeared on this earth:
>
>   May their soul ascend to Paradise
>   This very day.

2. The man and woman
    Who are the Fire of the Boiling Cauldron,

    Were born in the Year of
    Pyŏng-In Chŏng-Myo;

    The man and woman
    Who are the Star of Fire,

    Were wedded one to another
    And appeared on this earth:

    May their soul ascend to Paradise
    This very day.

3. The man and woman
    Who are the wood of the Great Forest,

    Were born in the year of
    Mu-Chin Ki-Sa;

    The man and woman
    Who are the Star of Wood,

    Were wedded one to another
    And appeared on this earth:

    May their soul ascend to Paradise
    This very day.

4. The man and woman
   Who are the Earth of the Roadside,

   Were born in the year of
   Kyŏng-O Shin-Mi;

   The man and woman
   Who are the Star of Earth,
   Were wedded one to another
   And appeared on this earth:

   May their soul ascend to Paradise
   This very day.

5. The man and woman
   Who are the Metal of the Sword's Apex,

   Were born in the year of
   Im-Shin Kye-Yu;

   The man and woman
   Who are the Star of Metal,

   Were wedded one to another
   And appeared on this earth:

   May their soul ascend to Paradise
   This very day.

6. The man and woman
   Who are the Fire on the Mountain Peak,

   Were born in the year of
   Kap-Sul Ŭl-Hae;

   The man and woman
   Who are the Star of Fire

   Were wedded one to another
   And appeared on this earth:

   May their soul ascend to Paradise
   This very day.

7. The man and woman
   Who are the Water Flowing Between Rocks,

   Were born in the year of
   Pyŏng-Cha Chŏng-Ch'uk;

   The man and woman
   Who are the Star of Water

   Were wedded one to another
   And appeared on this earth:

   May their soul ascend to Paradise
   This very day.

8. The man and woman
   Who are the Earth on the Great Wall,[11]

   Were born in the year of
   Mu-In Ki-Myo;

   The man and woman
   Who are the Star of Earth,

   Were wedded one to another
   And appeared on this earth:

   May their soul ascend to Paradise
   This very day.

9. The man and woman
   Who are the Gold of the White Wax,

   Were born in the year of
   Kyŏng-Chin Shin-Sa;

   The man and woman
   Who are the Star of Gold

   Were wedded one to another
   And appeared on this earth:

   May their soul ascend to Paradise
   This very day.

10. The man and woman
Who are the Wood of the Willow Tree

Were born in the year of
Im-O Kye-Mi;

The man and woman
Who are the Star of Wood,

Were wedded one to another
And appeared on this earth:

May their soul ascend to Paradise
This very day.

11. The man and woman
Who are the Water in the Well,

Were born in the year of
Kap-Shin Ŭl-Yu;

The man and woman
Who are the Star of Water

Were wedded one to another
And appeared on this earth:

May their soul ascend to Paradise
This very day.

12. The man and woman
    Who are the Earth in the House,

    Were born in the year of
    Pyŏng-Sul Chŏng-Hae;

    The man and woman
    Who are the Star of Earth,

    Were wedded one to another
    And appeared on this earth:

    May their soul ascend to Paradise
    This very day.

13. The man and woman
    Who are the Earth on the Wall,

    Were born in the year of
    Kyŏng-Cha Shin-Ch'uk;

    The man and woman
    Who are the Star of Earth,

    Were wedded one to another
    And appeared on this earth:

    May their soul ascend to Paradise
    This very day.

14. The man and woman
    Who are the Wood of the Pine Tree,

    Were born in the year of
    Kyŏng-In Shin-Myo;

    The man and woman
    Who are the Star of Wood,

    Were wedded one to another
    And appeared on this earth:

    May their soul ascend to Paradise
    This very day.

15. The man and woman
    Who are the Water of the Long Flowing River

    Were born in the year of
    Im-Chin Kye-Sa;

    The man and woman
    Who are the Star of Water

    Were wedded one to another
    And appeared on this earth:

    May their soul ascend to Paradise
    This very day.

16. The man and woman
     Who are the Gold in the Sand

     Were born in the year of
     Kap-O Ŭl-Mi;

     The man and woman
     Who are the Star of Earth,

     Were wedded one to another
     And appeared on this earth:

     May their soul ascend to Paradise
     This very day.

17. The man and woman
     Who are the Fire Neath the Mountain,

     Were born in the year of
     Pyŏng-Shin Chŏng-yu;

     The man and woman
     Who are the Star of Fire,

     Were wedded one to another
     And appeared on this earth:

     May their soul ascend to Paradise
     This very day.

18. The man and woman
     Who are the Wood of the Flat Land,

     Were born in the year of
     Mu-Sul Ki-Hae;

     The man and woman
     Who are the Star of Wood,

     Were wedded one to another
     And appeared on this earth:

     May their soul ascend to Paradise
     This very day.

19. The man and woman
     Who are the Earth in the House,

     Were born in the year of
     Pyŏng-Sul Chŏng-Hae;

     The man and woman
     Who are the Star of Earth

     Were wedded one to another
     And appeared on this earth:

     May their soul ascend to Paradise
     This very day.

20. The man and woman
     Who are the Gold of the Plaited Metal,

     Were born in the year of
     Im-In Kye-Myo;

     The man and woman
     Who are the Star of Gold

     Were wedded one to another
     And appeared on this earth:

     May their soul ascend to Paradise
     This very day.

21. The man and woman
     Who are the Fire of the Covered Lantern,

     Were born in the year of
     Kap-Chin Ŭl-Sa;

     The man and woman
     Who are the Star of Fire,

     Were wedded one to another
     And appeared on this earth:

     May their soul ascend to Paradise
     This very day.

22. The man and woman
     Who are the Water of the Heavenly River[12]

     Were born in the year of
     Pyŏng-O Chŏng-Mi;

     The man and woman
     Who are the Star of Water,

     Were wedded one to another
     And appeared on this earth:

     May their soul ascend to Paradise
     This very day.

23. The man and woman
     Who are the Field of the Government Post,[13]

     Were born in the year of
     Mu-Shin Ki-Yu;

     The man and woman
     Who are the Star of Earth,

     Were wedded one to another
     And appeared on this earth:

     May their soul ascend to Paradise
     This very day.

24. The man and woman
     Who are the Gold of the Lady's Hairpin,

     Were born in the year of
     Kyŏng-Sul Shin-Hae;

     The man and woman
     Who are the Star of Gold

     Were wedded one to another
     And appeared on this earth:

     May their soul ascend to Paradise
     This very day.

25. The man and woman
     Who are the Wood of the Mulberry Tree,

     Were born in the year of
     Im-Cha Kye-Ch'u;

     The man and woman
     Who are the Star of Wood,

     Were wedded one to another
     And appeared on this earth:

     May their soul ascend to Paradise
     This very day.

26. The man and woman
     Who are the Flowing Water of the Great Valley,

     Were born in the year of
     Kap-In Ŭl-Myo;

     The man and woman
     Who are the Star of Water

     Were wedded one to another
     And appeared on this earth:

     May their soul ascend to Paradise
     This very day.

27. The man and woman
     Who are the Earth in the Sand,

     Were born in the year of
     Pyŏng-Chin Chŏng-Sa;

     The man and woman
     Who are the Star of Earth

     Were wedded one to another
     And appeared on this earth:

     May their soul ascend to Paradise
     This very day.

28. The man and woman
    Who are the Fire above Heaven,

    Were born in the year of
    Mu-O Ki-Mi;

    The man and woman
    Who are the Star of Fire,

    Were wedded one to another
    And appeared on this earth:

    May their soul ascend to Paradise
    This very day.

29. The man and woman
    Who are the Wood of the Pomegranate Tree,

    Were born in the year of
    Kyŏng-Shin Shin-Yu;

    The man and woman
    Who are the Star of Wood

    Were wedded one to another
    And appeared on this earth:

    May their soul ascend to Paradise
    This very day.

30. The man and woman
    Who are the Water of the Great Sea,

    Were born in the year of
    Im-Sul Kye-Hae;

    The man and woman
    Who are the Star of Water

    Were wedded one to another
    And appeared on this earth:

    May their soul ascend to Paradise
    This very day.

II.

"Let us go and see
Let us go and see;

Let us go and see
The way to Paradise.

Let us go.
Let us go;

To the
Place of Reincarnation

Among the many things
In all of this universe,

Is there anything, really,
Other than man?

You there!
Thou who gives offerings;

Give ear to that which
I would speak:

The man of this earth;
Who gave him charity?

By Sakyamuni's[14] blessing,
By favor of the god of Life,[15]

From father's bone,
And mother's flesh,

From the life span bestowed
By the God of the Big Dipper,

And from the good fortune bestowed
By the God Sakrodevendra,[16]

At last,
He was created.

In his infanthood,
He knew nothing at all;

He knew even not
His parents' charity.

Yea,
Though he entered manhood,

He could not yet repay
His parents' favor.

The years pass by
Like a flowing stream,

And suddenly,
One becomes old.

When one becomes senile,
He's likely to be ridiculed;

In many places,
They laugh at me.

I am sorrowful,
I am sad;

I am wretched,
I am vexed;

Who would deny
This pitiful state of mine?

Ah, woe is me!
Pity this sorrowful state of mine.

I am wretched,
I am vexed;

I am old,
I am white-haired;

What can I do?
What can I do?

This world is so filled
With discontent.

Spring grass is green
Year after year,

But even the dead prince
Never returns.

We mortals too
If once departed,

To return again—
Ah, how difficult it is.

Though we might reach
The age of a hundred,

If the days we lie ill,
The time of sleep,

The time of worry and
The time of trouble

Are tallied and withdrawn,
Our life is really then

But a mere
Forty years.

Yesterday I was healthy,
And today, suddenly,

Unexpectedly
I am attacked by illness.

Sickness is upon me
Like a great mountain.

I cry out "Mother,"
And seek cool Water;

Though the ginseng and deer horn[17]
Are ministered to me,

My heavy illness
Cannot be cured.

Though the doctor is summoned
And medicine dispensed,

My heavy illness
Cannot be cured.

Though the "Shaman" woman is summoned
And a rite is held,

T'is of no avail;
I remain afflicted.

Though the blind auger is summoned
And a recitation is performed,

T'is of no avail;
I remain afflicted.

I offer sacrificial rice
To the monk;

We journey to the holy mountain,
And to the sacred river.

At the upper stream,
We wash and boil the rice;

At the midstream,
We wash our hands and feet.

Burning three sheets of
Sacred mulberry paper,

And, with pure heart and mind,
Placing incense burner and candle

On the sacrificial table,
I pray, I pray;

I pray to
The Big Dipper God, and

Before all Buddhist saints
I make offerings;

And though, too,
I make offerings before

The God of the Mountain,[18]
Which Gods shall give

Their divine response
To my supplications?"

III.

In this portion of the ritual there follows a graphic picture of Hell where the Ten Kings preside and where all the dead are judged. In the Korean concept, the dead are considered "criminals" and are treated accordingly until judged otherwise.

The *Sa-Ja* ("Messengers of Death") of the Ten Kings are therefore viewed as harsh, cruel policemen sent to fetch the "criminal" off to jail in the "other world" to await trial. For this reason, the family of the deceased leave them straw shoes, freshly boiled rice and smoking tobacco (or cigarettes) outside the front gate in hopes that the Sa-Ja will accept them (it being supposed that the Sa-Ja are hungry and tired from the long journey and that their straw shoes are worn out), and, in return, be more kindly disposed toward the deceased. The two Sa-Ja are referred to as the "Sa-Ja of the Day" and "Sa-Ja of the Month." In addition, when the soul reaches Hell, we also encounter the "Sa-Ja of This World" and "Sa-Ja of The Other World," who also must be treated favorably.[19]

Here, once again, we find our counterpart in the *Songs from the Bengali*,[20] in the part entitled *Nibedan*, a prayer to Krishna:

"Now
at the end, I fear
the Messengers of Death."

✢ ✢ ✢ ✢ ✢ ✢ ✢ ✢ ✢

"In the first palace is
King Chin-Kwang the Great;

In the second palace is
King Ch'o-Kang the Great;

In the third palace is
King Song-Je the Great;

In the fourth palace is
King O-Gwan the Great;

In the fifth palace is
King Yŏm-Na the Great;[21]

In the sixth palace is
King Pyŏn-Sŏng the Great;

In the seventh palace is
King T'ae-San the Great;

In the eighth palace is
King P'yŏng-Dŭng the Great;

In the ninth palace is
King Toshi the Great;

In the tenth palace is
King Chŏl-Yun the great.

Under the command of
The Ten Kings are

The Sa-Ja of the Day and
The Sa-Ja of the Month.

In one hand they carry
An iron whip;

In the other,
An iron hammer

And a mighty chain;
It is, indeed,

A most fearsome thing
To behold

To the front and back
And all around.

On every side
These mighty arms

They bear;
T'is indeed

A most fearsome thing
To behold.

The road is bent like
The arch of a bow,

But the Sa-Ja
Comes a'running

Straightaway—
Like the arrow.

He opens the gate
With a mighty kick,

And calls out the three-letter name[22]
With a mighty roar.

His voice rings forth
Like horrendous thunder.

Fate's order is unavoidable;
I cannot hesitate, I must obey.

My body is thin,
Like a piece of thread;

His chain is thick,
Like a man's arm;

He winds the chain round and
Pulls me away, so

It must needs be
That I

Give up the ghost
And die.

The Sa-Ja of the Day and
The Sa-Ja of the Month;

Like a great storm,
They gather up my soul.

'You there, Sa-Ja!
Hold on a bit!

Permit me to take along
Some money for the journey.'

Though I entreat by
Various means,

No Sa-Ja gives ear
To my voice.

Ah! Woe is me!
I am sorrowful;

I am wretched;
I am vexed; and so

I bid farewell
To this world.

Oh,
Wild Aronia,[23]

In ten leagues of
White gleaming sand,

Do not regret
The falling petals;

In the third month of
The newborn year,

And the coming of spring,
You'll blossom forth once again.

But our human existence
If once gone,

When shall it
Come again?

What shall I do?
My heart is pained.

A long, long way to go;
A road of endless journey.

'If you go now,
when shall you return?

When the cock on the painted screen crows,
Shall you come then?

When the boiled red bean in the cupboard sprouts
Shall you come then?'

Ah! Woe is me!
I am sorrowful;

I am wretched;
I am vexed.

I grasp the hands of my
Wife and child

And family
Gathered round me.

I entreat one and all
To help me; and,

Taking hold of myself
I gaze all around.

There sits the medicine pot,
With ginseng and deer horn a'brewing;

Though faithfully trying
To rescue my life,

How can they save
This dying frame?

I have heard
The old man say.

The way to the other world is
Far and away;

But now, on this very day,
When I face this time,

The other world lies
Just outside the front gate.

Though many neighbors gather round,
Which of them can accompany me?

Though many friends gather round,
Which of them can accompany me?

I open the door of
The family shrine,

And bow to the
Old ancestral spirits;[24]

And, bidding a final farewell
To the new ancestral spirits,[25]

I kick open the front door and
Forthwith pass out from the

Four Great Gates.[26]

Holding my coat in hand
And proclaiming the Ch'o-Hon,[27]

I hear the three-letter name[28]
And my sorrow springs forth.

The Sa-Ja of the Day
Grasps my hand;

The Sa-Ja of the Month
Shoves my back;

As they gruffly
Hasten me along,

The high place becomes low and
The low place becomes high.[29]

'You must be hungry;
How about some lunch?

Your feet must be sore;
How about some rest?

Aren't your shoes
In need of repair?'[30]

Though I desperately entreat them
To take some rest,

No Sa-Ja gives ear
To my voice.

With the iron hammer,
They strike my back;

'Quickly, be on your way!
Make haste!

Else we should fail
To be there on time!'

Pushing and driving the
Dead soul along,

They arrive before the gate of
The other world.

Fearsome and dreadful,
Awesome and horrible.

The Sa-Ja of This World is
Na-Du Na-Ch'al;

The Sa-Ja of The Other World is
Na-Du Na-Ch'al.[31]

Their voices are like
The sound of thunder,

And one can judge that
Their clemency is to be paid for.

When I lived on earth,
Fine clothes and good food

Did I myself deny
So that money could be saved;

Therefore even a penny
Can I not depart with.

An empty stomach, too
Did I endure

So that money could be saved;

Therefore even a penny
Can I not depart with.

What shall I do?
Shall I pay them

Or not?
I cannot decide.

Ah! Woe is me!
I am sorrowful.

I remove my clothes
And offer them as payment.

And we forthwith pass through
The Twelve Gates.[32]

Fearsome and dreadful
Awesome and horrible;

The Keeper of the Jail,
Waiting there!

The Keeper of the Dungeon,
Waiting there!

The Ten Kings summon me;

And thereby do I,
The Keeper of the Jail follow.

Taking hold of my self,
I gaze all around;

There,
Sitting before me,
The Ten Kings!

There,
Holding the trial docket before me,

The Judge!

There,
Standing all around,

The torture rack in readiness!

Swords, spears, banners, armaments,
Everywhere hanging in fearful array!

What poor soul would dare not
Bow his mind in fear.

Fearsome and dreadful,
Awesome and horrible.

The Ten Kings
Give the command;

The Jailer,
Hearing the order,

Grasps the prisoner and
Brings him forth.

The prisoner is asked:
'What is your crime . . . ?

(He answers not)

You there! You dog!
Listen here!

Whilst you lived on earth,
What good deed did you?

The principle of being a human
Is to do good deeds.

Did you follow this principle?

Were you loyal
To your country, and

Were you dutiful
To your parents?

Did you maintain good relationships
With your brothers, and

Did you establish a good life
For your home and family?

Did you give food
To the hungry, and

Did you give charity
To the poor?

Did your clothe the naked and
Show mercy to the unfortunates?

Did you build a bridge
Over deep waters,

So that all might pass over?

Did you give water
To the thirsty, and

Did you show mercy on those
Whose throats were parched?

Did you give medicine
To the dying man, and

Did you seek to revive him?

Did you plant melons
By the roadside, and

Did you offer them
To the thirsty traveller?

Did you build a house
In a good place

To benefit the homeless, and

Did you build a large temple
Atop a high mountain,

And offer prayers
To the *San-Shin?*

Did you build a temple
Deep in the mountains, and

Did you give your uneaten rice
To charity?

Did you with chants
Sing praises to the Buddha, and

Did you make offerings to Him?

Did you scandalize
The good name of others, and

Did you cause much grief—
Is your offense not grave?

Is not the sin you committed
Deep and unpardonable?

Off with thee then!
To jail,

In a lackluster Hell!'[33]

'Next, bring in the man of virtue;
Summon he who lived by righteousness!

Be gentle with him, and
Speak to him with kindness.'

(To the condemned prisoner)

'You there! You evil dog!
Take note of this scene!

Behold! Before you stands
A man of virtue!

A man of such merit
Is highly esteemed.

Behold this man of virtue
Who stands before you!

Those evil dogs who have gone before,
Their sins are many;

For them the end was prison
In a murky Hell.

But here is the way
A good man is rewarded.'

And, thereupon
He is taken and asked:

'What is your wish?

All that is your desire
You need but only speak.

Is it your wish to be
A mortal once again, or

Do you seek Paradise?

Is it your wish to go
To the Moonlight World, or

Do you seek
The World of Sunshine?

Is it your wish to be
A servant of Sŏ Wang Mo[34]

And tend the
Fairy Peach Tree, or

Do you seek to be reborn
As the most beautiful man?

And dwell by the side of
The Yo-Ji Pond?

Is it your wish to be
The leader of a million soldiers,

The commander-in-chief,
The most powerful of all; or

Do you seek to be
The one and only son of

A man of untold riches,
And know great wealth and fame?

What is your wish?

All that is your desire
You need but only speak.

Let us then chant Amit'a-bul,
And redeem the dead;

Let us then guide them,
To the Three Precious Ones,[35]

Na-mu Ami-t'a bul.'

'Bring forth the evil woman!'

With harsh and coarse voice
She is asked;

'You there! You evil bitch!
Listen here!

Whilst you lived on earth,
What good deed did you?

To your in-laws[36] and
To your parents,

Were you loyal and dutiful?

To your husband's younger brethren, and
Toward your own younger brethren as well,

Did you establish a firm kinship?

Did you create a congenial homestead, and
Did you respect your husband?

Disloyal and villainous wench!

Woman whose heart is ever changing
Throughout the twelve hours![37]

Speaking lowly of every man;
Yet,

Within his presence,
Ever smiling and cordial.

Evil woman!

Thou who hast accumulated
The worst of sins.

Detestable slut!

Thou who hast committed
Innumerable adulteries.

Damnable bitch!

Thou who hast alienated
True friendships.

Wanton whore!

Thou who hast committed
Sexual transgression.

Foul strumpet!

Thou who hast committed
Countless thefts.

Wicked dame!

Solely occupied with
Evil gossip.

Your sins are many and unpardonable!'

'Guards!
Make way!

I condemn this woman
To the One-Million Hells.[38]

To the Sword Mountain Hell;

To the Hell of Scalding Water;

To the Hell of Ice;

To the Sword Forest Hell;

To the Hell Where Tongues Are Pulled Out;

To the Hell of Poisonous Snakes;

To the Hell of Starvation;

To the Hell of Saws;

To the Hell of Hot Iron Floors;

To the Hell of Utter Darkness.

Na-mu Amit'a bul.

Off with thee then,
To the One-Million Hells!'

'Next, bring in the woman of virtue!

Be gentle with her,
And ask her;

What is your wish?

Pray, tell us,
What is your desire?

Is it your wish to be mortal once again, or
Do you seek Paradise?

Is your desire untold riches, or
Is it fame, fortune and rank?

Would you like to become a man, or
Do you seek lifelong marital bliss?

Do you wish to be a servant of
Sŏ Wang Mo, or

Do you wish to go to the
Lotus Blossom Peak?

Is it your wish to be
The wife of a great lord?

What is your wish?

Pray tell us,
What is your desire?'

When the Eight Angels are called
To guide her to Paradise,

She is addressed thus;

'You there,
Soul-bearing chariot;

Soul-bearing chariot,
Hear what I say!

Whilst you sojourned on earth,
What good deed did you?'

Kneeling on the ground
And folding her hands together,

The soul-bearing chariot
Begins to speak:

'I do hereby confess,
With every measure of truth in my heart.

Brought into this world
From my parents,

I knew not
What was pain; what was happiness.

Perchance I fell gravely ill, and
Found myself before

The Ten Kings.

Oh, Your Majesties,
Give ear to my words!'

'Virtuous thou art,
Yet, unfortunate indeed.'[39]

The scribe is ordered
To enter an inscription;[40]

'Send her on to Paradise!

Good Sa-Ja,[41]
Guide her along the way;

Good sailor,
Mend thee a ship and

Cross over into Paradise.' "

IV.

As in Part III, a graphic description of the Ten Kings is again given, but here the Buddhist names of the Ten Kings are also mentioned, it being understood that in China, Buddhism was fused with the prevalent Taoist belief at the time of its introduction.

1. First is the palace of
   King Chin-Kwang the Great.

   Chŏng-Kwang Bul-I[42]
   Is the Wŏn-Bul.[43]

   To the hapless soul-bearing chariot
   He affords passage over

   The Sword Mountain Hell.

2. In the second palace is
   King Ch'o-kang the Great.

   Yak-Sa Yŏ-Rae.[44]
   Is the Wŏn-Bul.

   To the hapless soul-bearing chariot
   He affords passage over

   The Hell of the Boiling Hot Bath.

3. In the third palace lives
   King Song-Je the Great.

   Hyŏn-Gup Ch'un Bul[45]
   Is the Wŏn-Bul.

   To the hapless soul-bearing chariot
   He affords passage over

   The Hell of Ice.

4. In the fourth palace lives
   King O-Gwan the Great.

   Amit'a Bul-i
   Is the Wŏn-Bul.

   To the hapless soul-bearing chariot
   He affords passage over

   The Sword Forest Hell.

5. In the fifth palace is
   King Yŏm-Na the Great

   Chi-Jang Bo-Sal
   Is the Wŏn-Bul.

   To the hapless soul-bearing chariot
   He affords passage over

   The Hell Where Tongues Are Torn Out.

6. In the sixth palace is
   King Pyŏn-Sŏng the Great.

   Taese-Ji Bo-Sal
   Is the Wŏn-Bul.

   To the hapless soul-bearing chariot
   He affords passage over

   The Hell of Venomous Snakes.

7. In the seventh palace is
   King T'ae-San the Great.

   Kwan-Ŭm Bo-Sal[48]
   Is the Wŏn-Bul.

   To the hapless soul-bearing chariot
   He affords passage over

   The Hell of Grinding Stones.

8. In the eighth palace is
   King P'Yŏng-Dŭng the Great.

   Nosana Bul-i,[49]
   Is the Wŏn-Bul.

   To the hapless soul-bearing chariot
   He affords passage over

   The Hell of Cutting Saws.

9. In the ninth palace is
   King To-Shi the Great.

   Ya-Kwang Bo-Sal[50]
   Is the Wŏn-Bul.

   To the hapless soul-bearing chariot
   He affords passage over

   The Hell of Iron Beds.

10. In the tenth palace is
    King Chŏ-Yu the Great.

    Sŏk-Ka Yŏ-Rae[51]
    Is the Wŏn-Bul.

    To the hapless soul-bearing chariot
    He affords passage over

    The Hell of Utter Darkness.

And thus we come round
To Paradise!

The rivers of this world[52]
Are thirty-three in number;

The rivers of that world[53]
Are thirty-three in number;

Three are ninety-nine rivers[54]
To cross.

For the deep water,
We make a bridge;[55]

For the shallow water
We make a bridge;

To cross the deep water,
We board a ship;

To cross the shallow water,
We board a ship.

Behold!
We come 'round to Paradise!

And with a pair of bluebirds
Holding a flag,

Behold!
We enter into Paradise!

V.

Herein, Paradise is vividly portrayed in accordance with the O-bang cosmology that associates the "Five Directions" of East, South, West, North and Center with the colors Blue, Red, White, Black and Yellow, respectively, and are coordinated, in turn, with the "Five Elements,"[56] the "Five Aspects of Wisdom," the "Five Great Ones," and the "Five Aggregates."

1. White = water, the light-path of the mirror-like wisdom (the *Vajra-Sattva* esoterically as a reflex of *Akshobhya*), the aggregate of consciousness;
2. Yellow = earth, the light-path of the wisdom of equality (the *Ratna-Sambhava*), the aggregate of touch;
3. Red = fire, the light-path of the discriminative wisdom (the *Amitabha*), the aggregate of feelings;
4. Black[57] = air, the light-path of the all-performing wisdom (the *Amogha-Siddhi*), the aggregate of volition;
5. Blue = ether, the light-path of the wisdom of perfected actions (the *Vairochana*), the aggregate of matter.[58]

And further, again from the *Tibetan Book of the Dead*:[59]

> *May the ethereal elements not rise up as enemies;*
> *May it come that we shall see the Realm of the Blue Buddha.*
>
> *May the watery elements not rise up as enemies;*
> *May it come that we shall see the Realm of the White Buddha.*
>
> *May the earthy elements nor rise up as enemies;*
> *May it come that we shall see the Realm of the Yellow Buddha.*
>
> *May the fiery elements not rise up as enemies;*
> *May it come that we shall see the Realm of the Red Buddha.*
>
> *May the airy elements not rise up as enemies;*
> *May it come that we shall see the Realm of the Green Buddha.*
>
> *May the elements of the rainbow colour not rise up as enemies;*
> *May it come that all the Realms of the Buddhas will be seen.*

✤ ✤

1. Look there
    To the East!

    To the East dwells
    The Blue General.

    There lies
    The Blue-Glass World.[60]

    Place the Blue Candle in
    The Blue Lantern.

    Light the Candle in
    The Blue-Fire Lantern.

    Hang the Lantern on
    The Blue-Dragon Gate,

    And guide her[61] on the road
    To Paradise.

2. Look there,
    To the South!

    To the South dwells
    The Red General.

    There lies
    The Red-Glass World.

    Place the Red Candle in
    The Red Lantern,

    Light the candle in
    The Red-Fire Lantern,

    Hang the Lantern on
    The Red-Phoenix Gate,

    And guide her on the road
    To Paradise.

3. Look there
   To the West!

   To the West dwells
   The White General.

   There lies
   The White-Glass World.

   Place the White Candle in
   The White Lantern,

   Light the Candle in
   The White-Fire Lantern,

   Hang the Lantern on
   The White-Tiger Gate,

   And guide her on the road
   To Paradise.

4. Look there
   To the North!

   To the North dwells
   The Black General.

   There lies
   The Black-Glass World.

   Place the Black Candle in
   The Black Lantern,

   Light the Candle in
   The Black-Fire Lantern,

   Hang the Lantern on
   The Black-Tortoise Gate,
   And guide her on the road
   To Paradise.

5. Look there,
   To the Center!

   In the Center dwells
   The Yellow General.

   There lies
   The Yellow-Glass World.

   Place the Yellow Candle in
   The Yellow Lantern,

   Light the Candle in
   The Yellow-Fire Lantern,

   Hang the Lantern verily on
   Dead Center,

   And guide her on the road
   To Paradise.

   And with a pair of bluebirds
   Holding a flag,

   Behold!
   We enter into Paradise!

VI.

Boating Song

The melody and rhythm of the Mu-ga is changed here.

The rhythm is in free-style and the melody is sung in a sorrowful tone while the devotees weep, as this is the final departure of the soul. It is here that a small boat, the *Prajna* Dragon Boat, here referred to by the Mudang as the "Dragon Phoenix Boat," gaily decorated with paper flowers and paper images, symbolic of the departed, which is suspended from strips of colored material strung across the ritual area, begins to move very gradually across the area from one end to the other. This is done by means of cords or wires attached to the boat which are slowly pulled.

1. "Ah-
   Uh-ya-di-yuh-

   Uh-gi-di-yuh-
   Uh, uh-,

   Uh-gi-ya-di-yuh,
   Ch'a.[62]

   The boat is leaving—

   Ten-thousand acres of sea—

   In a great expanse of water—

   A small boat,
   Like a leaf,

   Floating on the river.

   The soul-bearing chariot
   Rides on the boat—

The southeast wind[63]
Is a fair wind indeed—

Behold
We enter into Paradise!

2. *Uh-gi-yuh-di-uh*
    Uh-gi-yuh-di-uh,

    Uh-ya-di-ya
    Uh-ya-di-ya,

    Ch'a
    Ch'a!

    Anchors aweigh! and
    The sound of the oars

    Breaks my liver in two![64]

3. *Uh-ya-di-ya,*
    Uh-ya-di-ya,

    Uh-ya-di-ya; ch'a, ch'a!
    Ch'a, ch'a

    Ten-thousand acres of sea;

    A great expanse of water
    The moon shines so brightly;

    Can I not help think of
    My wife and child?

4. *Uh-yuh-di-yuh,*
   Uh-kŏ-ya-di-ya,

   I am going,
   I am going;

   I am on the road
   From whence I came.

   Were is the road
   From whence I came?

   I am on the road
   To Paradise.

   Think not of your wife,
   Think not of your child,

   Think not of your kinfolk either;

   I am on the road
   To Paradise.

5. Hear me,
   Men of this world!

   Whilst you sojourn
   On this earth,

   You too
   May go my way.

   I am going,
   I am going;

   I am on the road
   To Paradise.

Hear me,
Men of this world!

Thou of covetous deeds
Multifold,

Look upon me and
Mend thy ways;

Thou of unrighteous deeds
Multifold,

Look upon me and
Mend thy ways;

Thou who hast committed thefts
Multifold,

Look upon me and
Mend thy ways.

Men of this world,
I pray you

Again and again;
Do good deeds and

The road of afterlife
Shall be smooth.

I am going,
I am going;

(sobbing) *Euh, euh, euh*!

I am on the road
To Paradise.

If you go now,
When shall you return?

I am on the road
Of no return.

And with a pair of bluebirds
Holding a flag,

I am on the road
To Reincarnation.

6. *Uh-ya-di-ya,*
   Uh-ya-di-ya.

   The sound of the oars
   Breaks my liver in two!

   Hear me, good sailors!
   Mend thee a ship;

   To the Western Paradise,
   The West Country,[65]

   I ride on the
   Dragon-Phoenix Boat.

   Wait!
   We cannot go yet!

   Why do you hurry me so?

   But the tide is in,
   And the boat is turning round . . ."

Epilogue

"Owing to the virtue of
My descendants,

Owing to the sincerity of
My kinsfolk,

I return to Paradise.

And by virtue of
The sincere and earnest supplications

Of this Mudang,
Whose fame is known far and wide,

I return to Paradise."

The drums, gongs and cymbals play very loudly, and the Mudang dances.

Notes

1. The "Bridge" in the title refers to a bridge in the city of P'yŏngyang, the capital of P'yŏng-an Province. When a person died, his bier was carried across this bridge on the way to the burial grounds. The female members of the funeral cortege were, in accordance with tradition, forbidden to cross the bridge and enter the burial grounds during the funeral rites, and so they were compelled to bid farewell to the deceased at the entrance to the bridge, and it was here that the ritual for the safe and peaceful passage of the soul into Paradise was held. It was also held as a memorial ceremony for the dead. Symbolically, the bridge also represented the crossing over from this world into the next.

2. The Ten Kings of Hell, who sit in judgement of the departed soul and, according to Huhm (ibid., pp. 95-6) ". . . who assess the deeds of the dead while living in this world, during the first three years of death—that is, on the first seventh day, the second seventh day, the third seventh day, the fourth seventh day, the fifth seventh day, the sixth seventh day, the

seventh seventh day, the first hundredth day, the first anniversary, the second anniversary, the third anniversary—guide the dead, and are the examiners in charting the road to the other world for the dead as the Chinogwi Kut (the counterpart of the *Shi-Wang Kut* which is performed in the Seoul area and in Kyŏnggi Province) is performed for paving the road to the other world."

3. Sk: *Amitabha Buddha, Amitadha Buddha,* or *Amitayus Buddha.* According to the *Sukhavaricyuha Sutra,* he was an emperor before attaining Buddhahood. When enlightened by the *Bodhisattva Avalokitesvara,* he became a monk seeking Buddhahood. During his ascetic life, he made forty-eight vows. He also vowed that he would build a majestic paradise where those who call upon his name may dwell.

4. The boat that sails to Nirvana, otherwise known as the *"Prajna* Dragon Ship."

5. A place of great eternal happiness.

6. For a more detailed treatment of the Five Elements theory, see *The Tibetan Book of the Dead,* compiled and edited by W.Y. Evans-Wentz, Oxford University Press, London, 1971-4, pp. 8-10, Chap. IV, "The Esoteric Significance of the Five Elements."

7. *Songs from the Bengali,* "In Praise of Krishna." Translated by Edw. C. Dimcock, Jr. & Denise Leverton, Doubleday & Co., Inc., New York, 1967.

8. The philosophy of the cycle of years is believed to have been introduced into Korea during the early years of the Three Kingdoms (Shilla, Paekche and Koguryo) period (c. 37 B.C.-935 A.D.) from neighboring China.

9. Called *"Hwan-Kap"* in Korean, meaning "returning to *Kap,"* the first symbol of "Heaven."

10. According to Buddhist lore, the monkey was the ninth of twelve animals that hurried to the bedside of the dying Buddha to pay homage. First came the rat, then the cow, the tiger, rabbit, snake, horse, sheep, monkey, chicken, dog, and finally the pig. Thereafter, a year was named for each in order of this succession. The twelve animals and what they symbolize are said to influence the year and the personality and character of those born in that period.

11. A general term, not to be thought of as exclusively pertaining to the Great Wall of China.

12. The "Milky Way."

13. During the Yi Dynasty (1392-1910 A.D.), the government maintained various relay stations and outposts throughout the countryside. Attached to the station were government-owned rice fields whose yields were utilized for the purpose of feeding the messengers, soldiers and horses that were either posted at or passed through the station.

14. Sk: *Tathagata*.

15. The God *Ch'il-Sŏng*.

16. The God *Chesŏk*.

17. Ginseng is a medicinal herb; powdered deer horn is believed to have medicinal as well as aphrodisiacal powers.

18. *San-Shin*.

19. In a description of that section of the ritual known as the *Saja Samsŏng* of the *Chinogwi Kut* of Seoul and Kyŏnggi Province, Huhm (op. cit., p. 96) states the following:

> In this *saja kŏri* there are many interesting theatrical scenes such as tearing in two a piece of white hempen cloth which symbolizes the parting of relations between the *kut*-performing family and the departed; and mimicking the messengers taking the departed with them. The members of the *kut*-performing family give travel money to the messengers by way of placating them, and the messengers make threats with theatrical gestures.

20. Op. cit., p. 69.

21. Sometimes referred to as the "God of Hell."

22. Generally, personal names in Korea are comprised of three separate Chinese letters.

23. A wild pink rose.

24. In Korea, prior to setting out on a long journey, it was the custom to bow before the shrine of one's ancestors.

25. Those ancestors who have died more recently.

26. In ancient times, each city had four main gates, one each located at the north, south, east and west.

27. Immediately upon expiration, a mourner takes the coat of the de-

ceased out into the yard and twirls it around in the air, at the same time bellowing forth the deceased's name and address, after which it is cast up onto the roof. This also serves as a notice to the neighborhood that death has come.

28. Most Korean names consist of three Chinese characters.

29. An indication that he is being turned head over heels as he travels through the air.

30. In former times, straw sandals were worn which were not durable for journeys covering long distances.

31. Sk: *Yak-Sa.*

32. The "Other World," implying a very large palace or house.

33. The term "Hell" represents a Chinese compound (*Chi-Ok* in Korean) which literally translates as "Ground Prison."

34. A legendary fairy of China who possessed a pond called "*Yo-Ji*" beside which flowered a wondrous peach tree that blossomed once every 3,000 years. Consequently, those who partook of the peach were said to live 3,000 years.

35. Also known as the "Triple Treasure": Buddha, Dharma and Sangha.

36. In accordance with Confucian ethics, a wife must consider her husband's family before her own.

37. In ancient times, the day was divided into twelve hours.

38. In Buddhism, there are ten hells; however, those mentioned here are Musok derivations of the original Buddhist names.

39. In Korean folk belief, as of course elsewhere, long life is considered most fortunate and death resulting from sickness or accident a great misfortune.

40. Describing the woman's good deeds.

41. The Sa-Ja of Mercifulness.

42. Sk: *Dipamkara* ("The Buddha of Eternal Light").

43. The particular Buddha we pray to for a certain purpose.

44. Sk: *Bhaisajyaguru-Vaidurya* ("The Master of Medicine": "The Healing Buddha").

45. Sk: *Bhadra-Kalpa* ("The Buddha of Countless Wisdom").

46. Sk: *Ksitigarbha Bodhisattva.*

47. Sk: *Mahasthamaprapta.*

48. Sk: *Avalokitesvara* (the "Bodhisattva of Mercy").

49. Sk: *Vairocana.*

50. The *Ya-Kwang Bodhisattva.*

51. Sk: *Tathagata.*

52. From earth to the entrance of the "Judgement World."

53. From the "Judgement World" to Paradise.

54. Thirty-three rivers are unaccounted for, their mention being omitted in the song.

55. In a description of that section of the ritual known as the *Kilgarugi* (parting roads) of the *Chinogwi Kut* of Seoul and Kyŏnggi Province, Huhm (op. cit, p. 98) states the following:

> This (*Kilgarugi*) is said to mean parting of life and bridges of the ten kings. Cotton cloth represents the road from this world to the other world. Hempen cloth represents the entrance to the other world. It is also said that cotton cloth represents bridges on the road to the other world and hempen cloth the bridges of the ten kings.
>
> Cotton cloth and hempen cloth are cut into two strips of various length: 12 feet long by the traditional Korean measuring rod for a departed male, 9 feet long for a departed female, and 7 feet long for a departed unmarried boy or unmarried girl.
>
> The four corner ends of a piece of cotton cloth or hempen cloth are held by four people. Both end sides of the cloth are cut open a bit in the middle, and amid the playing of *tang'ak* (2/4) music with *changgo* and *chegŭm,* the shaman cuts the cloth by pushing her body from one cut end to the other cut end (symbolizing the parting of the deceased from the mourners). When cutting the cotton cloth the shaman holds a *chegŭm* in either hand with a hempen cloth strip draped around the waist. When cutting hempen cloth, the shaman holds a sword in either hand.

56. In accordance with Buddhist philosophy.

57. In *The Tibetan Book of the Dead* (op. cit., p. 202, Verse No. 10), the color used here is Green.

58. Ibid., p. xviii.

59. Ibid., p. 202, Verse No. 10.

60. In ancient times, glass was valued as a precious jewel.

61. The soul of the virtuous woman.

62. A rowing chant.

63. A mild spring wind, good for sailing.

64. We in the Western world more often refer to the heart in such instances.

65. Nirvana.

Kang Pu-Ja, a hereditary *Mudang*, chants a Buddhist invocation for the peace and good fortune of the family during the *Chesŏk Kut* ("The Ritual for the God Chesŏk") during a performance of the *Sshikkim Kut* ("Spirit-cleansing Rite") from Chŏlla Province. (photo: Kim Su-nam)

3. The Ritual Song of the God Chesŏk

Introduction

The Mudang appears in the trappings of a Buddhist monk, wearing a pointed hood, cloak and red mantle over one shoulder. Meat and fish are absent from the table of offerings in conformance with Buddhist vegetarian doctrine; however, this may be a vestige of ancient farming rituals in Korea that preceded the advent of Buddhism, but which present-day Mudangs mistake for Buddhist practice. Even the name *Chesŏk* itself may be of Korean Musok origin, different from that of the Buddhist *Chesŏk (Sakrodevendre),* but there is no evidence to substantiate this.[1]

Prologue

> "Here ye, here ye,
> One and all!
>
> The Ritual of Princess A-Wang and Yŏ-Yŏng[2]
> Is about to be held."

The drum and flute play in a slow rippling rhythm, and the Mudang then sings:

> "Today,
> At this time
>
> I begin this song;
>
> No mean song
> This.

'Tis the song of
Sakyamuni's blessing, and

The God Chesŏk.

From whence cometh
The God Chesŏk?

From the very highest place of
The Thirty-Three Heavens,[3]

Wherein one descends
The Twenty-Eight Stars;[4]

The place from whence
The moon and sun doth rise, and

The place where
The sun's rays and the moonbeams set.

Wind and clouds,
Fog and ice,

Are all dispersed
In this,

The home of Chesŏk."

I.

"Nine young noblemen from nine places,
Twelve young noblemen from twelve places,

To the Sŏng-Kyŏng Capital,[5]
To the Han-Yang Capital,[6]

They did journey
The Kwa-Gŏ to receive.[7]

But, alas! They did blunder, and
Returning their way,

A whisper overheard
In soft-spoken words:

'The beloved daughter of
Chesŏk . . .

Her beauty, ah 'tis most rare,'
The rumor doth say,

'Her talent, ah 'tis most notable,'
The rumor doth say.

'Her lack, ah 'tis but naught,'
The rumor doth say.

'Her spirit, ah 'tis most noble,'
The rumor doth say.

'Her nature, ah 'tis most gentle,'
The rumor doth say.

Before the gate of
Chesŏk,

Three years sitting,
Three years standing,

Three years lying,
They;

And if three years thus thrice counted are,
All tallied they be nine.

For naught but her,
Gave they of themselves;

Yea, a bud of her feature even,
Can they see not.

Yea, a mark of her footprint even,
Can they see not.

Their vigor having all been spent,
Their pulse now doth languish;

Alas . . .
Once again,

They do take up
Their homeward journey."

II.

The drum and flute are joined by the large gong and oboe in
ensemble; there is also a melodic and rhythmic change to a quicker
tempo.

"Down from the mountain,
Cometh there a monk;

Down from the mountain,
This monk he doth descend.

Take heed of this monk,
His aspect note with care;

Take heed of this monk,
His accessories note with care.

Pockmarked and black
Is his face,

Like the black sesame;

Pockmarked and black
Is his face,

Like the porous stone.

Were he to be thrown
From a lofty mountain cliff,

And roll down to the very bottom . . .

His body no impairment
Would know, and

His composure wholly unmoved
Would be.

Gazing upward,
The multifold peak;

Peering downward,
The white sand below.

Pines and cedars
Old and bent,

Row upon row,
Trees of endless sort;

A dense forest
Thick with trees.

Wild grape and berry vines,
Climbing everywhere;

Everywhere in profusion,
Hanging in the air.

Winding, ever winding,
Along the ever bending way;

Carefree, ever carefree,
This monk he doth descend.

Slowly, ever slowly,
He sways from side to side;

Carefree, ever carefree,
This monk he doth descend.

Slowly, ever slowly,
He sways from side to side;

Carefree, ever carefree,
This monk he doth descend.

Take heed of his raiment;
Ah, 'tis most splendid indeed!

How fine and straight his hat
Doth sit upon his head;

From strands of *song-nak* multifold,[8]
This way and that 'tis woven.

A silver-colored frock
Of cotton he doth wear, and

A red sash tightly bound
'Cross his body he doth bare.

A small knife sheathed
In a nickel case

Peers dangling 'neath his cloak;
'Tis from his blouse strings

It doth hang
By a lengthy cord suspended.

There 'cross his back,
A rucksack he doth carry; and

'Cross his shoulders
Left and right,

Of azure blue and precious white,
And of pure gold brocaded,

A mantle he doth wear, of which
His frame it doth envelop.

A rosary of beads one-hundred and eight[9]
Around his neck is hung, and

Unto his wrist a bracelet clings where
Polished nuts are strung.[10]

'Round his shoulder to the left,
A mental gong is slung;[11]

In his hand doth he hold forth,
Which from the root as yet uncut,

The six-ringed staff[12] that hath been from
The Circled Bamboo of So-Sang formed.[13]

Prodding the ground
As he ambles along,

"T'ang, t'ang,
T'ang, t'ang,"[14]

His staff the path doth tap,
From whence the red stones emerge.

Carefree, ever carefree,
This monk he doth descend

'Greetings,
Young noblemen!

From whence cometh thee,
That thou beith so distraught?'

'Ah yes
Ah yes . . .

To the Han-Yang Capital
We did journey,

The Kwa-Gŏ to receive.

But, alas! We did blunder, and
Returning our way,

A whisper overheard we
In soft-spoken words:

'The beloved daughter of
Chesŏk . . .

Her beauty, ah 'tis most rare,'
The rumor doth say.

'Her talent, ah 'tis most notable,'
The rumor doth say.

'Her nature, ah 'tis most gentle,'
The rumor doth say.

'Before the gate of
Chesŏk,

Three years sitting,
Three years standing,

Three years lying,
We;

And if three years thus thrice counted are,
All tallied they be nine.

Yea, a bud of her feature even,
Can we see not;

Yea, a trace of her shadow even,
Can we see not;

Yea, a mark of her footprint even,
Can we see not,

Alas . . .
Once again,

We did taketh up
Our homeward journey.'

'Young noblemen,
Know thee then

Where thou hast
Yon maiden failed to see,

This monk shall not.'

'Noble men
Such as we,

Three years thrice
Have we thus waited;

Yea, a bud of her feature even,
Can we not see.

How be it then
A lowly monk such as thou,[15]

The beloved daughter of
Chesŏk

Doth claim he can but see!'

'If the beloved daughter of
Chesŏk

This so-sŭng-i[16]
Can but see,

You, the twelve young scholars,
You, the twelve young noblemen.

His novitiate's
Shall be.

Yet,
Without seeing her,

Should so-s ng-i
Return,

He will the blood take from his breast,
Young noblemen,

And offer it to thee.'

Thereby, unto each other's blouse strings
A knot do they thus tie;[17]

Then turning about without a word,
And scurrying away,

The monk doth before
The gate of Chesŏk arrive

Take heed of this house;
Ah, 'tis most elegant indeed!

The master's chambers
Are thirty-three in number;

And at the four corners
The little wind bells doth hang.[18]

To the southeast wind they sway,
And the tinkling sound is heard;

"Chaeng-Kŭ-rŏng,
Chaeng-Kŭ-rŏng,"[19]

The tinkling sound is heard,

Straight and square,
The servants' quarters stand:

There, with servant and slave,
Doth every chamber abound.

Take heed of this house;
Ah, 'tis most elegant indeed!

Should flowers and trees, therefore,
In great abundance not abound?

In the outer garden,
Afore the main gate;

What flower and tree is it
That dwelleth there?

Huge and ancient pines,
Pines as flat as a table;

And the bush-shaped pine.

Their winding trunks be as like
Blue and black dragons ascending.

The black phoenix, the red phoenix
The indigo phoenix and the blue phoenix;

There, birds of every sort
Are singing.

Look to the East!

The plantain and
The green paulownia,[20]

The bamboo and
The tree peony,

The red azalea and
The flowering peony;

Ten-thousand kinds of flowers,
In full blossom everywhere.

Look to the South!

The apricot, the peach, and
The rose;

The winter plum blossom
That makes all seasons spring.

Deep golden azaleas, and
The wild aronia;

A pageant of beautiful flowers,
In full blossom everywhere.

Look to the West!

The fragrant smell of cedar,
The loftily towering fir.

In the deep blue forest,
A six-cornered pavilion;[21]

It stands as it were
A flying form.

Look to the North!

A lake filled with lotus blossoms,
Pink lotus, white lotus;

All the stems bearing forth blossoms
That blush at the sight of man.[22]

Goldfish large as serving plates
Frolic among the ripples;

Yea, though Pyŏn-San's beauty[23]
Be famed above all,

It cannot equal
That of this house.

The song-nak hat and cotton frock
Doth he now put off;

On the bough of the flat pine
Now worn with age,

They are hung.

The rucksack also
Doth he now put off;

On the bough of
The great pine,

It, too, is hung.

Gazing 'round the
Twelve Gates . . .

There, the fish locks,[24]
Each and every one,

That bind every door;

Surely,
They're most tightly secured.

'Ah,
Now let me see . . .

What sutra[25] is it fitting then,
That I should chant?

Shall it be the
Chŏng-Wŏl Kyŏng?[26]

For father,
The *Pŏp-Hwa Kyŏng*;[27]

For the conjugal husband and wife,
The *In-Nyŏn Kyŏng*,[28]

For the descendants,
The *Ae-Jŏng Kyŏng*;[29]

For the fraternal brothers and sisters,
The *U-Ae Kyŏng*;[30]

For the kinship,
The *Hwa-Nok Kyŏng*[31]

And when the twelve sutra
Had all been sung,

The Twelve Gates,
With but scarcely a sound,

Here, "*tŏng, t'ŏng*,"
There, "*tŏng, t'ŏng*,"[32]

Of their very own will,
Do fling open wide.

Entering the First Gate,
He strikes the *mok-t'ak*;[33]

"Tu-dŭ-rak,
Tak, tak"[34]

'So-sŭng-i salutes thee!

The monk of Ch'ŏng-Ke Temple
In Ch'ŏng-Ke Mountain.

On this, the 15th day of
The first month,

Doth come to beg the sacrificial rice
For the offering.'

But no answer whatever
Doth come from within,

And not a sign of life
Is to be seen at all.

Entering the Second Gate,
He strikes the mok-t'ak:

*"Tu-dŭ-rak,
Tak, tak!"*

'So-sŭng-i salutes thee!

The monk of Ch'ŏng-Ke Temple
In Ch'ŏng-Ke Mountain,

On this, the 15th day of
The first month,

Doth come to beg the sacrificial rice
For the offering.'

But no answer whatever
Doth come from within.

And not a sign of life
Is to be seen at all.

Entering the Third Gate,
The Fourth and the Fifth . . .

Entering the Middle Gate,
Entering the Inner Gate[35] . . .

And thereby,

Through all the gates
Having thus passed . . .

"Tu-dŭ-rak,
Tak, tak!"

'So-sŭng-i salutes thee!

On this, the 15th day of
The first month,

I do come to beg the sacrificial rice
For the offering.

If it be much,
Let it three bags be;

If it be little,
Let it three scoops be;
I pray thee
But a small offering.

The monk of Ch'ŏng-Ke Temple
In Ch'ŏng-Ke Mountain I be

The mountain o'er which I pass
Is only the famous mountain;

The river o'er which I cross
Is only the Silver River;[36]

The temple which I seek
Is only the great temple;

Such a monk am I.'

The beloved daughter of
Chesŏk,

The mok-t'ak sound doth hear;

'Sŏn-san-kŭm-a! [37]

Go and see who it is
That cometh here!

Hu-san-kŭm-a! [38]

Go and see who it is
That cometh here!

Neither crow nor magpie
Nay, nor any flying creature that be,

May this place enter.

Nay, nor any crawling creature either,
May these grounds defile.

The sound of a human, then;
How can it be!

The sound of a monk, then;
How can it be!'

'The rice for the morning sacrifice
Is nought;

So do I in the evening cometh,
The offering to beg.

The rice for the evening sacrifice
Is nought;

So do I in the morning cometh,
The offering to beg.'

The beloved daughter of
Chesŏk,

Thereby doth speak:

'My father's away,
The nation's affair to tend;

My mother's beyond the mountain afar,
The flower's loveliness to view;

My brothers nine to Seoul have hastened,
The capital's work to be done;

Of any man thereby,
This house doth vacant be.

What manner of speech is this,
That thou dost cometh,

The sacrificial rice to plead!'

The monk who seeketh offerings
Did thereupon reply:

'Were thy mother at home,
The pile of rice sheaves

Afore the house
She wouldst offer;

Were thy brothers nine at home,
The pile of rice sheaves

To the side of the house,
They wouldst offer.

If it be much,
Let it three bags be;

If it be little,
Let it three scoops be;

And if such be not thy desire,
One handful, two handfuls then . . .'

The beloved daughter of
Chesŏk,

Hearing these words,

'Aga toong toong,[39]
Sŏn-san-kŭm-a!

Fetch you the offering!'

'The offering brought by
Sŏn-san-kŭm-a,

The smell of fish
Doth bear;

Indeed, such a paltry amount
I cannot receive!'

'Aga toong-toong
Hu-san-kŭm-a!

Fetch you the offering!'

'The offering brought by
Hu-san-kŭm-a,

The smell of meat
Doth bear;

Indeed, such a paltry amount
I cannot receive!'

And then did the monk
Speak thusly;

'Whatever the amount
Be it great or small,

Yonder stands a maiden
Who need but offer little at all!'

The beloved daughter of
Chesŏk,

To the chamber
Doth retire.

Her tresses, long and beautiful,
Are like the sheaves of hemp;

Down through them ever gently,
Her comb she slowly draws.

A delicate ribbon of silk,
Her braid's end it doth grasp;[40]

So slightly is it tied thereon,
So subtly are its patterns formed.

The lovely braid is tucked inside
The back of her skirt;

Tis of the finest Hansan ramie cloth,[41] and
Pleats tightly at the waist.

Her double-breasted blouse is made
From silk of golden yellow;

The blouse strings doth she thereupon
A bow into unite.

Of plain silk, she doth,
Her many-layered garments adorn;

Of the very finest silk, she doth,
Her pantaloons adorn.

Her pŏ-sŏn[42] are like
The cucumber seed,

And with flowers
Are her leather shoes embroidered;

"*Jal-jal*,"[43] she goes,
Scuffling along.

Taking father's silver rice bowl cover, and
Washing it with clear water;

Taking father's most precious
White ground sparkling rice;

With Sŏn-san-kŭm-a to the fore, and
With Hu-san-kŭm-a to the rear,

Standing before the monk, she doth
The sacrificial rice offer.

Look here!

Say now,

What do you think
That monk did!

The offered rice
He taketh not;

But, instead,
The maiden's wrist doth grasp.

'Ah! What an insolent fellow,
This monk!

Thou art a monk out of the mountain;
A monk out of water![44]

Is the manner of all monks
As such?

If mother were here,
By a very large knife

A dead monk you'd be!

If father were here,
By a glowing red knife—

A dead monk you'd be!

If my brothers nine were here,
By a hay-cutting knife—

A dead monk you'd be!

That monk;
Begone with him!'

(The tempo of the drum quickens)

"'This monk,' 'That monk,'
Speak of me not;

Take me not for a
Streetwalking mendicant,

Begging alms afore
The wicket gate.[45]

The mountain o'er which I pass
Is only the sacred mountain;

The river o'er which I cross
Is only the Silver River;

The temple which I seek
Is only the great temple;

Such a monk am I!"

'Monk, oh monk,
Thou head-shaven monk!

What rubbish is this;
Thine offering take and begone!'

Take ye heed of this
Alms-begging monk;

In a bottomless sack
He doth the offering receive,

And thus do all the grains therein
Fall unto the ground.

'Sŏn-san-kŭm-a!

Hu-san-kŭm-a!

Fetch thee the brush, and
Sweep it up for him;

Fetch thee the winnower, and
Winnow it for him.'

And then did the monk say:

'The Buddha in our temple,
A supreme being of miraculous virtue doth be;

The rice that is swept and winnowed,
Defiled and unclean doth be;

To the Buddha
It cannot be offered.

Go thee up to the
Mountain yonder, and

Cut thee off a branch from the
Chinese juniper tree.[46]

Fashion for thyself
A pair of chopsticks from it,

Not unlike those of
Silver and brass,[47]

And from the yard lift thee up
The scattered rice,

Grain by grain.'

The beloved daughter of
Chesŏk,

The Chinese juniper branch
Doth cut and bring;

From it she doth
A pair of chopsticks fashion,

Not unlike those of
Sliver and brass, and

From the yard doth she lift
The scattered rice.

Grain by grain.

Then did the monk also from the yard lift up
The scattered rice,

Grain by grain.

The beloved daughter of
Chesŏk,

With a pair of chopsticks she doth,
From the ground the rice lift; and

Whilst gathering rice from here and there,
A mild wind from the southeast blew.

Then did the hem of
The monk's frock, and

The hem of
The beloved daughter's skirt.

One unto another,
Become entwined.

And thus did it come to pass,
Whilst gathering up the grains of rice,

That the sun did set in the west mountain,
And twilight was upon them.

And thus,
Did the alms-seeking monk say:

'Maiden, oh thou maiden,
O' beloved and beautiful daughter,

Allow me to pass
But a night;

Really, how many days
Is but a night?'

'This house of any man
Doth vacant be;

To pass but a night, thou sayest?

Most assuredly not!

If thou dost
To the uppermost place ascend,

The Mountain God Shrine
Thou shalt find;

If thou dost
To the lower place descend,

The school house
Thou shalt find.'

'In the Mountain Spirit Shrine,
I cannot sleep;

In the school house
There's the echo of recitation;

To such a noisy sound,
I cannot sleep.

Allow me to pass
But a night;

Really, how many days
Is but a night?'

The beloved daughter of
Chesŏk,

Alas,
What's to be done;

To father's room
He is guided.

'From stale tobacco
It doth reek;

I cannot sleep here.'

To mother's room
He is guided.

'From menstrual blood
It doth reek;

I cannot sleep here.'

To brother's room
He is guided.

'From the sound of recitation
It doth echo;

I cannot sleep here.'

The beloved and beautiful daughter,
Alas, what's to be done;

To the place apart,
Wherein her chamber lies

He is guided.

There, the fragrance of a lovely maid
Is filled with everywhere.

'This chamber, this room,
Whereof dost thou heretofore not speak?

To every place save this,
Whereof dost thou guide me?'

In the place apart is seated
The alms-seeking monk.

The song-nak hat and cotton frock
Doth he now put off;

The six-ringed staff
Is laid nearby, and

The metal gong
On the floor is placed.

The alms-seeking monk,
Here at this spot,

With calmness and equanimity,
Doth he be seated.

A distance far apart;

Between them,
In the center of the room,

There, filled with water,
Lies the large metal gong.

The six-ringed staff,
Lengthwise is placed;

Between them it doth
A boundary clearly form.

The cotton frock like
A curtain is hung;

Between them it doth
A boundary clearly form.

And thus, it came to pass
That sleep fell upon them.

At the first watch,[48]
She did come upon a dream;

Three precious jewels
Doth enter to her bosom.

At the second watch,
She did come upon a dream;

In the upper field,
Ordinary rice hath she planted.

At the third watch,
She did come upon a dream;

A blue crane, a white crane
Doth fly into the room,

Hither and thither,
Each other 'round and round!

And thus, it came to pass
That the night did end;

In the eastern sky the rising sun,
Brightening all round.

'O,' beloved daughter of Chesŏk,
How is it that
Sleep is yet upon you?

Quickly, quickly,
Awake thee from slumber!'

In such a way did
The alms-seeking monk

Wake her from sleep.

The beloved daughter of
Chesŏk,

Her eyes doth open, and
She waketh from slumber,

The night has ended,
The day becomes bright.

And thus,
Did the alms-seeking monk say:

'What dream hath thou dreamt?

Its message
Do I hereby offer:

The three precious jewels,
Which thou hast embraced,

Shall be three sons together,
Which thou shalt conceive.

The glutinous rice in the
Upper field planted, and

The ordinary rice in the
Lower field planted,

The food of all humankind
They shall thus be.

The blue crane, the white crane,
That doth 'round each other fly,

Verily, the blue and white crane,
Thy life's protector shall be.'

Then, a frock made of arrowroot,
To the maid he doth offer:

'Take ye this
And after a day,

When with trouble
Thou art beset,

This frock but place before you;

With burning incense,
Offer ye four bows,

And thou shalt arrive at
The path of survival.'

Then three seeds of the gourd,
To the maid he doth offer:

'Take ye this,
And after a day,

Should the three sons together,
Their father wish to see,

These gourd seeds three,
Thou shalt plant;

And their vines shall grow
A long, long way.'

Hardly three months
Had this monk been gone, when

Blemished
Was the lovely face, and

Widened
Was the slender waist, of

The beloved daughter of
Chesŏk.

The smell of cooked rice became
The smell of green rice;[49]

The taste of fresh water became
The taste of brackish water;

The smell of soybean sauce became
The smell of callow sauce.

That which be her dire wont
Is the very bitterest of wild apricots;

From beyond the mountain afar,
The child peach,[50]

Wild grapes and *ta-rae*,[51]
Pomegranate and citron—

Dozens upon dozens,
Doth she so desire.

The afore mountain,[52]
Becomes high and

The mountain yonder[53]
Becomes low.

The pink skirt of
Twelve *pok*,[54]

It can no longer be prevented
From opening here and there.

Father returns,
And speaketh thus:

'Say there,
My beloved daughter!

Thine aspect,
Why hath it so been changed?

It doth appear that
Thou hast entered upon

Thy very first contraction.'

Mother returns,
And speaketh thusly:

'Say there,
My beloved daughter!

Thine aspect,
Why hath it so been changed?

It doth appear that
thou hast entered upon

Thy very first contraction.'

The brothers nine return,
And speaketh thusly:

'Child, Child,
Our baby sister!

Thine aspect,
What hath it so been changed?

From out thy chamber there cometh
The smell of a monk;

Why is it so?'

'Oh Mother, Oh father,
Oh my brothers nine!

In this tiled-roof domain of
Thirty-three chambers and

Twelve Great Gates
Secured,

T'was I alone who
This house did attend;

That a monk should come
A'seeking alms,

Surely
I never did fancy.

No other guilt bear I
But that of giving alms.'

'Immoral and insolent wench
Thou art!

In what nobleman's house
Doth such misfortune occur?

Sŏn-san-kŭm-a,
Now what of her?

Whereof dost thou speaketh not
The offering to give?

Hu-san-kŭm-a,
Now what of her?

Whereof dost thou speaketh not
The offering to give?'

'The alms offered by
Sŏn-san-kŭm-a,

The smell of fish doth bear
And cannot be accepted.'

'Immoral and insolent wench
Thou art.

In what nobleman's house
Doth such misfortune occur?

Daughter who art beloved
As Heaven itself;

Daughter whom we
So preciously cared for,

As though she were
The blue firmament's solitary star . . .

Oh, this utter misfortune
That thou didst bring about!'

And thus it was decided
That she should be killed.

Into the herb potion
The *pu-ja*[55] is placed, and

In the medicine pot
The potion is boiled;

And, thereupon, is she offered
The medicine bowl.

The beloved daughter of
Chesŏk,

The bowl she doth
Set before her, and

On her bosom she doth
Rest her hands:

'Alas,

What's to be done,
What's to be done;

My fate is death,
What's to be done.'

A long, long sigh
Doth she breathe, and

Placing the arrowroot frock
Before her,

With incense burning, and
Offering four bows,

The southeast wind didst
From out of nowhere come;

And thereby was
The medicine bowl cooled.[56]

Though she did from
The cooled medicine bowl drink,

Yet she does not die—
But lives.

And thus,
Did Mother speak:

'Say there,
My sons of nine!

When we did this house settle,
A most fortunate place t'was said to be;

And t'was said that
The first daughter born

Would a monk to us bring
As a son-in-law.

Yet if this house were to be
By a carpenter of gentle breed built,

Surely would a nobleman
To us be brought

As a son-in-law.

Alas,
T'was by your father's insistence

That the carpenter of a monk
Be employed;

And thereby have we now
A monk for a son-in-law.

Say there,
My sons of nine!

Killing . . .
Yet do I not wish to see;

Living . . .
Yet do I not wish to see.

Make a thee a pit a thousand men's height
In the mountain yonder;

In a stone box
Let her body be sealed,

And into the hole thereby
Be laid,

If she die for lack of breath,
Let it thus be her fate;

If she die for lack of food,
Let it thus be her fate;

If she die for lack of warmth,
Let it thus be her fate.'

The beloved daughter of
Chesŏk,

In a stone box
Is her body sealed, and

Into a pit of a thousand men's height,
Is she thereby imprisoned.

Then down from Heaven flew
The blue and white crane;

One wing each
They spreadeth out beneath her, and

With one wing each
They covereth her.

The blue crane didst
Water to her bring, and

The white crane didst
Food to her bring;

Thereby doth she hunger not, and
Thereby doth she live.

Thus,

The days came to pass, and
The time came to pass, and

The three sons together
She did conceive.

As like the cucumber,
They did grow;[57]

Soon did they
The Four Books and Three Classics[58]

Come to know.

Thus,
It did come to pass

That the parents of
The beloved and beautiful daughter,

Their deceased one did
Long to see; and

To the pit of a thousand men's height
They did journey.

But dead is not
The beloved and beautiful daughter; and

Sitting before her
The three sons together,

Reading they the
Four Books and Three Classics.

'This . . . this . . .
But how can it be!

Surely 'tis not
The work of a human.

Quickly, make haste!
Quickly, lift them out!

Homeward
Let us carry them.'

Thereby mended they
A long rope, and

Down into the pit of a thousand men's height
T'was lowered.

The stone box then
They did raise up, and

The beloved daughter and
The three sons together

Homeward
They did carry.

Thus,

The days came to pass, and
The months came to pass, and

When the three sons together
Their father did long to see,

The beloved daughter of
Chesŏk,

The gourd seeds three
Did offer unto them;

'These gourd seeds three
Shalt thee take and plant;

The vines of this gourd
Wherever they may grow,

Thy father thou shalt see,
If you'll but follow.'

And thus did three sons together,
The gourd seeds take and plant.

The vines of the gourd,
Wherever they did grow,

They didst follow;

Far and away,
O'er hill and dale,

Into the mountain,
Ever deeper,

Until at a temple,
They did at last arrive.

A young novitiate
Before them did appear:

'Ah
How strange!

These three lads together fair,
My master doth surely resemble.'

Following the novitiate,
They before the master

Stood with head bent down;

Offering two bows;
They did thus cry out:

'Oh Father!'

And then did the master
Speak thusly:

'Whereof dost thou call me 'Father'?

I am, I am
Beyond all earthly desires;

This frame a son
Must surely be without.

From a man of this world
Thou surely didst come;

How is it then
That ye call me 'Father'?

If my sons
Thou truly be,

Adorn thyselves with
Hoods of paper,[59]

Garb thyselves in
Raiment of paper,

Place upon thyselves
Pŏsŏn of paper,

And in this pond,
Go thee a'swimming,

If thou dost without
A drop of water return,

My sons truly
Thou shalt be.'

The three sons together,
Upon themselves,

Hoods of paper,
They did adorn;

Raiment of paper,
Upon themselves,

They did garb;

Pŏsŏn of paper,
Upon themselves,

They did place;

And in the pond,
A'swimming they did go,

But not a drop of water even
Do they bear.

Seeing this,
The master did say:

'By this alone,

Thou hast no claim
My sons to be.

Go thee to the river and
Fetch a dead carp;

With a large carving knife,
Ŭ-sŭk ŭ-sŭk.[60]

Cut it up into several pieces,
Which, thereupon, thou shalt devour.

If thou canst then
A living carp heave,

My sons truly
Thou shalt be.'

The three sons together,
Did they a dead carp,

Into several pieces cut,
And thereupon devour.

Whereupon did they,
A living carp heave.

Seeing this,
The master did say;

'By this alone,

Thou hast no claim
My sons to be.

Set thee afore
The gate of this temple

A spider's thread, and,
Thereupon

Go ye forth and back
Upon it.

If the spider's thread
Breaketh not,

My sons truly
Thou shalt be.'

The three sons together,
Upon the spider's thread,

Forth and back,
They did go;

But the spider's thread
Breaketh not.

Seeing this,
The master did say:

'By this alone,

Thou hast no claim
My sons to be.

From the afore mountain yonder,

A cock of arrowroot
Thou shalt mend, and

A drum of straw
Thou shalt mend.

When the cock shalt crow,
And the drum shalt sound,

My sons truly
Thou shalt be.'

When the three sons together,

The arrowroot cock
Had made to crow,

The crowing of all fowl
Below heaven

Was to be heard;

And,

When the straw drum
Was beaten,

From all temples
Below Heaven,

The sounding of the drum
Was to be heard.[61]

Seeing this,
The master did say:

'By this alone,

Thou hast no claim
My sons to be

Gather thee the bones
Of a cow dead three years;

If thou canst from it
A living calf mend

And come upon it
A'riding,

My sons truly
Thou shalt be.'

The three sons together,

Of a cow dead three years,
The bones they did gather,

And from it,
A living calf did mend;

And, each upon his own beast,
They three did come a'riding.

Seeing this,
The master did say:

'By this alone,

Thou hast no claim
My sons to be.

Go thee afore
To the mountain yonder,

And build ye there
A castle wall of sand

Whose height in feet
Doth thirty-three be;

Then, o'er the castle wall,
Hop to and fro.

If ye the castle wall
Breaketh not, and

On thy bodies
Not a grain of sand I see,

My sons truly
Thou shalt be.'

The three sons together,

A castle wall
From sand did build;

Though hopped they o'er to and fro,
Not a grain of sand there be.

Seeing this,
The master did say:

'A pan with water
Let us fill,

And our fingers cutting,
Thereupon,

From out them
Blood shall flow;

Thy blood and mine,

If in one place gathered
It be congealed,

My sons truly
Thou shalt be.'

The three sons together
Their fingers did cut,

And blood did henceforth
From out them flow;

The master did
His fingers cut,

And blood did henceforth
From out them flow.

Into the water
'Round and 'round,

Their blood doth turn;

And lo!
To a drop in the center

Do the others
Gather 'round,

'Till all of them do
In one clot congeal.

And thus,
Did the blood of four men

Become one.

Then did the master
The three sons together call:

'My sons!
My lads! My sons!

Over life and fortune,
In this human world,

Thou shalt reign.'[62]

The beloved daughter of
Chesŏk

Is then summoned:

'Thou hast done well;
From this day forth

Thou shalt be called
The God of Birth.[63]

And in this human world,
Thou shalt bestow unto man

His generations.'

(The Mudang dances and the rhythm changes
to a faster tempo)

'You there,

The nine novitiates, and
My fellow monks twelve!

Get thee down to
An ordinary house,[64]

Take thee a wife
Unto thyselves, and

Live as other men
Would do.

I, too, this celibate life
Do hereby renounce, and

Seek but the happiness of
The human world.

The temple's main hall
Do I hereby dismember, and

A house of eight chambers[65]
Do I hereby build;

The temple's side hall
Do I hereby dismember, and

A house of five chambers[66]
Do I hereby build.

And the God of the Five Offerings[67]
Is the god I pray to . . .'

(The Mudang dances)

'The large frock
Do I hereby dismember;

For the single-cloth blanket,
It shall be suitable.

The small frock
Do I hereby dismember;

For the child's blanket,
It shall be suitable.

The metal gong;

For the rice pot,
It shall be suitable, and

The square-cornered hood;

For the rice scoop
It shall be suitable.

The wooden *mok-t'ak*

For dipping the sauce,
The one half shall be suitable.

And the other;

'To catch the child's urine,
It shall be suitable.

The six-ringed staff
I break in two;

For the fire poke,
It shall be suitable.

And the God of the Five Offerings
Is the god I pray to . . .'

[The Mudang dances]
[The Mudang sings a song of entertainment]

"Let us play.

Let us play,

At the house of P'al-sŏn-i,[68]
Let us go and play.

In P'al-sŏn-i's chamber,
There hangs the Black Crane Harp;[69]

We pluck this string,
And from here "*P'ung-dong*"[70]

We pluck that string,
And from there "*P'ung-dong.*"

Swaying to and fro,
Let us play.

And the God of the Five Offerings
Is the god I pray to . . ."

(The Mudang dances)

III.

(The Mudang speaks)

"Say there,
You musicians!

That fellow of a monk . . .

With neither chant nor blessing
Did he leave us;

Therefore am I impelled
This chant to sing:

(The tempo slows and the Mudang sings)

"Na-muya,
Namu roda,[71]

"Na-mu, na-mu
Na-mu na-mu roda,

Life and Fortune
Do I bring you,

Na-mu yam
Na-muro-da,

Na-mu, na-mu,
Na-mu, na-mu roda,

The purse of life
On one shoulder do I bear,

The purse of fortune
On the other;

The purse of household goods,
The purse of posterity,

The purse of the garden,
The purse of the servants,

The purse of the rice field,

Dangling in clusters from me . . .

Thus I come.

Blessed Sakyamuni and
The God Chesŏk,

Upon every virtue,
Their benediction doth bestow:

The life of Heaven,
The fortune of Chesŏk,

The posterity of Ch'il-Sŏng, and
The medicine of Chŏ-Sŭng.[72]

By offerings and charity,
Thou mayst them receive;

Then a multitude of offerings
Thou shouldst give.

Na-mu, na-mu,
Namu, na-mu roda,

Thy multitude of offerings
Do I now receive.

In the deep water,
I shall a bridge build;

The charity to those crossing over,
We are obliged to give.

By every wayside,
I shall a hostel build;

The charity to the wanderer,
We are obliged to give.

In the sacred mountain,
I shall a temple build;

The charity to piety,
We are obliged to give,

At the lower place,[73]
I shall a temple build;

The charity to piety,
We are obliged to give.

Na-mu ya,
Na-mu roda.

Na-mu ya,
Na-mu, na-muroda,

Which tree is it
That is well-fated?

It is that which
The roof beam becomes.

Which tree is it?
That is well-fated?

It is that which
The king's throne becomes.

Which tree is it
That is well-fated?

It is that which
The palace gate becomes.

Na-mu ya,
Namu roda,

Na-mu, na-mu
Na-mu, na-mu roda,

Na-mu Amit'a Bul.

Na-mu Amit'a-Bul."

(The Mudang speaks)

"Say there,
You musicians!

Blessed Sakyamuni and
The God Chesŏk,

Having thus received
Offerings multifold,

We thereby
Upon them do bestow

The reward of life,
The reward of happiness, and

The fulfillment of all
Which they desire.

And so, that they may realize
Great wealth and fortune,

Let us thereby
Appoint unto them

The fortune that is gathered,
The fortune that is received, and

The great fortune
Whose numbers countless doth be.

Though who but to the sight alone
Appeareth well,

Should he the piled rice lack,
His inners doth empty be.

Let us thereby, for one and all,
The bundles of rice summon:

(The Mudang sings)

Ŏ-ŏu-,[75]
Bundles of rice,

Ŏ-ŏu-,
Bundles of rice;

Let us go gather
Bundles of rice;

Let us go receive
Bundles of rice.

In the great and wide fields of
Kim-Je and Man-Kyŏng,[76]

From here and there,
Rice bundles are piled:

To this house alone,[77]
We do appoint them.

Ŏ-gi yŏng-ch'a,[78]
Bundles of rice;

Ŏ-gi yŏng-ch'a,
Bundles of rice.

Yonder,
Behind the house,

The bundles of rice
That lie beyond;

To the master of the house,
They do belong.

Yonder
Afore the house,

The bundles of rice
Which there be piled;

To the mistress of the house,
They do belong.

Yonder,
Aside the house,

The bundles of rice
That in the corner doth lie;

To the heir of this house,
They do belong.

Pile upon pile,
The bundles are heaped.

The owl and its brood,[79]
When one wing doth flap,

One-thousand bags of rice
Doth emerge;

Yet, when it doth
All of its body move,

Rice bags in countless numbers
Doth emerge.

Ŏ-gi yŏng-ch'a,
Bundles of rice."

(The Mudang speaks)

"Say there,
You musicians!

Until now,
Every fortune below heaven,

Upon this house,
One by one,

Hath been bestowed;
And,

In all the four directions,
Bundles of rice,

By our supplications
Hath been dispatched;

Thereby,
None need envy

The great riches of
Sŏk-Sung.[80]

'Neath the bundles of rice,
Should no talisman[81] be settled,

The rice pile shall
By accident, official misfortune and defamation

Disappear;
So it is written.

The talisman,
Thereupon,

'Neath the bundles of rice
Settled need be.

Let us, thereby,
The talisman summon":

(The Mudang sings)

"*Ŏ, ŏ-ru,*
Thou talisman,

Ŏ-gŭ yŏng-ch'a
Thou talisman;

Talisman,
Thou art.

Midst the clouds on high,
The flying kite talisman[82]

Is hereby most welcome.

In Namwŏn town,
At the Kwang-Han-Ryu Pavilion,

Under the O-Jak-Kyo Bridge,[83]
In the flowing water, the talisman

Bobbing up and down
Is hereby most welcome.

Ŏ-ŏ-ru,
Thou talisman,

Ŏ-gŭ yŏng-ch'a
Thou talisman;

Talisman,
Thou art.

In the great bamboo groves of
Sun-Ch'ang and Tan-Yang,[84]

P'u-dŭ-dŭng,
P'u-dŭ-dŭng,[85]

The startled cock-pheasant talisman
Is hereby most welcome.

In the great pool,
The pond wherein the lotus dwells,

Floating up and down,
The long-headed talisman

Is hereby most welcome.

Ŏ-ŏ-ru,
Thou talisman,

Ŏ-gŭ-yŏng-ch'a
Thou talisman;

Talisman,
Thou art.

The serpent talisman
We hereby do summon;

At the upper place[86] it is seated,
And thereupon revered.

The toad talisman
We hereby do summon;

'Neath the rice bin it is seated,
And thereupon revered.

The calf talisman
We hereby do summon;

At the shed it is seated,
And thereupon revered.

The phoenix talisman
Doth hereby fly in;

At the rear yard it is seated,
And thereupon revered.

Ŏ-ŏ-ru,
Thou talisman,

Ŏ-gŭ-yŏng-ch'a
Thou talisman;

Talisman,
Thou art."

(The Mudang speaks)

"Say there,
You musicians!

Having piled the rice bundles
Here and there, and

Having thereby summoned
The talisman multifold;

And, thereupon,
As this house

The fortune of Heaven,
The fortune of the domicile, and

The great fortune
May come to realize,

Let us now
The man of low station summon";

(The Mudang sings)

Ŏ-ŏ-ru,
Thou servant woman,

O-ŏ-ru,
Thou serving man;

Ŏ-gŭ-yŏng-ch'a
Thou serving woman,

Ŏ-gŭ-yŏng-ch'a
Thou serving man;

The servant woman and man,
We hereby do summon;

To their respective duties,
They are thereby appointed.

Ŏ-gŭ-yŏng-ch'a
Thou serving man;

Ŏ-gŭ-yŏng-ch'a
Thou servant woman.

When the servant woman and man
Are thereby summoned,

The serving man
Well the letter doth inscribe, and

The servant woman
Well the chores doth execute;

They who
Faithful and gentle be,

The serving man
Well the farm doth tend, and

The servant woman
Well the cloth doth weave.

Ŏ-ŏ-ru,
Thou servant woman,

Ŏ-ŏ-ru,
Thou serving man;

Ŏ-gŭ-yŏng-ch'a
Thou serving woman,

Ŏ-gŭ-yŏng-ch'a
Thou serving man;

(The Mudang speaks)

"Say there,
You musicians!

Until now,
Life and fortune

Upon this house multifold,
Have we thus bestowed.

And now,

To the Front Shrine Grandmother, and
To yonder Rear Shrine Grandmother,[87]

To the God of Earth, and
To the God of the Nation,

The great gong sound,
Five pounds heavy,

The oboe sound of
Ten leagues 'round, and,

The large flute sound of
Ten-thousand leagues 'round,

Let us play
For but a while . . ."

(The instrumental ensemble begins to the play
and the Mudang dances)

(The Mudang sings)

"To the Front Shrine and
To yonder Rear Shrine,

To the God of Earth and
The God of the Nation,

To blessed Sakyamuni and
The God Chesŏk,

The Ritual of the Shrine
Do we now hold forth.

Thereupon do we supplicate thee
To descend to this place; and,

Shouldst thou with pleasure
Our dedicated offering receive,

How fine a thing
Should it not be . . ."

(The Mudang dances)

(The Mudang sings)

"The god we pray to
The god we play to,

The God of the Five Offerings is
The god we pray to.

Let us go and play,
Oh god that we pray to.

Among the clouds of
Man-Kyŏng heights,

The Fairy Crane God is
The god we pray to;

The God of the Five Offerings is
The god we pray to.

If a man doth not speak,
How then shall he eat?

Yonder Rear Shrine Grandmother,
Should she not speak, then

She too, as a rule,
Of sustenance may be deprived.

Thereupon do we supplicate thee,
Our dedicated offerings and

Our devotional service,
Thou wilt receive;

Thereupon do we supplicate thee,
That which we do implore,

Thou shalt bequeath.

Thereupon, by virtue of this
Supplicatory rite,

Ten-thousand fortunes
Thou wilt descend;

One-thousand years
Ten-thousand years,

Years without number,
Thou wilt descend.

The god I pray to,
The god I pray to,

The God of the Five Offerings is
The god I pray to."

(The Mudang dances)

Notes

1. In a description of the *Chesŏk Kŏri* (Ritual of the God Chesŏk) section of the *Ch'ŏnshin-maji Kut* of Seoul and the northern part of Kyŏnggi Province, Huhm (op. cit., pp. 79, 80) states the following:

. . . *Chesŏk Kŏri* means a shaman ritual performed for the god enshrined in the loft at the back of the women's quarters of the family performing the *kut*. *Chesŏk* in Buddhism refers to Sakradevanam Indra but the *Chesŏk* god in the Korean *kut* refers to the procreation god, *Sam-Shin,* who is one of the three gods governing childbirth, and is responsible for the health and longevity of the family concerned. So the god is worshipped for the health and longevity of the offspring of the family.

Chesŏk Kŏri is a ritual dedicated to a procreation god, not a Buddhist god, but unfortunately the mistaken notion still persists that it is a Buddhist god.

The *Chesŏk* god is enshrined in a dark earthen jar, a white porcelain jar, a gourd, a rice bag or a box placed in the loft or wall closet at the back of the women's quarters of the family performing the *kut.* The spirits so enshrined are varied and include those of mountain, sea, water, commerce, fishery, scholar, money and monk. But they are all procreation gods of the families involved.

The *Chesŏk* god is a supreme god, clean and quiet, so the *Chesŏk Kŏri* is a clean *kŏri. Chesŏk* tables are clean and simple. For offerings, no animals are used; only produce is used, such as uncooked polished rice, cotton yarn, watercress, dates, chestnuts, apples, persimmon, pears, white rice cakes, steamed white cakes, tea, etc.

2. Legend says that King Yo of China, who ruled about five-thousand years ago during the "Utopian Age," had two daughters, A-Wang and Yŏ-Yŏng, whom he gave to Sun, a wise man, found after long searching. The two daughters, after ascending the throne, became the equivalent of *Mudangs,* and this ritual is believed to have originated with them.

3. In Buddhist cosmology, a very high and deep place.

4. Same as 3.

5. Presently called Kaesong, it was the capital of the Koryŏ Dynasty.

6. Presently called Seoul, it was the capital of the Yi Dynasty.

7. The National Government Examination, required of all who aspired to officialdom during the Yi Dynasty.

8. A type of moss or fern (*Cryptogamia*) which grows under pine trees deep in the mountains. It was used by monks for making hats.

9. An accessory worn by Buddhist monks.

10. Same as 9.

11. A small gong used to mark out the rhythm in chants and songs.

12. A gnarled crook that often accompanies monks on their journeys.

13. The bamboo which grows on the banks of Tong-Jong Lake in So-Sang near the Yangtze River in China. This particular bamboo, unlike others, has concentric circles on its exterior that grow naturally; for this reason it was highly valued and used only by persons of the highest rank.

14. The sound the staff makes when it hits the stones on the ground.

15. Under the Confucian-dominated society of the Yi Dynasty, Buddhist monks were held in low esteem.

16. This lowly Buddhist monk.

17. In ancient times, a vow was made by tying a knot in the blouse strings.

18. In large houses and temples, a small bell can be found hanging under the eaves at the corners and is rung by the motion of the breeze.

19. The sound of the bell, comparable to the western "ting-a-ling."

20. A very precious wood. It is planted in the gardens of noblemen because it is said the phoenix roosts on its boughs and eats only the seed of this particular tree. The flower is white and the fruit is an edible bean, which is rather tasty.

21. Korean pavilions ordinarily are hexagonal in form.

22. The lotus is thought to be a very modest flower of deep virtue that humbles itself in the presence of another.

23. A mountain in Chŏlla Province, famed for its scenic beauty.

24. Korean locks are traditionally shaped in the form of a carp.

25. It should be pointed out that the sutras mentioned here did not originate from the Buddha himself and therefore are not to be found in the *Tripitaka Koreana*—but were made by later monks and disciples.

26. The *Suddhacandra Sutra*. It is chanted at the beginning of the new year to bring blessings and good fortune to the home.

27. The sutra that summons obedience to the teachings of the Buddha. In this respect, the analogy is drawn to the father, who is head of the household. The *Um-No Kyŏng* may also be chanted here. This sutra dwells on the role of the mother as protector of the family.

28. The *Ha-Dae Kyŏng* may also be chanted here. This sutra calls upon the husband and wife to endure whatever adversities may come in life.

29. This sutra is chanted for love and protection, good breeding and education of the descendants.

30. This sutra calls for fraternal love between brothers and sisters, and toward all mankind as well.

31. This sutra calls for a peaceful relationship between men of the same kin as well as others, regardless of their station.

32. The sound the locks make as they snap open, comparable, perhaps, to the sound "twang, twang" in English.

33. A round wooden gong with a handle that is used by monks for rhythmic accompaniment in chanting. It is usually referred to as a "slit-gong" or "temple block."

34. The rhythmic sound emitted when the *mok-t'ak* is struck.

35. Large Korean houses of old had three main gates: the Outer (composed of the "Twelve Gates" mentioned in the song text), the Middle, and the Inner.

36. The Milky Way.

37. The 1st lady-in-waiting, or chamber maid.

38. The 2nd lady-in-waiting, or chamber maid.

39. A meaningless expression used in summoning servants.

40. In former times, maidens wore their hair in a single braid, at the end of which a long red ribbon was tied.

41. Hansan is the most notable place in Korea for the making of highly refined ramie cloth.

42. Bootees or padded socks that are worn mostly by women these days. The seed of the cucumber is small, white, and of a lovely shape, and is therefore likened to a dainty foot.

43. The sound which leather shoes make while scuffling along a path.

44. The reference is obviously a paraphrase of the expression "a fish out of water," which, coincidentally, is also used in Korean.

45. A poor man's house.

46. A very fragrant wood used for incense.

47. Chopsticks in Korea are ordinarily made of silver or brass.

48. Deep night.

49. Unripened rice.

50. An unripened rice.

51. The fruit of *Actinida arguta*.

52. The belly.

53. The breasts.

54. A very wide skirt worn by girls of upper-class families; it was made by fashioning twelve pieces of material together.

55. A poisonous plant.

56. When the poisonous potion is cooled, it is rendered ineffective.

57. An indication of rapid growth.

58. Confucian classics. The Four Books include: *The Analects of Confucius, The Works of Mencius, The Book of the Golden Mean,* and *The Book of the Higher Learning.* The Three Classics include: *The Book of Odes, The Book of Prose,* and *The Book of Changes.*

59. A monk's hat is shaped in the form of a triangular hood.

60. "Crunch, crunch."

61. In Buddhist temples, there is a large drum that is struck at certain intervals during the day and at sacred ceremonies.

62. And thus, according to *The Folk Treasury of Korea* (The Korean Oral Literature Society, Seoul, 1970, p. 92), they became the Three Chesŏk Deities. See Appendix I.

63. *Sam-Shin.*

64. According to Lee, Jung-young (op. cit., p. 31), "Samshin" (Sam-Shin) or the god of procreation seems to have its origin in Sansin *(San-Shin)* or the mountain god, who is one of the most popular and important shamanistic deities in Korea. He refers to the foregoing myth in this ritual song as "The Myth of Tangun Agassi," and gives the following account (p. 21):

> According to this myth or legend, Tangun Agassi (who can be compared with Pari-kongju or Pari-degi here) (see Appendix II) was a virgin who fell in love with a monk who came to beg for rice. In a dream, she had sexual relations with him; and as a result of this

dream, she actually conceived a child illegitimately. As a conse-
quence, she is punished by her nine brothers. She is placed in a
stone box and cast into the water. However, Tangun Agassi, with
heavenly assistance, gives birth to triplets, all boys. Later, they were
able to break the box and leave the water. They rescue not only their
mother but also search out their father. The story ends with the
elevation of their mother, Tangun Agassi, to the position of Samsin,
the god of procreation, who is also known as Sansin, the Mountain
God.

A narrative account of the myth (with variations) may also be found
in Arthur Kinsler's "A Study of the Fertility Cult for Children in Korean
Shamanism" (Yonsei University, Seoul, Ph.D. dissert., abstract reprinted in
The Idea of Soul in Asia, Association of Asian Folklore, Seoul, 1979), in *The
Folk Treasury of Korea* (op. cit., pp. 81-92), and in Appendix I. However, in
view of the fact that both Kinsler and the *Folk Treasury* refer to the heroine
as "Tanggŭm Agasshi" and "Tanggŭm-Agi," respectively, Lee's (op. cit., pp.
21, 32) reference to her as "Tangun Agassi" and his assertion (p. 32) that
"the literal meaning of Tangun Agassi is 'the wife of Tangun'" (the mythical
founder of Korea) is felt to be incorrect (the word "Agassi," or "Agasshi,"
itself means "virgin" or "young unmarried girl," and "Agi" means "child").
In addition, his assertions (pp. 31-2) that Tangun is ". . . the prototype of
shamans . . . who is also known as the great shaman," and that "It is no
doubt in the mind of shamans to elevate this god (Tangun Agassi) to the
highest position that the Korean people can think of" ('the wife of
Tangun') are both highly presumptuous and controversial. Further,
according to the way the myth is narrated in the above-mentioned sources,
and in the way that it is sung in the Mu-ga, Lee's assertion (p. 21) that
"Tangun Agassi . . . was a virgin who fell in love with a monk who came to
beg for rice" and that "in a dream, she had sexual relations with him" are
also felt to be inaccurate in that no "falling in love," as he puts it, is ever
intimated in the plot, and the so-called "sexual relations she had with him"
were only a symbolic interpretation of such by the monk himself after the
virgin had awoken from the dream.

65. The secular world.

66. The master's house; the main house.

67. The servants' quarters.

68. Flowers, rice, candles, lanterns and incense. The precise meaning
of this phrase has as yet not been fully established. It is always sung at the

commencement of the dance as a cue to the musicians that the dance is about to start.

69. The name of a beautiful girl or *kisaeng* (female entertainer; the Korean counterpart of the Japanese *geisha*).

70. The *kŏmungo* or *hyŏn-gŭm*; actually not a harp, but a musical instrument of six strings played with a plectrum. When not in use, it is hung on the wall.

71. The sound which emanates from the strings, somewhat comparable to the western "twang."

72. Namu Amita-Bul.

73. An imaginary king of the "other world."

74. The city, valley or any ordinary place.

75. Sacred Buddhist words in Sanskrit of undetermined meaning; *"sa-ba-ha"* refers to the Sanskrit word *svaha*.

76. A work chant.

77. Two place-names in North Chŏlla Province where large rice fields are found.

78. The house of the person holding the ritual.

79. Another work chant.

80. In Korean belief, the owl is a sign of affluence.

81. The wealthiest man in Chinese history.

82. In Korea, such creatures as weasels, large snakes and toads, to name but a few, were regarded as such.

83. A bird that dwells in very high places.

84. A town, pavilion and bridge in North Chŏlla Province that figure in the famous folk legend of *Ch'un-Hyang* ("Fragrance of Spring"). The O-Jak-Kyo bridge takes its name from a bridge believed to be formed by crows and magpies across the heavens on the seventh of July in the lunar calendar when the Plover and Weaver Stars meet.

85. Place names in North and South Chŏlla Province.

86. The sound the bird makes when it starts up suddenly.

87. In a Korean room, the most respected location is the warmest part of the heated floor, normally reserved for elders and honored guests.

88. In Korea, the goddess is always represented in the form of an aged female. Originally, all Musok gods were female; it was only with the introduction of Chinese culture into Korea that male gods appeared.

4. *The Ritual Song of the God Son-Nim*[1]

Prologue

> "Hear ye, hear ye,
> One and all!
>
> The Ritual of Princess A-Wang and Yŏ-Yŏng
> Is about to be held."

The drum begins to play and the Mudang sings:

> "In this year,
> The Year of the Dog,[2]
>
> In this month
> The very auspicious month of May, and
>
> On this day,
> The twenty-third of the month
>
> This ritual we hereby do
> Hold forth."

(In the following part, the Mudang tells of how the
ceremonial place was selected.)

> "By ordinance of the Thirty-Three Heavens,
> Was this house settled, and
>
> By ordinance of the Twenty-Eight Stars,
> Was it divined.

At the first hour,[3]
Heaven was opened, and

At the second hour,[4]
The earth was formed.

When man is born,
We pray before the God Ch'il-Sŏng;

For the good fortune,
We pray before the God Chesŏk;

For the good medicine,
We pray before King Chŏ-Sŭng; and

Thereby are a great multitude of humans
Born unto this world, and

Thereby do they
Multiply and prosper, and

Thereby must there
A national law be created,

So that all may
Under order thrive."

I.

The Mudang sings:

"Today,
At this time,

I begin this song;

No mean song
This.

'Tis none other than
The song of the God Son-Nim.

The master of this house,
The master of this ceremonial place,

Surely, of this ritual,
Doth he know not?

This house,
Throughout the countryside,

To one and all,
Be it not known?

In this province,
The province of Chŏlla,

In this county,
The county of Puan,

In this district,
The district of Ch'ul-P'o,

In this village,
The village of Ch'ul-P'o,

In this household,
The household of Sŏng,[5]

This ritual we hereby do
Hold forth."

II.

The Mudang sings:

"The home of the God Son-Nim,
Let us go and see;

The home of the God Son-Nim,
Where doth it be?

He doth from
Kang-Nam in

The Great Han country[6]
Hail;

He doth from
Our land,

The Small Han country[7]
Hail;

He doth from
P'al-Byŏn Mountain

In Chŏlla Province
Hail;

He doth from
The Ch'ŏn-Man nation[8]

In the barbarian country
Hail.

The Kang-Nam country,
Though it be great and wide,

The small law[9] only,
Do they keep;

Our Chosŏn country,[10]
Though it be small and narrow,

The great law only,
Do we keep.

The Great Country,[11]
Though it be great and wide,

Their food be poor:
Millet, three years aged.

Though their garments of
Silk brocaded be,

Wooden ships,
Wooden chariots, and

Wooden shoes,
They do employ.

Our Chosŏn country,
Though it be small and narrow,

The most precious white, ground and sparkling rice
That doth twice-over polished be,

With bowl and spoon of brass,
Do we partake thereof."

III.

The Mudang sings:

"When the God Son-Nim
Doth appear,

For his appearance,
Should there be no intent?

For his appearance,
Should he bear no name?

'Tek-i' is he surnamed, and
'An-Dŏk'[12] doth his given name be.

When he does in
Our Chosŏn country appear,

For his appearance,
Should his countenance not be fine?

For his appearance,
Should he be without ornaments?

From Kang-Nam in the Great Han country,
The Son-Nim Gods,

How many thereby
Do appear?

Fifty-three in all
There do appear, and

Fifty in all
There do return;

Thereby, only three among them
Do appear."

IV.

(Here, the song contains a description of the
male Son-Nim God's raiment.)

"The Honorable Son-Nim God;
Verily, how fine his countenance doth be!

His headband of wavelike threads,
The hawksbill tortoise-shell buttons doth bear,[13]

His finely-woven top hat from T'ong-Yŏng,
The amber chin strap doth bear;[14]

Pantaloons of the finest damask,
And leggings he doth wear;

A well-fitting blouse of
Indigo damask he doth wear; and

A crimson frock of free-flowing ends,
He doth wear.

A minstrel's sash 'round his waist
Tightly there is bound, and

Pŏ-sŏn like the cucumber seed,
With hu-ho-dŭng[15] embroidered,

His feet do adorn.

The palanquin that brings him forth,
Four bearers there do carry."[16]

V.

(Here, the song contains a description of the
female Son-Nim God's raiment.)

"The Lady Son-Nim!
Verily, how fine her countenance doth be!

Let us take a glimpse of her
From the rear:

Her tresses, wavy as the clouds;
Her comb, as like the crescent moon,

By which, here and there,
Her hair so gently hath been groomed.

Her braid,
Wide as an ironing board:

Ah, what a truly fine bun
It doth make.

The knotty bamboo hairpin,
Obliquely it is set, and

The golden phoenix hairpin,
Straightaway is placed.[17]

In her ears,
The laurel crown pendants;

On her hand,
The white jade ring.

The inner blouse doth of
Red damask be,

The outer blouse doth of
Red silk be, and

Her collar,
Like a gossamer doth be.

Ah, how truly fine
Her raiment it doth be!

The red damask skirt,
Tightly pleated 'round,[18] and

The silken pantaloons beneath
Of the finest silk are made[19]

Her very uppermost garments
Of the most precious silks are formed;

Ah, to her,
How so truly becoming they be!

Her pŏ-sŏn of cotton,
Like the cucumber seed they be, and

Her shoes of leather,
Embroidered all around . . ."

VI.

(Here, the song contains a description of the palanquin.)

"Let us now see
The palanquin.

A black damask curtain
'Round the palanquin there is hung, and

A white silk fringe
'Round the palanquin there doth be;

From gold and silver tacks there hangs
The silk-framed curtain of beads, and

A ball of red-painted paulownia wood doth
Atop the palanquin sit.

The retinue to the fore, and
The retinue to the rear;

The herald to the fore, and
The guards to the rear;

A pair of clarions, and
A pair of cymbals;

A pair of banners,[20] and
A pair of standards.[21]

The Honorable Son-Nim,
A blue flag doth bear;

The Lady Son-Nim,
A red flag doth bear;

Like an inferno,
They do come forth."

VII.

"When they did to
Our Chosŏn country,

The dark country,
The twilight country,[22]

Scaling mountain, and
Crossing rivers,

How many mountains
Did they scale?

How many rivers
Did they cross?

Yonder to the fore,
The mountain up ahead;

Yonder to the rear,
The mountain beyond

Over Ma-T'aryŏng and Chang-Dŏk San,
Ma-Ch'iryŏng and Chang-Po San.[23]

How many rivers
Did they cross?

Yonder to the fore,
The river up ahead;

Yonder to the rear,
The river beyond.[24]

Yonder to the fore,
The river of Ŭi-Ju,[25]

The Ch'ŏng-Ch'ŏn River,
The Tae-Dong River[26]. . .

With voice strong and clear,
They do all forth:

'Boatman, boatman,
You there, boatman!'

The mountains do their echo
Ring forth.

Then, with voice strong and clear,
Trice calling forth,

The waters do their echo
Ring forth

Then, with voice strong and clear,
Twice calling forth,

The boatman, at last,
Doth appear,

'Boatman, boatman,
You there, boatman!

Pray but a while
They boat do lend us!'

'Prithee, what procession is this,
That does at midnight go forth?

The ships which
I did thus own,

In the Japanese invasion
Of the Im-Jin year,[27]

The ships formed of sand,
They did all dissolve;

The ships formed of stone,
They were all sunken;

The ships formed of wood,
They did all float away;

The ships formed of iron,
They were all broken;

The ships formed of earth,
They did all crumble;

Yea, neither boat nor anchor,
Have I now.'

And then,

The wrath of the Son-Nim Gods
Was invoked;

The boatman's eldest son
They did capture, and

The cholera disease[28] upon him
They did inflict.

Then did the boatman
The Son-Nim Gods know.

'The ships formed of wood,
May I mend thee?

The ships formed of iron
May I mend thee?

Only I beg of thee,
My son do spare!

Pray thee,
Pray thee,

Before thou Son-Nim Gods,
I do beseech thee,

Merciful and generous
Son-Nim majesties!'

'Without the ship,
Can I not cross?'

To the southeast,
The Son-Nim God doth gaze.

When the Son-Nim God is seated,
One-thousand leagues can he see; and

When he rises up,
Ninety-thousand leagues can he see.

In ten-thousand leagues 'round under Heaven,
All things doth he know.

And suddenly,
From without,

There did
A willow branch flow down.

One leaf doth he pluck, and
In his mouth place;

In the twinkling of an eye,
A ship he doth mend.

A pair of banners
He does bring forth, and

The wind's course
He doth make;

A pair of standards
He does bring forth, and

The gently swaying sail
He doth make.

And thus,

The boat bridge,
The boat road,

He doth make, and

The retinue,
Fore and aft,

He doth make.

A pair of clarions,
A pair of cymbals,

A pair of shell-trumpets,[31]
A pair of conical oboes,

A pair of flageolets,
A pair of cross-flutes;[32]

A multifarious ensemble,
Does thereupon play forth.

The servants of high station
Be twenty and four in number;

The servants of middle station
Be ten and four in number; but,

The servants of low station
Be only four in number.

The servants who do
The writing table bear;

The servants who do
The inkstone bear;

The servants who do
The raincoat, rainhat and umbrella bear;

A multitude of servants
In attendance there do follow.

When they did to
Our Chosŏn make their way,

The first to cross was
The Lady Son-Nim, and

The second to cross was
The honorable Son-Nim.

To every country,
To every village,

All over the land,
To every nook and cranny;

To the teeming cities,
Unto households without number,

Unto each surname,
One and all, and

Unto each surname which be
That of another;

When night doth fall,
Unto the lighted household, and

When day doth brighten,
Unto the stirring household.

One day, two days,
Three days, four,

To the head, he does
Himself attach.[33]

On the fifth and sixth day,
The buds[34] do appear;

In the color of cochineal,[35]
The buds do appear.

Then, as if they were
With powder wiped,

The silver scab,
The bronze scab,

The cloud scab,
The fog scab,

The *jibi* scab,[36] and
The falling petal scab,

Are thereby formed.

'Say there
You Son-Nim Gods!

Long life,
We do beseech thee;

Good fortune,
We do beseech thee.

As like the pear cast from
Tŏn-Jin Mountain,[37]

From Tŏn-Jin Mountain,
Cast as like the string;

As like the string cast from
Tŏn-Jin Mountain.

From Tŏn-Jin Mountain,
Cast as like the pear.[38]

Upon this family,
Upon this house, and

Upon our most treasured descendants,
Thy blessing we do beseech;

For as like

A pearl in the stone mountain,
A flower in the snow mountain,

A carp swimming on frozen ice,
A bamboo shoot in snow,[39]

A boat gliding on the frozen ice, and
The Venus Star in the dawn,

To us they be.

From day unto day, and
Month unto month,

Their long life,
We do beseech thee;

Long life, wealth, rank and male descendants,
We do beseech thee.

> The measles Son-Nim,
> The tumor Son-Nim,
>
> The infant disease Son-Nim,
> The swelling disease Son-Nim,
>
> The cold Son-Nim,
> The infection Son-Nim,
>
> The typhus Son-Nim,
> The cholera Son-Nim,
>
> The left side Son-Nim,
> The right side Son-Nim,
>
> This family and this house,
> Receive our supplications,
>
> And gently, gently,
> Be on thy way . . .'"

Notes

1. *Son-Nim* means "Visitor"; the disease known as smallpox is held to be a visitation from the outside, as it was foreign to Korea in ancient times.

This is, therefore, a ritual for the exorcism of smallpox. It is also sometimes referred to as the *Mama* (Smallpox) Ritual and the "Ritual of Pyŏl Sŏng" ("Another Star"). Huhm (op. cit., p. 22) lists the *Mamabaesong kut* of the Seoul area as being ". . . performed on the thirteenth day after contraction of smallpox."

2. This would, of course, be in accordance with the time and date the ritual is actually held.

3. From midnight to 1:00 AM.

4. From 1:00 AM to 2:00 AM.

5. This ritual was held is the house of the Sŏng family in Ch'ul-P'o Village, Puan County, North Chŏlla Province by a Mudang from the same village.

6. Ordinarily understood to be an imaginary, undetermined place, but here thought to be Vietnam and China, respectively.

7. Korea is referred to by the Koreans themselves as *Hanguk*, the "Country of the Han."

8. An undetermined place name.

9. Laws of an insignificant nature.

10. Another name for Korea.

11. Kang-Nam.

12. The actual meaning of these names is unknown. The God Son-Nim, however, is never addressed by these names.

13. In ancient times, men in Korea wore a headband covering the forehead that bore two buttons on each side over the temples.

14. T'ong-Yŏng is a town in South Kyŏngsang Province famed for the weaving of highly-refined horsehair top hats, worn by gentlemen during the Yi Dynasty period. The chin strap hung down loosely beneath the chin; if it was made of amber, it was indicative of high rank and affluence.

15. Meaning undetermined.

16. The palanquin carried by four bearers was indicative of high rank and affluence.

17. During the Yi Dynasty, women wore their braid tied in a bun at the nape of the neck with a long pin running through it horizontally that had the head of a phoenix carved at one end, and a smaller pin of silver or gold running through it diagonally that was carved in the shape of knotty bamboo.

18. Girls of genteel households always wore their skirts tightly pleated.

19. Women of the upper classes wore silk; commoners wore cotton.

20. Signifying "Order" or "Protection."

21. Signifying "Commander-in-Chief."

22. In a description of that portion of the ritual known as the *Hogu kori* (*Hogu* is considered a smallpox god by some) of the *Ch'ŏnshin-maji Kut* of Seoul and North Kyŏnggi Province, Huhm (op. cit, p. 68) makes the following statements in regard to the words "dark country":

> In the message from the dead tributes are paid to dark countries such as Mongolia and Han Dynasty China.
>
> This practice refers to the tributes paid by the Koryŏ Dynasty in the declining days to Mongolia and China. Koryŏ maidens were part of the tributes and they died there longing for their homeland.
>
> The *Kori is* performed in supplication lest there be any more such misfortune.

However, other sources simply interpret "dark country" to mean "night" and "twilight country" to mean "evening."

23. Very high imaginary mountains believed to be somewhere in North Korea near China.

24. Here we may infer that it is the Yalu River, located between North Korea and Manchuria, that is referred to.

25. A city located on the Yalu River.

26. Rivers located in North Korea.

27. Japanese forces, headed by General Hideyoshi, invaded Korea in 1592.

28. "Wonder visitor" or "marvel disease" in the original Korean.

29. Astronomy or astrology.

30. Geography or geophysics.

31. Made from the shell of a large sea conch.

32. A large transverse flute of bamboo or jadeite stone.

33. Headache.

34. Smallpox.

35. A dark red color in which the smallpox manifests itself when the symptoms first appear.

36. Meaning undetermined.

37. An imaginary mountain.

38. A play on words symbolizing the hope for a facile casting off of the disease.

39. These expressions are related to two Chinese tales of filial piety.

An Sa-in, a Cheju Island *Mudang*, sings and dances during a performance of the *Yŏngdŭng Kut* ("Rite for the Spirit of the Wind") at a seaside shrine. (photo: Kim Su-nam)

5. The Shrine Ritual[1] Song of the Tutelary God Sŏ-Gwi-P'o[2]

Note: The Prologue to the ritual proper, having been lost to the memory of the Mudang, is not included.

I.

The Mudang sings.

"In the land of Cheju,
From the Snow Mountain Country[3] sprung forth,

Is the God
Il-Mun-Gwan-Param-Un.

His father's country,
Hong-To-Do[4] doth be; and

His mother's country,
Pi-Ut-Do[4] doth be.

His topknot[5]
Large as a fist;

His headband,
Of the most delicate texture;

And the strings that bind it,
Ah, how truly fine they be!

His black felt is
From the fur of the mountain beast made,[6] and

Inside, it is with
Sun-designed damask lined.[7]

The loosely tied chin strap,
Of black-colored damask is made, and

The firmly tied chin strap,
Of the finest woven black damask is made;

The dangling amber chin strap,
Of great beads is construed, and

At the crown there is affixed,
A 'heron's plume.

His broad pantaloons,
From the East do come,

His wide blouse
From the North doth come.

Of indigo damask,
His tunic is made, and

From *su-ri*[8] damask,
His waistband of doubled cloth is made.

His eyes, like the phoenix,
Do open wide, and

His long beard, his moustache and side-whiskers,
He doth stroke at length.

When he doth
A lone arrow let fly,

Three-thousand soldiers
Spring forth;

When he doth
Still another let fly,

Three-thousand soldiers
Sprout forth.

He does the Heaven's secrets know, and
The earth's secrets know.

From o'er the mountains and the sea,
O'er ten-thousand leagues,

The rumor,
He doth hear:

In the Red Soil Nation,
Red soil o'er a thousand leagues,

Where, when rain doth fall,
It falls o'er a thousand leagues,

There dwells a woman of beauty,
Who Ko-San-Guk is called.

Thereupon doth he,
The blue cloud grasp,

And upon it,
He doth ride;

And, in the twinkling of an eye,
He doth thereupon arrive.

Verily, it doth be!
There the beauteous woman doth reside.

Thereupon did
Ko-San-Guk bow and say:

'Noble guest,
From what place do you come?'

'From the land of Cheju,
From the Snow Mountain Country sprung forth,

The God Il-Mun-Gwan-Param-Un,
Am I.'

'Ko-San-Guk,
They do call me.'

Whereupon did they,
Their bows exchange,

And unto one another,
Their countenance take note;

And forthwith, unto one another,
They did enamored become.

'My adoration for thee is such,
The long road I think of no more;

So say I,
Here before you.'

'Last night's dream,
T'was most wondrous indeed;

Today I meet you, and
A great fortune is mine.'

And thus, lovers
They did become, and

Husband and wife
They did become.

Two, three days, they,
In wedded bliss did pass,

When a woman most beauteous
Did appear.

Her beauty did that of
Ko-San-Guk far surpass;

Under Heaven there be not
A virgin such as she.

'Yon maiden,
Who doth she be?'

'The virgin doth
My younger sister be.'

Seeing for the very first,
The younger sister of Ko-San-Guk,

His breast did
Heave mightily,

And his heart,
He could not contain.

His features masculine and heroic,
He did lose!

A body thinking of a woman only,
Did he become.

When she's nowhere to be seen,
The more he doth adore her;

When she comes into sight,
You'd think the man were an idiot.

Toward Ko-San-Guk he doth
A great sin commit;

Mind and body only do
Great anguish know . . .

And endless fear . . .

To herself alone,
Doth the younger sister of Ko-San-Guk,

The God Il-Mun-Gwan Param-Un,
Adore . . .

No different a mind of agony,
From Il-Mun-Kwan was hers.

Though for each other,
Their hearts were burning,

The anguish of Il-Mun-Gwan,
The maiden knew not; and

Of the virgin's agony,
Il-Mun-Gwan was unaware.

Though they did so
Each other adore,

When they perchanced to meet,
Their eyes with anxiety were filled;

Until, at last,
Their hearts turned cold.

In such torment they,
The days and months did pass.

Alas,
What's to be done;

Il-Mun-Gwan
May hesitate no longer

At the third watch
He doth,

The maiden's soft wrist,
Firmly grasp.

Though he so wishes to speak,
No words can he utter;

Ah,
How his breast tightens so!

Huge tears only,
From his eyes do fall; and

In the maiden's misty eyes are filled,
Tears with drops like dew.

In her heaving bosom is filled,
The sound of anguished breath;

The heart that can not cry out,
With but affliction only is filled.

Ah,
How her breast tightens so!

Days of torment,
They did pass;

Then, one day, they two,
In secret their escape did plan.

In the utter blackness
Of the night,

The blue cloud they did
Grasp and ride,

And in the land of Cheju they did
Into Yŏng-san Mountain[9] enter.

The night did thus pass,
And Ko-San-Guk did awaken.

Of Il-Mun-Gwan-Param-Un,
No stirring sound is heard:

'It must be that
He sleeps late.'

Going to the chamber of
Il-Mun-Gwan,

Not a soul is to be found;

'It must be that
For some fresh air,

He's out to the garden.'

Going out to the garden and
Gazing 'round,

Not even his shadow is
Anywhere to be seen.

Entering the chamber of
Il-Mun-Gwan,

She doth peer all about with care;

The belongings of
Il-Mun-Gwan,

Are nowhere to be seen.

And thereupon was Ko-San-Guk,
With astonishment overcome.

To seek the whereabouts of
Il-Mun-Gwan,

Does she
To younger sister's chamber hasten.

But yet too, younger sister,
Where has she gone?

And yet too, her belongings,
Where do they be?

'Those two, they've gone mad;
'Tis likely they've eloped!'

To her own chamber,
Ko-San-Guk doth retire;

Her clothes
She doth put off,

And a man's costume
She doth put on.

An iron bow of
A thousand pounds, and

Iron arrows of
A hundred pounds,

'Cross her back
She doth place.

'Where'er they've gone,
Those faithless ones,

I pray,
Thou wilt guide me.'

So to heaven she did pray,
And then a banner she did wave.

Though the wind doth
In the opposite direction blow,

The banner toward Mt. Halla
Doth violently flutter.

The banner's direction,
Ko-San-Guk doth follow, and

A shortcut,
She doth take.

The road that is
A hundred leagues,

In five leagues
Is traversed; and

The road that is
A thousand leagues,

In ten leagues
Is traversed.

To Mt. Halla of Cheju,
In a breath she doth arrive.

Sure enough,
Her younger sister and Param-Un,

In matrimony
There do dwell.

Ko-San-Guk
Who yet,

From the dream of marital bliss,
Hath not yet awakened,

With anger
Bursting unto the heavens,

By the sharpest arrow tip
She will,

With but one shot,
That wench and rascal kill.

Her younger sister,
Who as 'Ko-San-Guk' is also known,

A magic mist
Doth summon,

And a dense fog and rain
Doth make;

To the east, west, south and north
Darkness all around.

Ko-San-Guk did thereby
Her senses all but lose.

Alas, what's to be done,
She knows not;

Unto almighty *Hanna-Nim*[10]
She did pray.

Again and again,
Endless magic she doth conjure,

But the dark fog and rain,
She can not disperse.

To escape from the mist,
She knows not how.

Upon the stone cliff,
The eyes of Ko-San-Guk did fall;

There, a dead camphor tree
Doth stand.

The camphor tree
She doth remove, and

The rotted branches
She doth break off;

The remaining stem,
A cock doth resemble.

In the mid slope of the stone cliff,
The cock she doth place.

The cock doth his neck stretch out, and
His wings he doth flap;

With voice loud and clear,
He doth cry out:

'Cock-a-doodle-doo!'

To Heaven and Earth,
And the Four Directions,

His cry was
Everywhere heard.

And thus was the gathered fog,
In this way dispersed.

Then, from the east,
A most beauteous moon did arise.

Her senses all regained,
She doth gaze all about;

There, from afar,
The faithless ones do stand.

'Wench, I'll catch you!
Minx, I'll kill you!

Lecherous rake!

On a chopping board
I'll cut you to bits!

Oh beastlike Param-Un!
You rogue!

Even though
I should kill you both,

My wrath could I
Not suppress!

Though you be
My younger sister called,

By such plight
Do you wish,

Your elder sister
To make thin and die!

You there,
Param-Un!

Though you be
My husband called,

By a nail driving
In her breast,

Do you wish
Your wife to kill!

Below Heaven,
The most depraved and wicked ye be—

I'll kill you both!

The code of morality
Know ye not,

Beastlike wench and knave!

The sharpest arrowhead,
That like unto a turnip be formed,[11]

This lone arrow,
These debauchers can kill;

Yet will I forego,
To these disloyal ones destroy

My younger sister
Thou art no longer;

By the surname 'Chi,'
Hereafter shall ye be known.

My spouse
Thou art no longer.

Thou art no relation—

Nay, naught but a stranger
Shall ye become.

To Ko-San-Guk[12]
I should return;

Yet, in such disgrace,
Return can I not.

Alas, where'er these feet may carry me,
There I shall go.

Depraved devils,
Where'er it is your wish to go,

Begone!'

And thereby did Ko-San-Guk
Her relationships all sever,

And by herself alone,
Did she depart;

Unto Hallim town[13]
Did she descend.

And thus,
Chi-San-Guk and Param-Un,

In Halla Mountain,
Near the White Deer Pond,[14]

'Mongst the peaks therein,
Did wander.

And from the mountain without,
On a grassy plain they stand;

To the East, West, South and North,
They gaze in every direction;

No man, no house,
Nor song of birds there be.

Their dwelling place to settle,
Did they a spyglass and a compass bring forth.[15]

The village at the upper place,
A most favorable ground doth appear;

To the village at the upper place,
Do they thereby descend.

But when they did
To the village at the upper place descend,

The dwelling place,
'Twas not suitable, and

Once again, the compass
They did bring forth.

The Rice Mountain[16] summit,
A most favorable ground doth appear;

At the Rice Mountain summit,
A white tent they did pitch."

II.

(The Mudang sings)

"In Upper West Village,
There was a man called Kim Pong-t'ae.

From the land otter's hide,
His hat is made;

From the yellow dog's hide,
His coat is made.

On his back,
The narrow-necked hunting bag hangs;

From 'round his waist,
The hunting knife hangs.

The four-eyed dog,[17]
'Mok-Dong-Yŏni'[18] is called;

The blue shaggy dog,
'Po-Mae-Kka-Gi'[19] is called;

Four dogs in all
He does bring forth,

For 'tis a-hunting
He will go.

To the lower pagoda
He does ascend, and

On the summit of Rice Mountain,
The white tent he does spy.

'The white tent,
If not by fairy-gods pitched,

Surely then, by a holy man
It must be.

How strange indeed!'

To the middle pagoda
He does ascend;

The white tent,
Does yet remain.

'Truly, it must be
The gods themselves.'

Within a hundred feet
He doth approach;

Hands folded together,
Three times he doth bow, and

With head bent low
Remains.

'Who goes without?'
A voice he doth hear.

'It is I,
Kim Pong-t'ae,

Who in Upper West Village
Does dwell.'

'For what purpose
Do ye come here?'

''Tis for hunting
That I do venture out.

What gods be it, I pray,
That come here?'

'From the Snow Mountain Country sprung forth,
Il-Mun-Gwan Param-Un am I.'

'From the Red Soil Nation,
Red soil o'er a thousand leagues,

Where, when rain doth fall,
It falls o'er a thousand leagues.

Chi-San-Guk
Am I.'

'For what purpose dost thou
To this place descend?'

'The human world, the human race,
Do I observe,

And my human disciple,
Do I come to seek.'

'Ah, yes.
I see.'

'As fate would have it,
That you to us do belong,

Our pathway
Thou shalt guide.'

'To carry out thy wishes,
Thou dost honor me far too much.'

'What village is it
That nearest doth be?'

'I dare say, sir,
It is that which is called Upper Sŏ-Gwi,

And below is the place
Which is known as Lower Sŏ-Gwi;

To the west be the place
That is called West Hong-Ni.'

'Well then,
To Upper Sŏ-Gwi do guide us.'

And thus,
To Upper Sŏ-Gwi they did descend;

But there, in Upper Sŏ-Gwi,
No suitable dwelling place there be.

'As in Upper Sŏ-Gwi
A suitable dwelling place there be not,

In your house
Three months I'll dwell;

How be it?'

'By your words, sir,
You do me too great an honor;

The dwelling of a mortal
Is surely unclean.

The smell of dust, and
The smell of smoke;

The smell of cooking, and
The smell of a human;

For gods to there abide,
I dare say,

'Tis a place
Far too unclean.'

'Take ye no heed;

To thy house
Let's begone!'"

III.

(The Mudang sings)

"Well,

On the matter
We'll dwell no further;

Kim Pong-t'ae did
The two gods

To his home in
Upper West Village bring.

Yet, with the two gods together,
He dare not abide.

At the upper place,
The wood he doth cut;

And a house,
Small and clean,

For them to dwell therein,
He doth build.

'Begging your pardon, sir,

For but a short while,
Do at this place abide.'

And while the gods
There did three months abide,

Neither man on horseback,
Nor doglike creature,

Did they care to see.

'We, may, in this place,
No longer abide;

A suitable dwelling
We must seek out.

A few months hence,
Ye shall have word;

Until then,
Stay in peace.'

And with these words,
The two gods did

Take their leave.

Then did Il-Mun-Gwan Param-Un and
Chi-San-Guk

At a cavern called
The 'Black Cave' arrive.

And while they
Three months there did abide,

The voice of rushing waters
In a brook nearby, and

The deep forest
All around;

Hearing thus and
Seeing thus,

They were with
Loneliness overcome.

The two gods then
A new dwelling place did ponder.

'Though we did by strife
From Ko-San-Guk depart,

It be a good principle,
Her to meet once more;

And after meeting
Once again,

The dwelling place to decide,
More favorable will be.'"

IV.

(The Mudang sings)

"Ko-San-Guk doth
O'er the West Hong-Ni[20] people reign;

At the Thornhead-Hawk Rock,[21]
They did with her

A meeting arrange.

And thus,
On the appointed day,

At the appointed place
They did together meet.

But the wrath of Ko-San-Kuk
Yet hath not subsided:

'For what purpose be it that
Ye do seek me out yet again?'

'How long should we then
By this state exist?

The division of the land,
Let us in harmony deliberate;

To reign over the land,
To reign over the people,

Be it not thus
A far better thing?'

We once and for all
Our relation did sever;

'. . . in harmony,' you say?
'. . . deliberate,' you say?

Yet did Il-Mun-Kwan Param-Un
Her generosity pursue.

'Alas,
What's to be done . . .'

Then did Ko-San-Guk
The sharpest arrowhead,

That like unto a turnip be formed,
Let fly through the air; and,

At the lower pagoda,
It did fall.

'The people,
They be mine;

The land,
It be mine;

The water,
It be mine;

The trees in the mountain,
They be mine;

The beasts of the mountain,
They be mine;

From this day henceforth,
Ask of me no more!'

Then did Il-Mun-Gwan Param-Un
The arrow let fly;

To the Isle of Mosquitoes,[22]
To the huge rock it did fall.

'Get thee then
To Upper and Lower Sŏ-Gwi

To the north of Mosquito Isle,
And reign over all therein.

The man of West Hong-Ni
Shall not the East Hong-Ni woman wed,

Nor shall the man of East Hong-Ni
The West Hong-Ni woman wed;[23]

The Mudang of East Hong-Ni
Shall to West Hong-Ni not go,

Nor shall the Mudang of West Hong-Ni
To East Hong-Ni go.

The people over whom thou dost reign,
Mine enemies all do be;

The people over whom thou dost reign,
For a house to build,

Shall ne'er my trees cut down;

The people over whom thou dost reign,
I shall all destroy,

Should they my trees cut down.'[24]

And thereby did Ko-San-guk
To West Hong-Ni journey.

Then did Param-Un
The compass bring forth;

The uppermost branches of
The sacred wood of Lower Sŏ-Gwi,

A most favorable place
Doth be.

To there they did descend,
And a dwelling did establish;

Yet doth no man,
Nay, not even one,

To that place come
And give worship.

Then, one day,
In Upper Sŏ-Gwi,

The lineal descendant of
The O family,

With illness was taken;

And of a severe nature,
Did the illness become.

'Param-Un and Chi-San Guk,

Though in the uppermost branches of
The sacred wood dwell,

All who pass by
Indifference do pretend.

An unpardonable offense
It doth be;

Thereby have they
This illness laid upon me[25] . . .'

These words did murmur

The lineal descendant of
The O family,

As he did of
Param-Un and Chi-San-Guk relate.

Hearing this in amazement,

The O family did
To Lower Sŏ-Gwi descend.

At first did they
The Sŏng family seek out,

And all did relate
Of that which they'd heard.

The Sŏng family then
The lead did take, and

The inhabitants of Upper and Lower Sǒ-Gwi
Soon all did gather;

And it was thereupon decided
The dedication of a shrine.

Many trees they did cut,
And with them a shrine did build.

A Mudang was thereupon chosen, and
They did then up to Seoul proceed;

The moonlit damask,
The sunlit damask,

The plain-cloth silk,
Silk of all kinds,

The broadcloth silk,
The green silk,

A double silver ring,
A double gold ring,

A large bead,
An amber chin strap,

All these they did buy,
And as sacrifice did offer.

And, on the first day of
The year,[26]

They did, in a great ritual,
Their greetings offer;

On the fifteenth day of
The second month,

They did, in a great ritual,
Their welcome to the Dragon God[27] offer;

On the thirteenth day of
The seventh month,

They did, in a great ritual,
The devil exorcise;

On the first day of
The birthday ritual;[28]

And thereafter,
For Param-Un and Chi-San-Guk,

Was Kim Pong-t'ae
Revered.

Under the two gods,
A disciple he became; and

Thereby was he
By all the people worshiped.

And so, were
Param-Un and Chi-San-Guk,

As the gods of Upper and Lower Sŏ-Gwi
Settled."

V.

(The Mudang sings)

"From ancient times
There dwelled,

In Sujin-P'o,[29]
At the southwest tip,

A lady who was called
Kŭm-Sang-Hwang-Je.

The sacred wood of Upper Sŏ-Gwi
One day she did view;

There a god's dwelling
She did spy,

Whereupon she did exclaim:
'What god can this be?'

'Param-Um and Chi-San-Guk
Are we.'

'What matter is it
That to this place brings ye?'

'The populace of
Upper and Lower Sŏ-Gwi,

To reign over
We do come.'

'Upper and Lower Sŏ-Gwi
My kingdom doth be.'

'Oh!
We have sorely erred.

Had we but known
Upper and Lower Sŏ-Gwi be thy domain,

Surely, such a thing
We'd not have done;

Out of ignorance did we,
Such offense commit.'

Hearing this,
Lady Kŭm-Sang-Hwang-Je did say:

'My power is weak;

The danger from East and West,
I can not thwart;

The populace to the East and West,
I have no power to rule.

If it be your want,
The land and people

Of Upper and Lower Sŏ-Gwi
To occupy and reign,

I shall the
Dragon Palace[30] enter, and

The departing ship,
The incoming ship,

The departing woman diver,[31]
The incoming woman diver,

The departing passenger,
The incoming passenger,

All these shall I possess,
And over them shall I reign.'

The Lady Kŭm-Sang-Hwang-Je
The Dragon Palace did enter, and

Il-Mun-Gwan Param-Un and
Chi-San-Guk,

The land and people of
Upper and Lower Sŏ-Gwi,

Did reign over;

And by all the inhabitants therein,
Were they duly worshiped,

And so did they,
The tutelary Gods of Sŏ-Gwi-P'o become."

Notes

1. This ritual, known as a *Tang Kut,* is comprised of a *Pon-P'uri,* a legend telling the origin or history of the guardian deity shrine of the town or village. On the mainland of Korea, there is no known tutelary god shrine *Pon-P'uri* in existence at present, although there may have been at one time, having long since passed into oblivion. For a further discussion of the shrine ritual and a narrative description of the myth that is sung here, see *The Folk Treasury of Korea* (op. cit., pp. 10, 11 and 98-6). See also Sect. III, Chapter 5 of this work, "An Explanation of the Shrine Ritual Songs (*Mu-ga Pon-p'uri*) of Cheju Island," p. 333, and Appendix III.

2. Sŏ-Gwi-P'o is a seaport located in the southern part of Cheju Island, off the southern coast of Korea.

3. Refers to Mt. Halla, a large volcanic mountain in the center of Cheju Island.

4. A place of undetermined origin.

5. In ancient times, Korean men wore their hair tied up in a knot at the top of the head.

6. An indication that the hat is of a very soft texture.

7. Indicative of high rank and affluence.

8. Meaning undetermined.

9. A holy mountain; another reference to Mt. Halla.

10. God, the Almighty, or Heaven.

11. Makes a whirring sound as it flies through the air.

12. The name of Ko-San-Guk's native country and her own name are the same.

13. A town in West Cheju.

14. Located at the summit of Mt. Halla.

15. To choose the most favorable spot in accordance with the rules of geomancy.

16. A mountain in Cheju.

17. A dog with black spots above its eyes.

18. The dog's name means "wide-necked," indicating that the animal is brave and strong.

19. The dog's name means "horselike," indicating that the animal resembles the pony native to Cheju Island.

20. Formerly a village; now a street in Sŏ-Gwi-P'o.

21. A place-name in Sŏ-Gwi-P'o.

22. Located off Sŏ-Gwi-P'o.

23. It is interesting to note here that even to this day this edict is strictly adhered to, the people believing that to do otherwise would result in a marriage ending in unhappy circumstances.

The Folk Treasury of Korea (op. cit., p. 14, no. 6, "The Guardian Deities of Sŏgwipo") relates the following:

> It is said that a long time ago there was no communication nor marriage between the villagers of Sŏ-Hong-ni (West Hong-Ni) and Sŏ-Gwi-ri (West Gwi-ri) in Sukwipo (Sŏ-Gwi-P'o). It was ascribed to the discord between the guardian gods of the two villages.
>
> This myth is recited during the "Danggut" (*Tang Kut*) for the guardian god of the village.
>
> The villages on Cheju Island each have their own guardian gods. The gods have their own lineage, and some of them are on friendly

terms and others are not. This fact is responsible for the concord or discord between the villagers, according to tradition.

24. This edict is also still strictly adhered to, the people believing that to do otherwise would be to invite misfortune.

25. An interesting parallel may be found here in a paper written by Brian Wilson entitled "Kut: Catharsis, Ritual Healing or Redressive Strategy?" (*Conference on Korean Religion and Society*, Mackinac Island, Aug. 25-29, 1980, pp. 8-12), in which he relates an incident whereby a murder and three suicides in a village near the town of Hong San in Ch'ung-Ch'ŏng Province are attributed to neglect of the village shrine (*sŏnang-tang*) ritual and the cutting of trees in the area.

26. In accordance with the lunar calendar.

27. The god of the sea.

28. This may actually refer to the anniversary of the shrine's establishment.

29. The name of a seaport at the southwest tip of Cheju Island.

30. The sea.

31. Cheju Island is famous for its women divers who collect seaweed and shellfish from the sea bottom.

Section II

Ogu Kut:
The Musok Ritual of the Dead
A Description of the Ritual Practice

Part I

The Ogu Kut[1] in Tong-Nae[2] is a K'un Kut, one of the largest Musok rites typical of the east coast region. Although it generally falls under the South Han classification, many of its traits are quite different from those of the kut performed in the South Han region, leading some to classify it separately under the category of "Eastern Seaboard."[3] Some of these differences are listed as follows:

1. The musical instruments employed in the Ogu Kut consist of a large and small gong, a changgo drum, and occasional cymbals. Although no wind or string instruments are used, the conical oboe is played in processional and some preliminary sections. At the opening of the ceremony, all the instruments are played louder and more nosily than in other areas of the southern region, and the rhythms are more varied and numerous.

2. The Mudang's costume is simpler. It consists of a *quaeja,* a traditional military costume, worn over an ordinary blouse and skirt. No hat is worn, but the Mudang's hair style is unique. She dresses it up in an antique style and ties a white band around her head with a blossomed flower-shaped knot on the left side. When she sings, she holds a fan in her left hand and a kerchief in her right. Sometimes she also holds in her hand a cluster of small bells which jingle as she moves to and fro, swaying slightly while singing.

3. The melodies of the Mu-ga are quite different from those of other areas and are not as varied. In addition, the singing

231

style is different. In other regions, the Mu-ga is sung from beginning to end without a pause, but in the Ogu Kut, the Mudang pauses often, alternating her performance with that of the accompanying musicians. While she sings, the Mudang is accompanied by the changgo and the large gong, although the latter is played softly. Coming to the end of a line in the song, all the instruments are played loudly and the Mudang stops her singing. During this pause, she dances slowly and gently, calmly raising her hands slightly and continuing to move them while stepping to and fro and turning her body around. This alternation of singing and instrument playing, which continues throughout the song, is never found in other regions of Korea. Similarly, the dance performed during the pause lacks the jumps, quick turns, kneebends and waistbends which are characteristic of the northern region.

4. The player of the changgo must be the husband of the Mudang who is in charge of that section of the kut at which he plays. While the Mudang sings and dances, her husband plays the changgo and watches her. He may also sing, briefly or at length. This optional singing, called *paraji*,[4] has various purposes: sometimes it helps the Mudang to recall parts of forgotten lines or to correct her mistakes, serves to give her encouragement, or breaks up the long verses of the song. The husband may on occasion shout out such calls as "My darling is the best singer!" or "What a great wife I have!" or simply "Well done!" In addition, the husband sometimes performs comic gestures, intones syllables in a falsetto voice, and swaps quips with his wife. In so doing, he makes the audience laugh and heightens interest in the performance.

5. After the mudang finishes singing the main Mu-ga appropriate to the given section of the kut, she proceeds to recite various Buddhist scriptures such as the *Ch'ŭn-Sŭ-Kyŏng* (the "Dharani of the Great Compassionate One"), *Panya-Shim-Kyŏng* (the "Heart Sutra") or *Podhemaduagortha* (the "Forty-Eight Great Wishes"). She also performs ritual dances and recites spells such as the *Ch'uk-Won*. Such

elements are structural features of each section of the kut;
after they are performed, the Mudang continues with elements of a more complex nature. Depending upon the
section of the kut, these more complex elements include
such things as Buddhist scriptures, group dances, spells
for obtaining a blessing, short comic dramas, a flower
dance, a lantern dance, holding a rite for various demons,
asking the participants for an offering, or singing folk or
popular songs.

6. An altar is erected inside the hall (really a large tent)
   where the ritual is performed. Both sides of the altar are
   decorated with various kinds of flowers made of colored
   paper. Various kinds of colored lanterns are hung inside
   the hall: octagonal lanterns, long lanterns, and miniature
   figures of the Buddha as well as the eight Bodhisattvas.
   Imitation iron nets made of paper are also hung about the
   hall as well as ten long strips of paper on which is written
   "Ten Gods (Kings) of Hell! We dare to ask you to come."
   On the center of the altar, the deceased's mortuary tablet
   and soul basket are placed. On the front of the altar are
   plentiful offerings of various kinds of foods, but neither a
   cow's head or hooves nor a boiled whole pig are to be
   found. Outside the hall, the *quettae,* which announces the
   holding of the ceremony, the post of the guardian god,
   gold and silver-colored paper money, a miniature *Panya*
   ship (the *Prajna* Dragon Boat), and a long white cloth are
   hung in the air. The presence of these objects indicates
   that the Musok ceremonies in Tong-Nae have adopted
   more Buddhistic elements than the kut found in other
   areas of Korea.

7. The Mudang makes every attempt to perform the blessed
   fortune spell for the members of the general audience
   as well as for the sponsor of the kut. This provides her
   with several opportunities to request monetary offerings,
   although the offering from the sponsor is larger than any
   of those received from the members of the general audience. The Mudang requests offerings several times during
   each section of the kut. In other areas of the south, the
   Mudang does not use this method to request offerings,

and the occasions for requesting them are fewer. In Seoul and its surrounding areas, the method of obtaining offerings is similar to the one found here; however, another method, called *mugam* (see Introduction, p. 31, fn. 47), is also used whereby the Mudang watches for an appropriate moment to tempt a volunteer from the audience to dance. The volunteer must then pay a fairly large sum of money for the privilege of dancing. She borrows one of the ceremonial costumes of the Mudang and wears it while dancing to the musical accompaniment until she becomes tired. It seems as though mugam serves as a means of emotional catharsis for oppressed females.

8. The Mudang in Tong-Nae calls the female members of the audience "*posalnim*,"[5] a Buddhist expression, and calls their monetary offerings "*shi-ju*," another Buddhist expression. These audience members come to the ritual not only as spectators, but also to utilize it as an opportunity to pray for their own personal happiness.

9. The Ogu Kut is a rite for consoling a dead soul and for guiding it to its eternal resting place. In Tong-Nae, however, the rite may also be performed for the soul of a living person. In such instances it is called *Saeng Ogu Kut*, meaning "living Ogu Kut," and its purpose is to console and bring good fortune and happiness to the sponsor of the ritual while he or she is alive, as well as to guide the sponsor's soul to its eternal resting place after death. Therefore, the Saeng Ogu Kut may be viewed as an advance Ogu Kut.[6]

10. Although the Ogu Kut in Tong-Nae is ostensibly a religious rite, it exhibits many elements of a feast or festival. Interwoven with the religious elements, the amusement aspects of the performance dominate not only each individual section of the kut, but its entire gestalt or pattern as well. Although the ceremony has religious meaning and function, it is also regarded as a way of demonstrating the sponsor's personal fame and prestige. In order to sponsor the ceremony, a person must spend a good deal of money and provide a large amount of food and other goods. He or she must purchase the various items which are needed

for the rite, must pay a substantial fee to the Mudangs and musicians, and must also provide food and drink for the audience. Thus, the Ogu Kut could be viewed as the Korean equivalent of the potlatch.

11. The chief Mudang employs in turn many co-workers. She pays them their traveling expenses from the contract fee which she receives from the sponsor. The remainder of the fee is divided in half between the chief Mudang and all of her co-workers. Ninety percent of the offerings received during a given section of the kut is kept by the Mudang in charge of that particular section, and the remaining ten percent is given to the musicians. During the time that the ritual is in progress, the sponsor provides food and lodging for the Mudangs and their co-workers.

12. Early in the morning of the day on which the Ogu Kut is held, the chief Mudang holds a simple ceremony for the guardian god of the house and for the mountain god, and she prays that the soul which is entering its new home will be allowed to receive its descendant's offerings.

Part II

The K'ŭn Kut generally consists of twelve sections, but the Ogu Kut in Tong-Nae contains nineteen.[7] These sections are listed below in the order of performance. The first three are performed in the sponsor's house, and the remainder are held in the ceremonial hall specially erected outside.

1. *Pujong Kut* (Purification Rite)
2. *Songju Kut* (Rite for the Main House God)
3. *Chosang Kut* (Ancestor Rite)
4. *Kolmaegi Kut* (Guardian God Rite)
5. *Ipmun Kut* (Rite for Entering the Gate)
6. *Mun Kut* (Gate Entertainment Rite)
7. *Ch'ornangju Kut* (Rite for the Dead Soul)
8. *Palwŏn Kut* (Wishing Rite)

9. *Ogu Tae Wang P'uri* (Legend of King Ogu)

10. *Kang-Shin Kut* (Rite of the Descending God)

11. *Nŭk-Irŭkigi* (Soul-Raising Rite)

12. *Yŏnga Mokyŏk Shikigi* (Soul-Bathing Rite)

13. *Ch'uk-Wŏn Kut* (Petition Rite)

14. *Saeng Ogu Kut* (Living Person's Ogu Kut)

15. *Shi-Wang Kut* (Rite for the Ten Gods–or Kings–of Hell)

16. *Panya-Sŏn Taeugi* (Rite for Launching the Deceased's
    Soul in the Panya Ship)

17. *Kkot Nori* (Flower Entertainment Rite)

18. *Tŭng Nori* (Lantern Entertainment Rite)

19. *Subu Shishik* (Rite for Serving Demons)

Each of these sections has its own characteristics. Some are very simple, comprising only singing with drum accompaniment; others are more complicated and include not only singing with instrumental accompaniment, but also short skits, requests by the Mudang for an offering, singing of folk and popular songs, and paraji all woven together for the sake of a more interesting performance. In addition, the time required to perform each of the sections varies. Shorter ones are completed in about an hour, but the longest one takes more than six hours.

In every section, just before the song begins, the musicians strike up a rhythm called *punŭri* and the Mudang begins to dance slowly. She then faces the altar and bows reverently four times. Then the rhythm changes to one called *ch'ŏngbo*, and a few minutes later, the Mudang begins to sing the Mu-ga appropriate to that section. Every Mu-ga, except the Legend of King Ogu, is sung by the Mudang in a standing position.[9]

While the Mudang sings, the large gong is played lightly, the small gong not at all, and the changgo is more highly accented. During the pause, all the instruments are played and the Mudang dances. Here, the dance form is simple: she merely moves her hands and feet slightly, steps to and fro, and turns around slowly. In the Gate Entertainment Rite, however, the dance is characterized by a highly unique form of dance step not found in other regions wherein arms are held high and the fingers and hands move in and out in conjunction with very slight and graceful skips, jumps and kicking steps. Here the dance is vibrant and is performed by two Mudangs facing each other.

The ch'ŏngbo rhythm has five tempos. The first one is slow, the second a little faster, and as the song advances toward the end, the tempo becomes even faster. The Mudang's singing keeps pace with the music so that by the end of the song she scarcely has time to interrupt her singing in order to dance.

After singing the Mu-ga, the Mudang recites various Buddhist scriptures, accompanied by the rhythm of *sakong-jaebi* or *chŏng-ch'i*. Next, the Mudang prays to Amitabha accompanied by the *chang-yuk* rhythm while she accompanies herself on a small slit-gong or temple block. The prayer is followed by the *kasam* rhythmic pattern which is done without singing, and this in turn by a song about a monk in the *chasan* rhythm. Next, the Mudang dances to the rhythm of either *tong sal-p'uri* (a rhythmic pattern in 12/8 time) or *puchŏng chak kongi* while holding up a small dried codfish in a small basket. The rhythm picks up to a rather brisk accelerando here as the Mudang starts dancing about, going to and fro in the hall where she is performing. During this time, she approaches the sponsor of the kut and imitates the coming of the ancestral spirits, induces the sponsor into a deeper emotional state, and asks for a special offering. Upon completion of this dance, the Mudang recites a *Ch'uk-Wŏn* to the accompaniment of the *sal-p'uri* (12/8) rhythm.[10] The Ch'uk-Wŏn is a prayer or spell which is spontaneously composed. Its text consists entirely of expressions which encourage the coming of good fortune and urge the expulsion of evil. At first, the Ch'uk-Wŏn is recited for the sponsor and his or her family members, in return for which the Mudang receives an offering. Then she recites one for the audience in general, and they too give offerings. Sometimes a member of the audience will request a personal Ch'uk-Wŏn, and a special offering is received for that as well. The Ch'uk-Wŏn recitations afford an opportunity for momentarily changing the solemn atmosphere of the religious ceremony to one of amusement and entertainment whereby the Mudang mimics, tells jokes, and finally may even interpolate folk or popular songs not in any way related to the Mu-ga. Upon completion of the Ch'uk-Wŏn, a given section then progresses for the service of the demons. These are thought to be the vengeful spirits of those who have died a miserable death. They have no eternal resting place and so they wonder about from place to place. Hungry and naked, they are constantly seeking satisfaction of their needs. Places crowded with people and where music is being played attract them, since such places are thought to be those where food is plentiful. So the demons visit as uninvited guests. If neglected, they take revenge by bringing about various types of disasters. Even though a ceremony is performed very well, its good effect may be spoiled by not treating the demons properly.

In the Ogu Kut, almost every song is sung in a solo capacity except those of the following section: the Gate Entertainment Rite, the Rite for Launching the Deceased's Soul in the Panya Ship, the Flower Entertainment Rite, and the Lantern Entertainment Rite. In these four sections, the mudangs sing together. The dance is also performed in a solo capacity except in the above four sections where group dancing is executed. Although the Mudang imitates the gods in other ways (e. g., voice, facial expressions), none of the dances in any of the sections display any indication or imitation, symbolic or otherwise, of the actions of the gods, nor do they reveal any narrative account of the god's behavior.

When interviewed, the Mudang in Tong-Nae named many kinds of rhythms employed in the ritual, but upon actually hearing them, her designations of particular rhythms were often found to be inaccurate. Instances were found where the names of the rhythms were different but the rhythms themselves seemed to be identical (e.g., *kŭ-mum* and *chakkongi* rhythms). In addition, the dance which is performed while holding up a dried codfish is sometimes performed to a chakkongi rhythm and sometimes to a *sŭchang chakkongi* rhythm. Thus, it appears that the actual names of the rhythms are of little significance to the Mudang, and, irrespective of their names, she substitutes similar rhythms rather freely. Despite this inaccuracy in terminology, however, it is obvious, as stated previously, that the rhythms found in the Tong-Nae area are more varied and numerous than those of other regions, and more complex as well.

The Mudangs of Tong-Nae enter their profession by hereditary succession, not by experiencing possession. They do not act as prophets or fortunetellers, nor do they provide remedies for illnesses. In their rites, they never employ such properties as broadswords, three-pronged spears, or tridents, sharp tools for chopping animal fodder, or five colored flags for telling fortunes, as are found, for example, in the rituals of Seoul and the North Han region, nor do they perform acrobatic feats.

Since the Ogu Kut has adopted many Buddhist elements, one might be tempted to think that it, and Musok in general, has no traits of its own, and that it is no more than a Buddhist imitation. However, closer examination of the Musok rites reveals that while Buddhism advocates the renunciation of worldly desires, Musok is concerned with the satisfaction of them. Musok may have absorbed various Buddhist elements, but it has adapted them to its own purposes without impairing its own essence.

Notes

1. The Ogu Kut is a rite performed by a Mudang for the purpose of consoling the soul of a dead person and for ensuring its safe and peaceful passage into Paradise.

2. During the spring and summer of 1971, three such ceremonies were observed in Tong-Nae, South Kyŏngsang Province, an area which lies partly within the city of Pusan and party adjacent to it.

3. Huhm, op. cit., p. 10.

4. Different in melody, rhythm and method of singing than that of the *mansubaji* of the Seoul area ritual (see Huhm, ibid., pp. 23-4).

5. "Goddess," not in the real sense of the word when directed to a female member of the audience, but merely an expression used by female Buddhist believers when addressing each other.

6. Huhm (op. cit., p. 93), in a description of the *Chinogwi Kut,* "The *kut* performed to pave the way for the spirit of the dead from the Seoul area of Kyŏnggi province . . ." states the following:

> In the Kyŏngsang provinces, the kut performed immediately after death is known as *Chin ogu kut,* meaning wet, or the tears are still wet. The *kut* performed some time after death is called *marŏn ogu kut,* meaning dried. The kut performed for old people while still alive to pave their way to the other world is called *Saeng ogu kut.* Thus, there are people who contend that the *Chinogwi kut* in Kyŏnggi province is the same as that performed in the Kyŏngsang provinces.

The above stated may be true except for *Saeng Ogu Kut,* which is unique to the Kyŏngsang ("Eastern Seaboard") area.

7. For the *Chinogwi Kut*, the counterpart of the *Ogu Kut* in Seoul and Kyŏnggi Province, Huhm (ibid., pp. 93-9) mentions twenty-six sections, which for comparative purposes, are listed as follows:

1. A purification ritual *(Pujŏng kŏri)* – All greater *kut* begin with the *Pujŏng kŏri*, a ritual to purify the site of the *kut*. *Pujŏng* means the cleansing of everything unclean. It is performed by the *kidae*, which are the assistant shamans.

2. Invocation of gods

3. Singing of a song of divination

4. Pouring of wine for gods, bowing

5. Singing of *manura norae karak* (a short Mu-ga)

6. Invoking the supreme god and receiving divination

7. Ch'o yŏngsil. It refers to the ghost of the departed, and this is a ritual for the transference of the ghost to the shaman.

8. A *kŏri* invoking the ghosts of ancestors as far as four generations back.

9. A *kŏri* in which is invoked the ghost of General Ch'oe Yong of Tongmul Mountain.

10. A *kŏri* in which the ghosts of feudal princes are invoked and which is performed for the living rather than for the dead.

11. *Shinjang Kŏri*. It refers to the divine generals of the five compass directions–east, west, south, north, and center. This is performed to purify the family in mourning and pray for its well-being and good fortune rather than for the dead.

12. *Wŏn yŏngshil kŏri*. This is a *kŏri* in which the spirit, now transferred to the shaman, narrates what happened when the departed was alive.

13. *Taegam kŏri*. The *taegam* in this case is the god of wealth who oversees and helps the living, that is, those in mourning, rather than the dead. *As* such, the *Taegam kŏri* is performed spiritedly and joyously even though it is a *Chinogwi kut*, which is essentially sad.

14. *Ch'angbu kŏri*. In *Chinogwi*, this is known as *Shiwang Ch'angbu* and is performed for the good fortune of the living—that is, those in mourning—until the end the three-year mourning period.

15. *Twitchŏn kŏri.* Following the *kut* performance at the hall of the *kut,* this *kŏri* is performed to feed and send off assorted demons.

16. *Chinogwi Ch'ŏngbae.* This is performed to invoke the relevant *Chinogwi* gods, to placate the departed spirit, and to invoke the ten kings and messengers with well-wishing remarks.

17. *Shiwang Kamang.* This is a *kŏri* in which the invoked god or gods pray to the Ten Kings of the Hall of Hades . . . and in which prayers are offered for the dead to safely reach the other world without any untoward incident between the dead and the living during the journey of the former to heaven.

18. *Shiwang malmyŏng.* This is performed to determine if there is a deceased member of the *Chinogwi*-performing family not given the benefit of *Chinogwi,* and to give blessings to the surviving members of the *Chinogwi*-performing family.

19. *Saja sam-sŏng. Saja* means messengers, messengers from the Hall of Hades, who, on orders from the Ten Kings, come to this world and take back with them the dead to the other world.

20. *Malmi (Pari Kongju*–the mythological forsaken princess). Known as "offering *Malmi,*" malmi in performing *Chinogwi kut* is designed to provide a time of rest to comfort the ghost of the departed, for the departed to realize his journey to heaven, and for the surviving family members to realize the family business. Offering *Malmi* also takes the form of telling narratives of the mythological *Pari Kongju* (see Appendix II).

21. *Toryŏng Kŏri.* This *kŏri* shows how *Pari Kongju* leads the ghost of the departed to the other world.

22. *Kilgarŏgi* (parting roads). This is said to mean the parting of life and the bridges of the Ten Kings.

23. *Sangshik.* This is a *kŏri* in which the ghost of the departed enjoys the last meal in this world before embarking on the road to the other world.

24. *Twit Yŏngshil.* In this *kŏri,* the ghost of the departed bids its family, relatives, and friends farewell and speaks out about everything that it wanted to do but failed to accomplish while living.

25. *Shiwang kunŭng.* This martial god of the Ten Kings is not the *kunŭng* god of an ordinary *kut,* but the martial god of the Ten Kings who is in charge of the road the ghost of the departed travels, and who oversees the ghost so it travels the road without incident.

26. *Chinogwi Twitchŏn.* The primary function is to placate, feed, and send off the last stragglers of assorted demons.

8. A narrative account of the legend may be found in Appendix II.

9. In the Tong-Nae rite, this is executed in a combination of song and narrative by the musician-husband of the chief Mudang.

Huhm, (op. cit., p. 97) relates how this particular section is performed in the *Chinogwi kut* of the Seoul and Kyŏnggi Province area:

> . . . the shaman sits in a chair holding the *changgu* vertically with the hand-beating side up (the other side is played with a bamboo stick).
>
> The shaman then beats the hand-beating side of the *changgu* with a folding fan held in the right hand while the left hand shakes the bells.
>
> As she performs in this way, the shaman offers *Malmi* or the narrative about the mythological forsaken princess.
>
> This epic mythological narrative is long, covering the events in the life of *Pari Kongju* (in the *Ogu Kut,* the myth is the same but it is called the legend of King Ogu; see Appendix II)—events such as how the princess was born, then forsaken, and later returned to her parents. The epic goes on to describe how the princess goes to countries bordering on Western China, finds the elixir of life, and saves her father.
>
> This narration is intended to depict the arduous journey of the departed to heaven.

10. The same rhythm is used to accompany the *Sal-P'uri* Dance (see Introduction, p. 30, fn. 38).

Section III

1. The Structure of Religions in Korea

A. Statistical Information on the Various Beliefs

Name of Religion	No. of Practicing Clergy	No. of Believers
1. Buddhist	18,629	7,990,000
2. Protestant	17,562	3,460,000
3. Catholic	3,478	790,000
4. Confucian	11,832	4,420,000
5. Ch'ŏn-Do-Kyo[1]	1,526	720,000
6. Wŏn Buddhism[2]	805	680,000
7. Tae-Jong-Kyo[3]	55	150,000
8. Miscellaneous	4,102	1,410,000
Total	57,997	19,610,000

In 1972, the Ministry of Culture & Information of the Republic of Korea released a set of data covering religious beliefs in Korea, which is set forth in Table I above.[4] Out of a total population of 35 million, the Buddhist and Wŏn Buddhist sects comprise a total of 8,670,000 followers, the Protestant and Catholic a total of 4,250,000, the *Ch'ŏn-Do-Kyo* and *Tae-Jong-Kyo,* religions that were founded in Korea, a total of 870,000, and various other types of religions; that is to say, newly-formed beliefs, the total of which is indicated in the above table.

Confucianism, which was propagated among the people after the establishment of the Yi Dynasty, was, in its essence, a political ideology really more than it was a religion. Moreover, since the Confucian "clergy," so to speak, whose number is estimated to be around 11,831, are not discernable as clergymen in any manner of dress or form,[5] it is impossible to know who they are.

Data relating to folk religion is, however, entirely absent from this compilation due to the fact that it is regarded as superstition and therefore cannot be regarded as religion in the regular sense. Foreign scholars, rather contending that every religion contains some element of superstition within it, cannot accept a compilation such as this from which folk religion is rejected on the basis of its being regarded by people in Korea as mere superstition.

In another sense, the writer would like to refer to the fact that, in 1973, members of an organization comprised of Mudangs and fortunetellers, known as the *Kyŏng-Shin Hoe,* which claims a total membership of 48,980, stated that there are estimated to be a total of 208,424 practitioners (Mudangs and fortunetellers) around the country; however, a member of the management staff asserts that because 80 percent are uneducated, guidance and organizational structure are difficult to maintain.

The writer discovered a Mudang who served between 100 and 200 households, or regular "clients," so to speak, which is equal to that of a church minister in a large town; however, this is an exceptional case, and because a religious organizational structure is lacking, it is difficult to know who the believers are. Nevertheless, the previously quoted total estimate of the 50,000 Mudang-fortuneteller membership and the 200,000 around the countryside is a surprising figure.[6] Because Musok is beginning to disappear and the reality of Korean folk religion today is a lamentable one, it is felt that a more detailed understanding and grasp of the real situation is needed, and measures on how to cope with the problem must be established.

B. Structure of Folk Religion

(1) *Confucian Ceremonials*

Here, consideration of Buddhism, Protestantism and other established religions will be set aside, and the phenomenon of folk religion and its relation to Shamanism will be observed.

First, in regard to Confucian ceremonials, there is the ceremony held by the blood relatives of the upper-class, male dominated paternal family line. On traditional holidays, all male descendants, including first, second, and up until third cousins, gather together and hold a brief ceremony for four generations of departed grandparental ancestors, a memorial ceremony also being held for them on the day of their death; for the fifth generation and over, a combined gravesite ceremony is held at each grave during the tenth month of the year. The eldest grandsons participate in these gravesite ceremonies for about ten days, and descendants on the whole are expected to participate in brief religious services and memorial ceremonies about ten times a year. The women of the family prepare the things to be used in the ceremony, such as the food and wine offerings, and serve guests, their participation in the ceremony proper ordinarily being prohibited.

The Korean psyche of maintaining respect for ancestors and the aged, and the separation of men and women, is a custom that is indeed rare to find among the peoples of the world today. Aside from this, Confucian practice as a whole has its merits as well as its defects. In former times, the Confucian literati themselves were responsible for the flunkeyism,[7] factionalism,[8] the ill-effects of the family-centered system, rank-consciousness, effeminacy, and contempt for industrial capacity[9] that existed, their critical attitude of everything also, along with the aforementioned, contributing to the defects that outcrop in the multifaceted society of today.

(2) *Beliefs as Practiced by the Women of the Household and Musok*

In spite of what was said in the preceding section, the womenfolk of Korea have always lived to serve their husbands and sons with the utmost sincerity and to fulfill their every wish and desire, this being the object of their supplications and prayers before the various icons that adorn the household. Though some differences may be found in accordance with various localities, in the kitchen it is the fire god, who is known as Cho-Wang, that is revered, and in the household proper, other gods are supplicated to in order to keep out misfortune. In the inner chamber, it is Sam-Shin, the god of birth, or Ch'o-Yong, who must be attended upon if the children are to grow well and the crops are to be abundant. In the wooden-floor room,[10] it is Sŏngju, the god of the household, who must be served if family and household peace are to reign. The back of the house is the place where the talisman[11] is set and supplicated to for good fortune. Before the food storage area, T'o-Ju, the god of the ground, is worshipped, and T'aekji-Shin's (the god of the house grounds) appeasement is sought. In the past, then, the character of the Korean mother was that of one who devoted her life to sincere supplication for the well-being of the family. Though this type of spiritual practice has generally been disregarded by the Korean father, the Korean mother, when the situation warrants such, and also on special festival days or traditional holidays, is accustomed to prepare special foods and offer them to the various icons first before they are given to the family to consume.

The religious practice of women in revering these various gods adheres very closely to the Musok ritual, specifically that of the more important procedural steps of the aforementioned Cho-Wang, Sam-Shin, and Sŏngju rituals, and also that of the Tae-Gam Nori.[12] Here too may be found such rituals as that for keeping away the evil spirits which bring measles and smallpox, and supplication to the god who wards off various demons in all the five directions; the ritual to the ancestor spirit Tangun,[13] and that to the god who wards off evil throughout the twelve months of the year; the rituals to the god of good fortune, the mountain spirit, and the god of long life; the rituals to Ch'il-Sŭng,[14] to the god of the sacrificial food for the dead soul, to Pari-Kongju,[15] to the god of birth, to the Ten Kings,[16] to the *Sa-Ja*,[17] and to various other deities, depending on the particular locality; also, rituals for good fortune, for curing illness, and for the departed soul—rituals of all different types depending on the purpose for which they are held. It should be mentioned also that the Korean Musok ritual is structured as such so that it begins with the devotee entreating the various gods to reveal the cause of the present unrest that has come about and ends with her supplication for appeasement.

(3) *Village Ceremonials*

The village festival in Cheju Island or in parts of other miscellaneous regions is made upon the agreement of the people who dwell in the same village with those from neighboring communities; and today, almost every village on the mainland elects a so-called master of ceremonies (the chief ceremony holder) from among themselves. This tradition has been handed down since the days of the ancient Tribal States period; the ceremony, held by the villagers together with participants from neighboring communities, being both one of reverence and devotion, and at the same time, a joyous festival, indicates that it also functioned as the fountainhead of folk art as we know it today.

As stated previously, under the Confucian precepts of rationalism, formalism, and male domination, that which was thought to contain superstition of any sort or form was unconditionally rejected, thereby establishing a prejudice in the minds of Korean people; and so, the 500-year reign of the Yi Dynasty, the succeeding Japanese annexation, the advent of Christianity and communism, the desire of the younger generation of today to break with the past and modernize, and the present streamlined government administration, all have contributed to the gradual destruction of Musok. Yet, despite all, a tradition that has so long a history and whose roots penetrate so deeply as that of the village folk religion continues to endure, despite the severe ill-treatment that has been accorded it, simply because it is so inseparably tied to the folk culture itself; and, also, due to the painful oppression it has had to endure, it naturally has been forced to undergo change. However, now, a certain portion of the younger generation along with scholars, researchers and the Ministry of Culture and Sports have recognized that folk religion is a worthy cultural property and are making every effort to preserve its tradition.

Whereas about half the villages in the nation today still hold the village rite, in large cities like Seoul, the ratio is such that if there are almost a hundred ceremonial shrines, one can expect that there will be over ten million worshippers. The most important characteristic of the village rite is that of the village tutelary god, who is, more accurately, a goddess, for whom a ceremony is held on the fifteenth day of the first month (in accordance with the lunar calendar) at midnight when the first full moon of the year rises up in the sky. From the very beginning, the moon, the tutelary goddess, and the earth, all negative elements,[18] are supplicated to for good harvests. According to a written survey made in 1968, it was found that each village household contributes an average of approximately 50 *won* (less than 10 cents US) annually toward the ceremonial expenses, which may be compared to the weekly church offering of a typical elementary school student in Seoul.

When the ceremony is about to be held, the selected master of ceremonies purifies himself by bathing, the village site is made calm and quiet, and the god is supplicated to.

Upon the completion of the ceremony, the men consume the sacrificial foods and wine and enjoy themselves in convivial comradeship, discussing various events and making resolutions among one another for the year to come. While the conviviality is going on, some men of the village also perform farmers' festival music and dance (*Nong-Ak*),[19] the music and dance itself sometimes consisting of the "road ritual" (*kŏri-kut*) and "well-water ritual" (*u-mul-kut*), marking the end of the village ceremony proper with a festival whose atmosphere is that of one which overflows with vigor.

The Korean village ceremony represents the largest scale combination of a holy sanctification and festival-like atmosphere by groups gathered together from neighboring village communities for this gala event. However, since the Korean people in general regard this ceremony as nothing else but mere superstition, it remains a problem in Korean religious society.

Notes

1. The religion of the "Heavenly Way," founded in Korea in fairly recent times.

2. A newly-created sect of Buddhism that does not believe in the use of icons; further, the clergy do not don the traditional garb of Buddhist monks, and the chants and sacred songs that are sung are in the Western tempered scale, sounding much like that of Christian hymns.

3. A religion based on the teachings of Tangun, the mythical founder of Korea.

4. For an update on these statistics see Republic of Korea, Ministry of Culture and Sports, Religious Affairs Office, General Religious Affairs Division, "Religious Culture in Korea," Jeong Moon Sa Munhwa Co., Ltd., Seoul, 1996, pp. 8-10.

5. They are usually elderly scholars garbed in traditional Korean attire.

6. "The 1978 official yearbook for Hong-San (a medium-sized city of 100,000 in Ch'ung-Ch'ŏng Province) lists only 34 *manshin* (Mudang), 30

female and 4 male. However, the former chairman of the Kyŏng Shin Hwa (*Kyŏng-Shin Hoe*) (Shaman's Association) assured me that there were at least 400 *manshin* and *paksu* (male shaman). If that figure is correct, then it means that there is one *manshin* for every 250 people, compared to one medical doctor for every 3500 people, and one herbal doctor (*han-yak*) for every 12,500 people. I mention these figures to indicate that the manshin is still a very important specialist in the problem-solving strategies resorted to by the citizens of Hong-San."—Wilson, op. cit., p. 5.

7. Manifested in Korea's vassal state posture toward China.

8. Among different clans.

9. Merchants and laborers were looked down upon by the upper-class literati, who regarded manual work of any sort as being mean.

10. Korean-style houses are composed of two types of rooms: that of "hotfloor" rooms heated from beneath, and "wooden-floor" rooms which are unheated.

11. See the Ritual Song of the God Chesŏk, p. 170, fn. 81.

12. A Musok ritual of the Seoul area; see Ogu Kut–The Musok Ritual of the Dead, p. 240, fn. 7, no. 13.

13. See the Ritual Song of the God Chesŏk, p. 168, fn. 63.

14. See Introduction, p. 27, fn. 24.

15. The god of the dead who consoles the departed soul; she is also regarded by some as the founder of Musok, and, according to Lee, Jung-young (op. cit., p. 20) ". . . the ancestor of modern shamans . . ." See also Appendix II, fn. 1.

16. See the Ritual Song of the Bridge, p. 59.

17. See the Ritual Song of the Bridge, p. 59.

18. The Yin-Yang theory, which contends that all things are composed of either negative (female, passive, etc.) or positive (male, active, etc.) elements. See the Ritual Song of the Bridge, p. 37.

19. See Introduction, p. 5.

2. The History of Musok

Of all the religious phenomena that exist, or coexist, in Korea, including Buddhism, Taoism, the Confucian ceremony, etc., that which boasts the longest history and the fact that it is the only native religion is Musok. Though it has long suffered under the designation of "superstition," thus creating for it a great problem, still today the roots of folk religion lie deeply, not only of Musok itself, but embodying also the basis of the entire religious thought of the Korean people.

The very beginnings of Korean Musok are uncertain; however, the first piece of clear evidence we have is the gold crown of Shilla. Professor Kim, Won-ryong[1] asserts that the gold crown of Shilla is of the same style as that worn by the Siberian Shaman, and it appears that all through the early Shilla period the gold crown was worn by the kings who were also thought to be Shaman high priests.[2] The *Sam-Guk Yu-Sa* (the "Reminiscences of the Three Kingdoms") provides us with further evidence in the passage which explains that the second king of Shilla, Nam-Hae Ch'a-Ch'a-Ung, was also referred to as "Ch'a-Ch'a-Ung," "Mudang," "Chŏn-Jang-ja," and "Wang-Ho."[3] Also, in the *Sam-Guk Sa-Gi* (the "History of the Three Kingdoms"), there is a passage which tells us that there was a fortress in the Koguryŏ Kingdom called Yŏ-Dong Sŏng (located in what now is a part of Manchuria) that was attacked time and again by the army of the Su (Chinese: Sui) Dynasty under the leadership of the emperor Yang-Jae, but that the attacks were continually repulsed until finally the great Su empire was destroyed. This fortress was again later attacked four times by Emperor T'ae-Jong of the Tang Dynasty leading a huge force of about a million men employing a "human wave" attack-like strategy, but the attack was again repelled, and it was said thus that Yŏ-Dong Sŏng was the strongest fortress in all of the Orient. The *Sam-Guk Sa-Gi* tells us further that the fortress was also the shrine of the founder-god Ko-Ju-Mong, and because the female Mudangs held a ritual dedicated to the god, it was prophesied that the fortress would be perfectly safe. In all probability, it is thought that the superior fighting ability of the soldiers defending the fortress was primarily the result of the accomplishment of the Musok religion, the function of Musok in the past, as was mentioned previously, having been a household religion that unified the people and gave rise to various forms of art.

Though the Musok of the Koryŏ period was well-harmonized with the state religion of Buddhism, Confucian scholars of the time had already begun to voice opposition to it. Though some Mudangs outside of the court were banished for having deceived the official title of *Sŏn-Kwan*.

At the time of the establishment of the Yi Dynasty, the policy of "Respect Confucianism–Oppose Buddhism" was in effect, it being prescribed in the first book of rule, entitled *Kyŏng-Guk Tae-Jŏn* ("A Compilation of the Laws of the Land"), that the wife of a nobleman shall not visit a shrine or tomb, nor participate in any form of supplication in the mountains or other outdoor areas, penalties being asked for violators, and it further ordained that Buddhist monks, Mudangs, *kwangdae* (male entertainers, e. g., actors, singers acrobats, clowns, etc.) *kisaeng* (female entertainers) artisans, butchers, funeral pallbearers (a special profession), servants and the like be designated the "Eight Outcasts" of the society. And though Confucianism permeated to the level of the common people, the so-called "brief religious service," the memorial service, and the tomb ceremony, though well-organized and well-ordered, suffered from over-formalization, and, as a result, the common people's desire for a pure religious feeling could not be fulfilled. Not only this, but because women were disregarded in this strongly paternal blood-line relative oriented religion, natural religious feeling was oppressed.

Therefore, the ordained penalties outlined in the Kyŏng-Guk Tae-Jŏn could not, of course, be enforced, Musok having sunk too deeply into the common folk; moreover, it being an inseparable part of the religion of the womenfolk, this (so-called) superstitious belief has survived oppression even until this very day. In addition, under the policies of Yi Dynasty Confucianism, women's education was neglected. As a result, Musok, during the 500-year reign of the Yi Dynasty, was mainly practiced by uneducated women and thereby became transformed. In the beginning of the Yi Dynasty, there was absolutely no trace of Musok ever being thought of as a national religion. In addition, the women believers themselves do not think of their religion as being superstition—though it really is to some extent—but only a creed that, in executing its various rituals, is followed by natural human instinct and desire, this being the element of realism that makes up the basic structure of Korean Musok.

Apart from this, until now, naturally, Korean Musok has been devoid of any form of religious theory, scripture, organizational or ethical code, the form of religious thinking being directed only toward the invocation of blessings, longevity, wealth, the exorcism of evil, and the things of everyday life that are wanting—that is to say, it is only these phenomena of desire that exist foremost in the mind of the supplicant. In addition, numberless gods are supplicated to with modesty and sincerity.

When we analyze the Mu-ga, we can find many instances where the *Chŏ-Sŭng Sa-Ja* are mentioned.[4] The Chŏ-Sung Sa-Ja and the ten kings who dispatch them are phenomena borrowed from Buddhism. As it is almost impossible, to say the least, for the dead man to return to earth once again from the "World of the Dead," or "Hell," or wherever it may be, Korean Musok concerns itself with reality and the pragmatic; that is, the present—not the afterlife. Of course, this is not to say that this realistic, pragmatic basis as the prime object is confined to Musok alone, for this type of religious thought often appears in the minds of those who follow Christianity, Buddhism, and Confucianism as well, people in Korea as a whole being basically very realistic in character.

So, from the beginning of what has been written up to this point, we can understand much about the history and the realistic character of Korean Musok; however, it should be mentioned here that from the time of the Three Kingdoms period, Buddhism was imported for the purpose of protecting the nation, thereby also providing another realistic basis for adopting a religion. On this point, therefore, India differs with the three countries of the Far East—Korea, China and Japan—whose reason for adopting Buddhism was the same. Also, though Confucian culture thoroughly conquered Korea, it too was a thoroughly realistic religion. Though realism exists as a strong basic factor throughout all of the Far East, the foremost representative of it today appears in Korean Musok.

Notes

1. Professor of Archaeology, Seoul National University, and author of several books and tracts on Korean art.

2. For a very excellent photograph of this crown, see Lee, Sherman E., "5,000 Years of Korean Art," *Korean Culture,* Vol. 1, No. 1, New York, 1980, p. 25.

It is notable that the shape of this crown bears a remarkable resemblance to the ritual headdress worn by the Mudangs of the Seoul area and the northern regions.

According to Kim, Won-yong ("Three Royal Tombs," *Korean Culture,* ibid., p. 37), "The crown consists of a circlet of cut sheet gold with three tall uprights at the front, and with stylized branches like a tree. The uprights are flanked by two upright ornaments shaped like antlers. The tree form and the antler symbols reflect shamanistic beliefs widely spread across the Siberian steppe."

3. See Introduction, p. 22, fn. 5.

4. The *Sa-Ja of* "that place." See Sect. I, Chapter 1, p. 24, fn. 9; and Sect. I, Chapter 2, p. 94, fn. 19.

3. The Function of Musok

D. Banzaroff is a Siberian Shaman who also, at the same time, is said to function as a Shaman doctor and fortune-teller. In Korea, there are many small islands and mountain villages where hospitals, doctors, pharmacies, and even Mudangs are not to be found. It is in these places that one finds people who function much the same as the case mentioned above. On small islands off the western sea coast are women between the ages of fifty and sixty called *Sŏn Kŏri*[1] and in mountain villages of Kangwon Province there are god-possessed men between the ages of fifty and sixty who are called *Pok-ja*[2] whose main occupation is farming; but, when called upon by villagers to do so, act in the capacity of Shaman and fortuneteller. These individuals are not only empowered to tell fortunes, but, when there is a sick person to be treated, also conduct small-scale rituals, intone prayers of supplication, and indulge in acupuncture as well. In addition, they are called upon to conduct ritual supplications at lunar new year for the peace and prosperity of the homes. These prayers of supplication for the villages and the practice of acupuncture are done for less than 100 *won* (about 15 cents US) plus the cost of a cheap pack of cigarettes as a gratuity, and all-night rituals for the peace and prosperity of the home (called *An Taek Kut*) are done for somewhere between 500 to 1000 *won* (between one and two dollars US).

However, though Korea is not Siberia, neither is it only a country of small villages and mountain villages. As early as the time of the Three Kingdoms period, Musok was combined together with the people and functioned as the nucleus of the society, and, as evinced in the splendid gold crown of Shilla mentioned previously, in the creation of works of art. These works of art may have been extended to include such art forms as the *P'an-sori*,[3] the singers (kwangdae), who laid the foundations for its creation having originally been, so it is debated, the male members of the Mu family line.[4] It is also advocated that the mask dance-drama was created originally as a part of the village ceremony; indeed, the Hahoe mask dance-drama, which has been designated a national treasure, appeared as early as the Kŏryo Dynasty as part of the village ceremony of Hahoe village in North Kyŏngsang Province, and was thereby a product of folk religion.[5] In this manner, thereby, did the religious foundation of the folk directly and indirectly exert its influence.

In the neighboring countries of China and Japan, one can find about ten different genres of art which, in their creation, have been subject to change and development, the performers of the dances and music which have continued until the present time, such as the Chinese opera and the Japanese Noh drama, taking great pride in their own companies and theatres. In Korea, however, though genres like the mask dance-drama and P'an-sori have been designated "Intangible Cultural Properties" by the Korean government to be protected and preserved, and though there has been a movement toward the formation of national drama companies, as has been previously stated, there has always been a tendency to look down upon these art forms, the players themselves never being able to establish a reputable name for themselves in the society at large; the end result being that folk drama companies are, for the most part, in reality not able to maintain their own theatres.

It should be mentioned, at any rate, that in Korea the functions of artistic creativity and dance and music entertainment, other than that of serving Musok, the village ceremony, and the long-enduring folk religion, are not few in number. The many Buddhist temples, pagodas, sculptures and paintings are religious works of art that are also created by the hand of the Korean people. In the case of Confucianism, however, which is difficult to regard as a religion in the strict sense of the word, it is no exaggeration to say that almost nothing new in the way of religious art was created for it by the Korean people.

Finally, in summarizing the basic aspects of Musok, in regard to the so-called "ecstasy" phenomenon presented by M. Eliade[6] and others, the majority of the people in Korea think, in the narrow sense, that all practitioners of the Musok ceremony are inspired by "ecstasy," when, in fact, it exists primarily among the Mudangs found in the central and northern areas, it being entirely absent from among orthodox practitioners, that is, those who are such by heredity and not by possession. When an individual acquires the so-called "possession sickness," that is, when his or her body is possessed by the guardian deity (*Mom-Ju* or *Su-Ho Shin*), a Mu initiation ritual is held, and, in the ritual proper, each god is called upon to receive supplications, whereupon the god enters the Mu's body and the two become one.[7]

It is at this point then that oracles are told. However, in the southern areas, this experience of "possession sickness" is, for the most part, absent, the profession of Mudang proper being such by heredity.[8] The practice of telling oracles is also not to be found. It is only by the possessed Mu, who have spread out to every corner of the nation, that it is claimed that the gods descend unto them and teach them their skill and not the practitioners of Musok proper, who maintain an established ritual form that includes song and dance, and who do not engage in fortunetelling.

In the following section, we will observe that the myths of Cheju Island are to be found only in the Mu-ga and that the Mudang function as the sole transmitter of these myths. Though diverse archaic forms are found to be preserved within their contents, the Cheju Mu-ga are especially significant in that they retain the essence of the myth in its complete form, including its origin, transmission, development, and relation to the ritual itself. In addition, together with the aforementioned, the function of its scientific origin, artistic and religious forms are all to be found contained therein.

The writer will now turn his attention to the shrine ritual (*Tang-Shin Pon-P'uri*) songs of Cheju Island, presenting illustrations of several examples, the significance of which will be examined.

Notes

1. Sŏn Mŭdang: see Introduction, p. 19.

2. "Fortuneteller."

3. See Introduction, p. 18.

4. See Introduction, p. 29, fn. 34.

5. For a description and excerpts from parts of this drama, see Lee, Du-hyun, "Korean Mask Drama," transl. by Alan C. Heyman, *Traditional*

Performing Arts of Korea, Korean Nat'l Commission for UNESCO, Seoul, 1975.

6. Eliade, Mircea, *Shamanism: Archaic Techniques of Ecstasy*, Princeton: Princeton University Press, 1964.

4. The Shrine Ritual Songs of Cheju Island

*1. The Shrine Ritual Song of the Tutelary God of Mun-Su-Mul-Tang.[1]
Sung by KANG In-kwŏn[2] (male Mudang, age 56, of Ha-Myo-Ri, Tae-Jŏng-Eŭp). Recorded August, 1959.*

Here, in this ritual, the first 25 lines of the song explain the function of the god, lines 26-31 offer a description of the devotees, lines 34-39 outline the days on which the ritual is held, and lines 32, 33 and 40 comprise the words of supplication. These four elements form the composition of the shrine ritual.

" To the great shrine of Mun-Su-Mul
The god[3] doth descend.

Of the Ko-Nang Rock,[4]
The departing ship takes hold;

The arriving ship takes hold.

The upper ship does
At the upper place fish;

The center ship does
At the central place fish;

The lower ship does
At the, lower place fish.

The hae-nyŏ[5]
At the upper place,

The hae-nyŏ
At the central place,

The hae-nyŏ
At the lower place;

In-Jŏng[6]
Sa-Jŏng;[7]

This offering, we beseech thee,
Do receive.

Su-Kŭm,
Ch'e-Ro;[8]

This offering, we beseech thee,
Do receive.

The elder devotee[9]
Forty and eight years doth be;

The central devotee
Thirty and eight years doth be.

This offering,
We beseech thee,

On the third day and
The seventh day,

On the thirteenth day and
The seventeenth day,

On the twenty-third day and
The twenty-seventh day."

2. *The Shrine Ritual Song of the Tutelary God of On-P'yŏng-Ni.*[10] *Sung by HAHN Ki-shin*[11] *(male Mudang, age 45, of On Pyŏng-Ni, Sŏng-Sam-Myŏn). Recorded August, 1959.*

I.

> "The daughter of
> MYŎNG Ch'ŏn-ja,
>
> Three daughters bore
> Did she.
>
> In erudition
> They did excel; alas,
>
> Compelled were they
> To flee.[12]
>
> Mother and Father then,
> A boat they did so mend;
>
> With foodstuffs piled on high,
> Their daughters in exile did send.

II.

> Awaiting first,
> At the shrinc adjacent to
>
> The Chŏng-Pyŏng Shrine[13]
> Of Cho-Ch'ŏn[14]
>
> The first daughter
> The Lady CHŎNG, Jǔng[15]
>
> Is seated.
>
> The second daughter,
> The lady

Chim-Ryŏng Hwang-Se[16]
Doth be, and

The third daughter,[17]
At Shin-San-Ni,[18]

In Ko-Jŏng-Nam-Pat,[19]
The Lady MYŎNG doth be.

III.

The vassal,[20]
Old-man[21] MUN.

At the age of seven,
In Hawang-Al,[22]

Did the water enter;
And there,

Down under,
For seven days lived he;

And there,
Upon the water's surface,

For seven days
Lived he.

On the seventh day of
The fourth month,

As the moon was setting[23]
In the afar-off sky,

From the surface of the water,[24]
The head of a dragon

Did suddenly
Appear.

The god[25] did thus
The inauguration[26] begin.

A glass cup,
A glass table; and,

From behind the Sam-Myŏng,[27]
The vassal[28]

Did suddenly
Appear.

And, above the wind,[29]
Three-thousand cavalrymen[30]

Did suddenly
Appear."

3. *The Shrine Ritual Song of the Tutelary God of Kŭm-Ryŏng-Ni.[31] Sung by YI Dal-ch'un[32] (male Mudang, age 70, of Yul-Ip-Ni). Recorded December, 1959, by Hyŏn Yong-jun.*

The first part of this ritual song explains the origin of the god's name, the second part explains the function, and the last part explains the ritual day. The day of recording and the day of transcribing this ritual song are different; however, the three goddesses' names, the order in which they appear, and the place of their establishment coincide with the original.

"In the country of
Kang-Nam-Ch'ŏn,[33]

In the country of
Chŏng-Ja,[34]

In the village[35]
Did appear

The three Sisters,[36]
Who,

The isle of Cheju
Did enter.

At Cho-Ch'ŏn-Gwan[37]
The first sister,

The Lady CHŎNG, Jung,
Is seated.[38]

The second sister,
Who is the Lady

Chim-Ryŏng-Kwan-Sa-Jun,
Kaek-Sae-Jun,

The Heavenly Princess[39]
Doth be.

A book of gold
Too huge to embrace,[40]

A brush of gold[41]
Too huge of grasp,[42]

And three-thousand inkstones[43]
Do appear.

All things,
When created,

Of use may be;

All things,
When destroyed,[44]

Of no use may be.

The morning of
The thirteenth day

Of the first month
Is the day we choose

For thc great ritual
Of the new year;[45]

The thirteenth day of
The seventh month

Is the day we choose
For the great ritual

Of the mold;[46]

The thirteenth and
The fourteenth day of

The ninth month
Are the days we choose

For the great ritual
Of the harvest;[47]

Mudang one and all,
These great rituals three,

Before the shrines of the gods,
Do hereby hold forth.

The third sister,[48]
The Lady MAENG, Ho

Doth be:

At Yul-Nu-Ri[49] and
Ko-Jang-Nam-Pat,[50]

Is she thus seated."

4. The Shrine Ritual Song of the Tutelary God of Tari-Tang.[51] *Sung by KIM O-saeng*[52] *(male Mudang, age 53, of Sam-Do-Ri, Cheju City). Recorded August, 1959.*

The first part of this ritual song explains the lineage of the gods and the second part deals with their establishment; the third part explains the function of the gods and the fourth part deals with various gods other than that of the tutelary. The remainder of the myth is composed of an explanation of the ritual day and the words of supplication.

I.

"At the Upper Shrine
Is Kŭm-Baek-Jo;[53]

At the Center shrine
Is Saeng-Myŏng-Jo;[54]

At the Lower Shrine
Is Soro-Ch'ŏn-Guk.[55]

Eighteen sons and
Eighteen daughters, and

Grandchildren[56] three-hundred
And seventy-eight.

The first son,
Chi-Mŏ-Mun-Kok-Sŏng[57]

Doth be;

The second son,
The tutelary god of

Tae-Jung-Kwang
Doth be;

The third son
Mu-Mae-Gi[58]

Doth be;

The fourth son
Kwang-Yŏng-Tang-O-Hu-Jŏng[59]

Doth be;

The fifth son
The twelfth god[60]

Of Nae-Wat-Tang[61]
Doth be;

The sixth son
Sŏ-Nang-Tang[62]

The seventh son
Koe-Ro-Pon-San-Guk[63]

Doth be;

The eighth son
Kul-Mŏ-Ri-

K'ŭn-Do-Han-jun[64]
Doth be;

The ninth son,
Neither erudition

Nor skill at war
Hath he;

Three-thousand cavalry[65] and
A four-eyed dog,[66]

Day after day
Up the mountain

Taketh he.

In the mountain,
The *tang-kol-ma-ri* plant[67]

In one toss,[68]
To T'iuk-Jang-O-Ri[69]

Does he throw;[70]

In one toss,
To Kam-Ok Kan-Dong-San[71]

Does he throw;

In one toss,
To Han-Puk-ŭn-O-Rŭm[72]

Does he throw;

In one toss
To Sa-San-O-Rŭm[73]

Does he throw;

In one toss,
To Pul-Kŏn-Dae[74]

Does he throw;

In one toss,
To T'ae-Uk-Jang-O-Ri[75]

Does he throw;

In one toss,
To Mul-Jang-O-Ri[76]

Does he throw;

In one toss,
To Hae-Ku-Mu-Ni[77]

Does he throw;

In one toss,
To Tae-Na-O-Rŭm[78]

Does he throw;

In one toss,
To Tom-Bae-O-Rŭm[79]

Does he throw.

At Tom-Bae-O-Rŭm
He is seated; and,

Gazing all around
Here and there,

Cho-Raet[80] village
He does spy.

Yet,
Ground there is not;

Water there is not.

The village chief[81]
Chaeng-Min-Jang[82]

Is called.

The day of his birth and
The day of his death,[83]

In the family register
Are recorded.

To Tom-Bae-O-Rŭm
He is guided;[84]

'Tis there, above all
That Han-Jip[85] is revered;

'Tis there
In the Kul-Kuk[86] tree,

The Lady OK-Tang[87]
Is seated,

'Tis there,
In a hollow above the mountain,

That Grandmother Ko[89]
Is seated.

'Tis there,
At the children's village,

At the upper village,
At the "children's shrine,"[90]

That Grandmother[91]
Does appear,

Together with
The child-carrying maid,[92]

Before the shrine of Han-Jip,
Does she the god summon."[93]

II.

"The last day of
The twelfth month

Is the day we choose
For the ritual of the water;[94]

The fourteenth day of
The first month

Is the day we choose
For the great ritual

Of the new year;

The fourteenth day of
The seventh month

Is the day we choose
For the cattle-breeding ritual;[95] and,

Before the shrine of
The beneficent Han-Jip,

Do we pay homage."

5. *The Shrine Ritual Song of the Tutelary God of Sŏng-Tang.*[96] *Sung by Ko Pong-sun*[97] *(male Mudang, age 74, of Se-Hwa-Ri, Ku-Jwa-Myŏn). Recorded February, 1959.*

I.

" At the upper shrine is
Kŭm-Baek-Jo,[98]

At the center shrine is
Shil-Ryŏng-Jo,[99]

At the lower[100] shrine,
So-Ch'ŏn-Guk[101] and

Grandmother Paek-Jo[102]
Doth be.

From South Mountain
In Seoul,[103]

From Song-Ak Mountain
Did

The granddaughter of
Im, Jung-guk

Appear.[104]

With So-Ch'ŏn-Guk
Did she

Husband and wife[105]
Become;

And together
When they did

Eight sons bear,
At last,

The ninth one
Did appear.

For the rice bowl
Do

The children[106]
Call;

For mother's milk
Do

The infants
Call.

At Yu-Pung-Ni Kul-Wat,[107]
Gazing 'round,

A field of deep mud[108]
They do spy;

And,
Wide as such

That ninety-nine days
Must the plowshare[109] till;

The proper field,[110]
It too—

Ninety-nine days
Must the plowshare till.

When Sŏng-Jin-San-i[111]
To the field did go,

The servant,
Nŭj-Ŭn-Dak-Jung,[112]

The lunch
Did bring.

'Put it on the dike[113]
And begone!'

Then the wife of
Sam-Jin-San-i[114]

To the field did go,
Her husband to find.

'Beloved,
Why dost thou not

Of the rice
But a spoonful or two[115] taketh';

Yet,
Sam-Jin-San-i

Of the rice
Partaketh not.

'Why is it
That thou dost but

Of the rice
So very little taketh';[116]

For
When he did

Of the rice partaketh,

T'was his want
To take all.[117]

'The plowshare ox[118]
Did I

In So-Ch'ŏn-Guk's field
Strike and kill;[119]

And though
Consume it all

I did,

T'was yet not
But enough.[120]

Up yonder,
At a grassy[121] pond,

A plowshare ox
Stood by;

And though t'was of
I know not whom,[122]

Strike and kill[123]
And all consume

It, too,
Did I.'

Then did
Grandmother Paek-Jo speak:[124]

'When thou didst
To the field of

So-Ch'ŏn-Guk
Go,

Was it not
Thy want

So-Ch'ŏn-Guk
To see

With his stomach[125]
The field a'plowing?

What then
Didst thou[126]

With the plowshare ox,
Pray tell.'

'The plowshare ox
In So-Ch'ŏn-Guk's field

Strike and kill
And all consume

Did I.'

Then did Grandmother Paek-Jo speak:

'The plowshare ox
Strike and kill

And all consume
Didst thou?

Is that not then
Like the way a fox

Who does
A swine devour?

The plowshare ox
Of another man,

To strike and kill
And all consume;

Is that not then
The way of a cattle thief

Or a horse thief
To be likened?'

Like fighting[127] children[128]
So angry[129] they become.

Then did
Grandmother Paek-Jo speak:

'Thy plowshare ox
Strike and kill

And all consume
In revenge[130]

Shall I.'

Then did
Husband and wife

With one another
Into conflict enter;[131]

And,
From one another,

Did they depart."

II.

"The daughter of
General O-Baek,[132]

Who by the name of
'Concubine' is called,

Yu-Pung-Ni-Kul-Wat[133]
Did enter,

Hae-Nang-Kul-Ch'im-Pat[134]
Did enter,

And there
Did she dwell.

To the youngest son
Did she give birth; and

When he did
The age of seven become,

To Sam-Ch'ŏn-Tang[135]
Was he dispatched.

'Fatherless and
Untutored snipe[136]

That thou art;[137]

Come here,
To thy mother!'

'Oh, Mother dear,
My father,

Where has he gone?

Thereby
Am I

"Fatherless and
Untutored snipe"

Thus called.'

'Whilst thou naught but
A sapling[138] were,

Thy father and I
Did

Into conflict enter;

And,
From one another,

Did we depart;

Hence, into
Hae-Nang-Kul-Ch'im-Pat

Did I enter,

And there,
Did I dwell.'

To Mang-Dong Mountain[139]
He doth go,

And there,
Hae-Nang-Kul-Le-Je[140]

He doth spy.

After he did
To Father's shrine[141] depart,

With Father's beard
He doth sit and play.[142]

'You little snipe,
Naughty little snipe . . .

To thy mother's embrace,[143]
When thou didst return,

Her breast so gently
Thou did stroke,

She wouldst say:

"Fatherless and
Untutored snipe

Thou art."'

And thus,
For himself he did

A sack[144] prepare;

And thus,
With his bag,[145]

Into exile
Did he go.

Down beneath the sea,
To the land of

The Dragon Emperor,[146]
He did venture;

And there, above
A branch of a

Black coral tree,[147]

Were his clothes
Ensnared.

'What matter is it
That brings ye here?'

'Tis the factional strife of
Kang-Nam-Ch'ŏn-Ja-Guk[148]

Thy help I seek
In thwarting;

'Tis for this matter[149]
That I come.'

'Go ye then to
The eldest daughter.'

But to the eldest daughter
He goeth not.

'Go ye then to
The second[150] daughter.'

But to the second daughter
He goeth not.

'Go ye then to
The chamber of

The youngest[151] daughter.'

With his lips spread
Far apart,[152]

Like a woman
He smiles,[153]

And unto the chamber of
The youngest daughter

He enters.

The *o-yŏp-bang-sang*[154]
Doth she prepare,

But of it
He taketh not.

'Of what maker is it
That ye taketh not?'

'As I do
In So-Guk[155] dwell,

The meat I taketh
Be that of a general's; and

The wine I taketh
Be that of a general's.'

'Be it such then that
Mine guest[156]

I treat not well?'

One month,
Two months,

Three months thus
Did pass; and

The food stored
In the east, and

The food stored
In the west

Did he all
Consume.

'My country
Is ruined!

To thy country[158]
Return!'[159]

But he
Returneth not;

Then did
The youngest daughter speak:

'Father,
Oh, Father!

When a woman doth of
Eighteen years become,

Into marriage
Shouldest she

Not enter?

Unto the house of
Her in-laws

Shouldest she
Not go?

And there,
With her husband,

Shouldest she
Not dwell?

Thereby,
Shouldst I,

With mine husband together,
Away not sail?

With mine husband.

To the
White sands of

Kang-Nam-Ch'ŏn-Ja-Guk,

And there
Seated,

Shouldst I not be?

Shouldst I not
In a place

Near the sea
Dwell?

Shouldst I not
In a hamlet[160]

Near the sea
Dwell?

A stone box,[161] then,
Shall I place over;

From mine abode,[162]
The Kap-Se-Mu-Dŏk,[163]

Shall I withdraw;
and,

To the messenger of
Kang-Nam-Ch'ŏn-Ja-Guk

Shall I give greeting.'"

III.

"And when the stone box
Was opened,

Lo and behold,
There sitteth

A boy-child
Made of jade;

Yes,
There sitteth

A most wond'rous child
Of jade.

'In what country is it
That thou dost dwell?'

'Tis in

The land of Chosŏn,
In Ut-Son-Tang,[164]

In Paek-Jo-A-Dŭl Tang,[165]
In Mal-Jat A-Dŭl Tang,[166]

That I dwell.'

'For what purpose
Dost thou come?'

'Tis the factional strife of
Kang-Nam-Ch'ŏn-Ja-Guk

To cease
That I come.'

'For what reason
Be there strife?'

'On the 'morrow,
Or the next day to come,

Ye shall know;

'Tis then that
An event shall take place,'

Thus did he speak.

'Make haste
The factional strife of

So-Ch'ŏn-Guk
To cease

We pray.'"

IV.

"The two-throated strong man,
Who,

The twice stronger[167] strife
Hath ceased,

Doth now approach.

'Be it thus

Tae-Juk[168] or
Chi-Juk,

What country
Shall we not

Take for ourselves?[169]

Shall I
The governor

Of Cheju Island[170]
Be?

The island governorship
I wish not.

Rather,
Let us

A fisher's boat
Ready;

My fatherland,
My motherland,

Do I long
To see,'

Thus did he speak.

'Twas late in the evening[171]
When,

By a long promontory,[172]
Cow Island

He did enter;

To the port of
Chŏng-Dal-Li,

Ever slowly,
Did he enter; and

In the land of
Chŏson,

Upwards,
To Son-Tang,

Did he venture.

O'er the small mountain,[174]
O'er the great mountain,[175]

Ever higher,
Goeth he.

Then did
Tŭk-Jŏng,

The old servant,
Speak:

'Sang-Jŏn dear,
My dear Sang-Jŏn-a![176]

When thou wast nought but
Seven years of ago,

A great illness
Fell upon thee . . . and

Near death[177]
I knew ye to be.

But now,
My dear Sang-Jŏn-a,

Thou comest . . . !

Oh, child;

That I find[178] ye here,
How can it be?'

'Father doth at
The lower shrine be; yet

Hath Ko-Bun Mountain[179]
Greatly eroded.[180]

Mother doth across from
The Son-Tang be; yet

Hath the great nettle tree,[181]
With the passing of each day,

Leaned further
To the side;

Ah,
Woe is me,

How things[182] have changed;

A melancholy[183] god[184]
Is this,

Who doth here
Be seated.'"

V.

"The first god doth
In Kŏ-Mŏ-Mun-Kok-Sŏng[185]

Be seated;

The second god doth
In Tae-Jŏng,

In what now be called
Kwang-Jŏng-Tang,[186]

Be seated;

The third god doth
In Ae-ŭi

Be seated;

The fourth god doth
In Sŏng-An-Nae-Wat-Tang[188]

Be seated;

The fifth god doth
In Kwi-Nae-Kit-Tto[189]

Be seated;

The sixth god doth
In Kat-Mŏ-Ri-Mŏng-Dŏng-Kuk[190]

Be seated;

The seventh god doth
In Tari-San-Shin-Tto[191]

Be seated;

The eighth god doth
His seat to find,

To T'o Mountain[192]
To Nam-U-Mŏm-To[193]

Doth venture;

And there,
He doth be seated.

And thus
Did he,

To the place
From whence he came,[194]

In T'o Mountain,
Besides the Great Shrine,

Return;

And thus

Did all the sons of
Grandmother Paek-Jo,

To the place
From whence they came,

In Pon-San-Guk[195]
Besides the Upper Shrine,

Return."

6. The Shrine Ritual Song of the Tutelary God of Koe-Nae-Kit-Tto.[196] *Sung by KIM O-saeng*[197] *(male Mudang, age 65, of Sam-Do-Ri, Cheju City). Recorded August, 1971.*

KIM O-saeng, the singer of this ritual song, maintains that the sons of the Sŏng-Tang-Shin, the ritual god of the Kŭn-Ryŏng Snake Cave Shrine of Koe-Mae-Kit-Tto, were seven in number, whereas singer KO Pong-sŏn asserts the number was five. Though these differences do exist and each claims to be right, one can see, anyway, that they do, at least, possess a bit of theology.

In Cheju Island, within a radius of 400 leagues, one can find about 300 shrines and 300 Mudangs, and it is interesting to note that, within such an area, the mythological world (of the ritual songs) is, in general, fairly homogeneous; however, among the various parts, differences to be found are not few in number, in this particular case it being a question of lineage (seven sons as opposed to five).

I.

"At the upper Shrine is[198]
Kim-Baek-Jo;[199]

At the Center Shrine is
Sae-Myŏng-Jo,[200] and

At the Lower Shrine
So-Ro-So-Ch'ŏn-Guk[201]

Doth be.

With a masa musket[202]
O'er his shoulder slung,

So-Ch'ŏn-Guk doth
The mountain ascend.

Up and down
Doth he trod;

To the left and
To the right.

The deer path[203]
Doth he ascend;

The deer path
Doth he descend.

To Su-Jang-Ol[204]
Doth he ascend;

To Tae-Ak-Tan[205]
Doth he ascend.

To Hwa-So-Ak[206] and
Sae-Sol-Wat[207]

Doth he,
In one volley,[208]

The musket fire;[209]

And,
To the Spirit Mountain Peak

Doth he,
In one volley,

The musket fire.

To T'o-Jŏk-Ak,[210]

To Great Pyŏng-Dŭ-Ru,[211]

And,
To Little Pyŏng-Dŭ-Ru[212]

Doth he traverse;

And,
High up

In the lofty mountain,[215]
To Son-Tang,

Doth he ascend.

And there,
Is he seated."[216]

II.

"Misbehave
Did he,

The little seventh son;

Father's eye
Caught[217] he,

The little seventh son;

Mother's eye
Caught[218] he,

The little seventh son;

In a pig-iron box
Shall he,

Unto the
Dragon Emperor

Of the Four Seas,[219]
Be cast;

And there,
He shall die.

And
Thus was

The pig-iron box
Cast;

And
Thus did it

On the
Upper branch of the

Black coral tree[220]
Hang." [221]

III.

"A dream did come upon
the Dragon Emperor of the Sea;

The Blue Dragon,
The Yellow Dragon,

About each other
Entwined,

In battle,
He did see.

And,
At a start,

He did awaken;

And,
Then he did know,

'Twas only a dream.

'You there,
Eldest daughter,

Go out and see
What there be!'

'Oh Father,
There only be

In the heavens

A great multitude
Of stars.'

'You there,
Second daughter[222]

Go out and see
What there be!'

'Oh Father,
There only be

In the heavens

A great multitude
Of stars.'

'You there,
Youngest daughter,[223]

Go out and see
What there be!'

'Oh Father,

In the upper branch of
The black coral tree,

A pig-iron box
Doth hang.'

'You there,
Eldest daughter,

Take the box down and
Bring it here!'

Yet,
The eldest daughter

The box
Can not move.

'You there,
Second daughter,

Take the box down and
Bring it here!'

Yet,
The second daughter

The box
Can not move.

'You there,
Youngest daughter,

Take the box down and
Bring it here!'

Yet, when
The youngest daughter

The box to fetch
Did go,

The box did
Of itself,

In a twinkling[224]
Descend.

'You, there,
Eldest daughter,

Open the box!'[225]

Yet,
The eldest daughter

The box
Can not open.

'You there
Second daughter

Open the box!'

Yet,
The second daughter

The box
Can not open.

'You there,
Youngest daughter

Open the box!'

Yet, when
The youngest daughter

The box to open
Did go,

The box did
Of itself,

In a twinkling
Spring open.

And,
When the box was opened,

Lo and behold,

There sat a
Most beauteous child!

Noble of birth
Was he;

And,
Like precious white jade

Was his countenance;

Surely,

A loyal retainer
He shall be.

Then did
The Dragon Emperor speak:

'Child
From whence cometh thou?'

'From the isle of
Cheju Chŏl-Do

Is the place
That I come.'

'What brings ye here,
To a place so far as this!'

'Tis the factional strife
To cease

That I do come.'

Then did
The Dragon Emperor speak:

'Ah,
Most wond'rous

The people of
Cheju Chŏl-Do

Doth be.

Pray
The chamber of

Mine eldest daughter
Do enter.'

But yet,

With not even
A glance,

He doth refuse.

'Pray,
The chamber of

My second daughter
Do enter.'

But yet,

With not even
A glance,

He doth refuse.

'Pray
The chamber of

My youngest daughter
Do enter.'

Then slowly,
Ever slowly,

The chamber of
The youngest daughter

He doth enter.

Then did
The Dragon Emperor speak:

'Little son-in-law;

Mine only
Son-in-law

Thou dost be.

Thereby
Thou shouldest

Of some food
Partake.

What be thy wish,

Pray tell.'

'The rice I taketh
Be that of a general's;

The meat I taketh
Be that of a general's.'

'Open up
The food storage bin

In the east;

Open up
The food storage bin

In the west;

Open up
The food storage bin

In the south!

Mine only
Son-in-law,

Well fed
Must he be!'

Four months and
Ten days

Thus
Did pass; and

The food storage bin
In the east

Empty doth be;

The food storage bin
In the west

Empty doth be; and

The food storage bin
In the south

Empty doth be.

Then did
The Dragon Emperor

The youngest daughter
Summon;

And thus
Did he speak:

'A grave concern
Indeed

Thou dost
Cause me;

Be it not
On thy husband

That thou
Shouldst depend?

Get thee
To his country, and

With him
Begone!'

Then did
The youngest daughter

To her mother
Thus speak:

'When I
To mine bridal home,

To mine husband's land
Depart,

Silver
I desire not;

Gold
I desire not;

But rather,

The blue fan,[226]
Which

Beside Father
Doth lie,

Is that which
I desire.'

Mother doth
Her head gently nod, and

Father doth
The blue fan bestow;

And,
Into the world of mortals,

Above the waves,[227]
They do emerge.

To Son-Tang,
High

In the lofty mountain,
Their gaze doth

Fix upon;

To Son-Tang,
In Pae-Jin-Ko-Dal-Do,[228]

They do enter,
And,

To Son-Tang,
Their gaze doth

Fix upon."

IV.

"Mother[229] doth
In the Upper Shrine

Be seated,
And

Little Mother[230] doth
In the Center Shrine

Be seated.

Then did
The son speak:

'Where doth
My father be?'

'Thy father
Doth himself

In the Lower Shrine
Hide,[231]

To the Lower Shrine
In the Hidden Mountain[232]

Doth he venture;[233]

And there,
Like the

Pack saddle[234]
Of an ox,

Father,
All shriveled up,

Doth be.'

'Father,
Oh, Father;

Where shall I go?'

Thus did
The son a'frightened

Of a sudden
Inquire.[235]

'To the
Snake Cave of

Kŭm-Ryŏng
Go,

And there
Ye may dwell.'

And thus
Did he

To the
Snake Cave go,

And there
He doth

Be seated."

V.

"A child was born,

Then another,
And another,

Eleven,
Twelve,

Then another,
And another.

Then did
The wife

To the husband
Speak:

'The children have
Nothing to eat.

Oh, To-Sŏ-Nim-a,[236]
To-Sŏ-Nim-a;

Idle
Thou art.

How shall
The children eat?

Think thou[237]
Upon the children.'

'Ah,

What's to be done,
What's to be done?'

'The soil to till
The earth's foundation

Doth be.

Till the soil[238] then,
Let us;

Our field
Great and wide

Doth be.'

And thus,

To the Mudang's house[239]
Up yonder

They did venture;

And there,
In a twinkling,

The bull
Of a thousand pounds[240]

They did borrow;

And then,

Away
To the field

They did go.[241]

The wife
To the husband

Then did speak:

'Go thou
Into the field,

And I shall
The lunch prepare.'

When she did
Thus

The lunch prepare,

To the field
She did go.

But, alas,

The field
Tilled not be;

Man nor beast
Also,

There not be.

Then,
Gazing upward,

Above a mountain of stones,[242]
She did spy

Deep red strawberries[243]
In great abundance

A'ripening.[244]

'Make haste
Must I,

Up yonder
Quickly to go.'

When she did
Up yonder go,

Deep red strawberries
Were there

Not at all;

But rather,
A deep red fire

O'er which
The flesh of a

Slaughtered[245] bull
Lay.

And there
Sat he,[246]

The flesh of
The slaughtered bull

Devouring.

Then did she
To her husband

Quickly go,[247]

And,
In deep rage,

The lunch[248]
Cast down.

'Rascal
That thou art!

Oh,

What's to be done,[249]
What's to be done!

Cattle thief
That thou art!'

Then did
The husband retort:

'Bitch
That thou art!

Didst thou not
A louse

Kill and eat!

Didst thou not
A louse

Kill also!'

Then did they
Into conflict

With each other
Enter; and,

Then did
The daughter of

The Dragon Emperor
Speak;

'With thou
Can I no longer

Live together;

To the land of
The Dragon Emperor

Shall I return.'

And when they did
From one another

Take their leave,[250]

Not even her clothes
Did she change.

To Pat-Sŏng-Se-Gi[251]
Did she thus

Depart,

And there
Doth she

Be seated.

Then did she
Her children

Think upon.

'Wherefore
Didst I not

Mine children
Take with me.'

And then,
As she

Did burst out
A'weeping,

Her husband did
A'running come,

Her wrist
He doth grasp,

And then
He doth speak:

'A thousand pardons
I beg,

For that which
I have done.'

To the daughter of
The Dragon Emperor,

Forgiveness
He doth implore.

'Never again
Shall I

An act so thoughtless
Commit.'

'Return
Dare I not;

My face in shame[252]
A'fore the neighbors

I shall not
Bare.

Henceforth then,
Here shall I

Be seated;

And,
Before me,

Many
Shall appear,

The departing ship,
The arriving ship;

Hae-nyŏ
Ten-thousand strong.

And thus
Shall I,

Ever after,
Here

The offerings
Receive.[254]

You,
Mine husband,

Shouldst you
Return,

Henceforth,

On the first day of
The first month,

At the great ritual of
The new year,

Once again
Let us meet;

And,

On the fourteenth day of
The seventh month,

At the great ritual of
The mold,[255]

Once again
Let us meet.'

Thus,
On the seventh day,

At the children's village,
At the upper village,

At the neighboring village, and
At the center village,

The mountain boar
Is snared;

For the ritual offering,
To seven places,

Doth his flesh,
On the day of rites,[256]

Be sent.

To Ta-Rit-Han-Jip[257]
In Pat-Sŏng-Se-Gi,[258]

To the
Mountain Spirit also,

Shouldst the offering
Be sent,

To Hyng-Il-Han-Jip[259]
In Na-Mu-Rit-Kal,[260]

And in
Ka-Mi-Rit-Kae[261] also,

Shouldst the offering
Be sent."

Notes

1. The tutelary god shrine of Ha-Myo-Ri, Tae-Jŏng-ŭp.

2. As was predicted by a fortuneteller, he recovered from a long serious illness at the age of 29 and became a Mudang. Thereby, he was not a Mudang by heredity.

3. *Han-Jip.* An honorific suffix of a god.

4. A rock which contains a hole through which food is offered to a god in small doses.

5. Women divers.

6. Money or rice offered to a god.

7. A meaningless word, employed here merely for the purpose of keeping in rhythm with the aforementioned word *In-Jŏng.*

8. Meaning unknown.

9. The family holding the ritual; in this particular instance, that of the SŎNG family.

10. The tutelary god shrine ritual of On-P'yŏng-Ni, Sŏng-San-Myŏn. The tutelary god here is also the tutelary god and the sister god of the shrine ritual which immediately follows, that of Kŭm-Ryŏng-Ni (No. 3).

11. A nonhereditary Mudang who entered the practice at the age of 22.

12. In former times, women were not permitted to engage in scholarship; to do so, and particularly to excel in such an endeavor, would arouse the irate jealousy of the male populace.

13. The shrine at which the Lady CHŎNG is revered, located at Cho-Ch'ŏn-Myŏn, Se-Kun.

14. A place-name.

15. The most important of the three entering goddesses. The motif of the three entering goddesses is similar to that of the *Sam-sŏng* ("Three Names") myth.

16. The second of the three entering goddesses. In the following ritual, that of the Great Shrine Ritual of Kŭm-Ryŏng, this goddess assumes the leading female role.

17. The wife of MYŎNG, O.

18. A place-name; a village near On-P'yŏng-Ni.

19. A place-name; Ko-jŏng means Ko-Jang-Nam-Pat.

20. *Shin-ne.*

21. An aged servant.

22. A place-name; Hwang-Nal.

23. At the time the moon was setting.

24. A more precise translation would be "near the water."

25. See no. 3.

26. *Kŏ-Ung-Ha-Ne.*

27. Basic implements symbolizing the Three Sisters, who are the ancestors of the Mudang. These include the god's sword, the san-ban (a bowl with some large coins used in fortunetelling), and a hand bell.

28. *Kŭ-Ung-Shin-Ne.*

29. The god above the wind.

30. The god of three-thousand cavalrymen, or just three-thousand cavalrymen.

31. The tutelary god shrine of Kŭm-Ryŏng-Ni, Ku-Jwa-Myŏn.

32. A third-generation hereditary Mudang; a famous Mudang who conducts rites all throughout Ku-Jwa-Myŏn.

33. An imaginary place; a paradise.

34. A mythological place, imaginary place-name of a country, village, or other place; also, it is often used as the suffix of a god's name.

35. Or "inside the village."

36. The same Three Sisters who appeared in the previous ritual.

37. A place-name.

38. Is seated in front of Cho-Ch'ŏn-Kwan.

39. Or so it appears as such.

40. Or "an embracing movement of the arms."

41. A manifestation of the prefix of a fairy spirit.

42. Or "too huge to hold."

43. *Pe-rit-tol* or *yŏn-sŏk.*

44. Executed; killed.

45. The new year ceremony; the ceremony for greeting the new year.

46. After the monsoon season, a cleansing ritual is held to the god for the purpose of drying out and cleaning away the mold caused by the heavy moisture of the monsoon rains.

47. The ceremony of new grains; the ceremony of thanksgiving.

48. The last daughter.

49. A place-name; On-P'yŏng-Ni, Sŏng-Sang-Myŏn.

50. Travelling to and from Hwa-Mu-Jŏn, a place-name.

51. The tutelary god shrine of Kyo-Nae-Ri, Cho-Ch'ŏn-Myŏn.

52. A second-generation hereditary Mudang.

53. The maternal god.

54. A meaningless word improvised by the Mudang extemporaneously for rhythmic purposes only.

55. The paternal god.

56. *Kaji jil so shing.*

57. The tutelary god of Sa-Kye-Ri, An-Dŏk-Myŏn, Nam-Bu.

58. The tutelary god of Ha-Chŏn-Ri, P'yo-Sŏn-Myŏn, Nam-Bu.

59. The tutelary god of Kwang-Yang, Cheju City.

60. *Yŏl-tul-shi; ship-i-shin-wi.*

61. The shrine of Ch'ŏn-Woe, Cheju City.

62. The tutelary god of Sŏng-Hwan, Cheju City.

63. The tutelary god of Han-Tong-Ni, Ku-Jwa-Myŏn.

64. The tutelary god of Kŏ-No-Ri, Cheju City. Until now, the eight gods named are believed to be maternal and paternal ancestor spirits whose descendants, the tutelary gods, were scattered all throughout Cheju Island.

65. *Sam-ch'ŏn-paek-maet-dael.*

66. A hunting dog; appears to be an improvised word.

67. The name of a plant in the mountain.

68. *Il-shi.*

69. T'ae-Ak-Tam (Cho-Ch'ŏn-Myŏn); a place-name.

70. *Pot-t'-ku.*

71. Kŏ-Mun-Ak (Cheju City); a place-name.

72. To-Juk-Ak (Cho-Ch'ŏn-Myŏn); a place-name.

73. A place-name in Cho-Ch'ŏn-Myŏn.

74. A place-name in Cheju City.

75. T'ae-Ak-Tam (Cho-Ch'ŏn-Myŏn); a place-name.

76. A place-name in Cheju City.

77. A place-name.

78. Tae-Ch'ŏn-Ak (Cho-Ch'ŏn-Myŏn); a place-name.

79. Chŏng-Ak (Cho-Ch'ŏn-Myŏn); a place-name.

80. Kyo-Raet Village, Cho-Ch'ŏn-Myŏn, Puk-Kun. In the song, the village's name is pronounced "Cho-Raet" for smoother pronunciation.

81. In former times, the chief of a self-governing group in a rural area.

82. Kyŏng-Min-Jang; the name of a high-ranking position.

83. *Mul-ku* or *mul-ko.*

84. Here, as in the previous song text content, the most important motif is that of the god being established after entering the hunting grounds, and also the entrance into the village, as in the case of the *Sam-Sŏng* origin myth.

85. An honorific suffix of a god.

86. The tree's name.

87. A god other than the tutelary god.

88. *Pun-ji.*

89. A god other than the tutelary god.

90. *Sŏ* here means "Children"; *Sŏ-Tang* is thus the "Children's Shrine."

91. The guardian spirit of Children; the god who wards off various diseases of Children; the so-called *Yong-Ki-Nyŏ*; also referred to as *Ch'il-Il-Shin* (the "Seven-day" god).

92. A servant who bears the child on her back.

93. A mother prays to the "Grandmother God" for a safe birth.

94. The ritual for cleansing water.

95. *Paek-Jung* or *Mok-Ch'uk-Je.*

96. The tutelary god shrine of Sŏng-Tang-Ni, Ku-Jwa-Myŏn. This particular god assumes a very high position and Sŏng-Tang is regarded as the most important shrine on Cheju Island.

97. An hereditary Mudang, now deceased, who was widely acclaimed for his skill.

98. A maternal god.

99. A meaningless word, used only for rhythmic purposes.

100. The Sŏng-Tang at the very bottom; a word contraction.

101. A paternal god.

102. A maternal god.

103. The "South Mountain" (Nam-San) in Seoul here is thought to mean the one either in Hanyang (the old name of Seoul) or in Songdo (located in Inchon).

104. Here, also, we may observe that the female gods enter the island from the outside. Particularly in this shrine ritual song, rhythm takes precedence over meaning throughout.

105. The maternal and paternal gods.

106. *K'ŭn aegi*; children aged from two to three.

107. A place-name; "Kul-Wat" here means "Tae-Jŏn"("Great Field").

108. An especially muddy field.

109. A field so wide that it would require, with a plowshare drawn by an ox, 99 days to till.

110. A field whose soil is in good condition.

111. The name of a god.

112. An improvised word for a servant.

113. A dike located in a rice field.

114. Sŏng-Jin-San-i.

115. A small amount.

116. *Je ban sam sul.*

117. *Chŏn bu.*

118. *Nong-wu.*

119. The original text actually here reads "strike and eat."

120. *Puŏk ha ni.*

121. A mountain grass.

122. Actually, ". . . because it was there . . ."

123. Actually, "caught." Eating large amounts of meat is a special characteristic of the male gods of the Sŏng-Tang lineage, whereas the female gods are especially characterized by their consumption of grains.

124. To another.

125. Pok-pu.

126. Or, "Where did you put it?"

127. Pin nea kan da.

128. *Aegi te re.*

129. *Hwa.*

130. *Sang-jaeng.*

132. General O-Baek Peak west of Paek-Nok ("White-Deer") Lake (in Mt. Halla) personified.

133. A place-name.

134. A place-name.

135. A place-name.

136. A fatherless and uneducated child.

137. The mother speaking.

138. Or "growing up."

139. This particular mountain served as a point from which all places could be observed. Its main purpose was to warn the populace of an attack by Japanese pirates.

140. A place-name.

141. *An-bang shin-dŭi kan hu jen.*

142. Or "grasp."

143. *P'um an-e.*

144. *P'o-dea.*

145. *Chŏn-dae.*

146. *Yong-Wang Hwang-Je.*

147. *Hŭk san-ho namu.*

148. The name of a mythical country.

149. Or "event."

150. Or "middle."

151. Last.

152. Revealing the upper and lower gums.

153. *Pung kŭt.*

154. A set of bowls, trays and dishes of a minute size used to serve rice and soup; it consists of three very small bowls, five dishes, one small table and one rice bowl.

155. The name of a mythical country.

156. A large portion.

157. *Sa-wi-son*—an improvised word ("my son-in-law guest").

158. *Ne nara ro.*

159. The Dragon Emperor speaking.

160. *P'o-yu-su.* Similar to *ka-yu-sŏ* in meaning; used here merely for rhythmic purposes.

161. Appears to be a stone box with pig iron bent around it.

162. The neighboring area.

163. Meaning unknown.

164. A place-name.

165. The shrine of the son of the god Paek-Jo.

166. The shrine of the son of the god Mal-Jat.

167. *Yi-bae naeng-kyŏ.*

168. Meaningless words; used here merely for rhythmical purposes.

169. After putting an end to the strife, the two-throated strong man takes the spoils of the warring factions for his own country.

170. At the time of the Japanese annexation of Korea, the governor of

Cheju Island was referred to as *Cheju-Do Sa,* which actually means "Minister of Cheju Island."

171. *Sa-mut.*

172. Or "long cape."

173. An island located in the vicinity of Sŏng-San P'o, Tong-Buk.

174. So-Wŏl-Nang-Bong ("Small Moon Peak"); the name of a mountain in Se-hwa-Ri, Ku-Jwa-Myŏn.

175. Tae-Wŏl-Nang-Bong ("Great Moon Peak"); same as above.

176. The name by which the servant addresses his master's son.

177. Or "became ill and almost died."

178. Precise meaning unknown; however, it is thought to be "meet suddenly."

179. A mountain located in Sŏng-Tang-Ni, *Ko-Bun* means *sum nŭn da,* "to hide"; *ko-bu-rak-je-ri* means "to play hide-and-seek"; *sum* means "a mountain ridge."

180. *Sum-ŏ.*

181. *Tae-p'aeng namu.* The factor of the nettle tree leaning to the side is symbolic of the movement against superstition during the Japanese annexation of Korea (1910-46).

182. The state of things.

183. *Sŏ-rŏ-un;* an improvised word.

184. The actual word in the text is "elder brother"; however, the person speaking is construed to be a god.

185. The tutelary god of Sa-Kye-Ri, An-Dŏk-Myŏn, Nam-Kun.

186. The tutelary god of what was formerly known as Tae-Jŏung Hyŏn and is now called Tŏ-Su-Ri, An-Dŏk-Myŏn.

187. The tutelary god of Ha-Chŏn-Ni, P'yo-Sŏn-Myŏn.

188. Ch'ŏn-Woe-Tang, Cheju City.

189. In the following ritual song (No.6), the most important god.

190. The tutelary god of Ip-Du-Dong, P'yŏng-Dae-Ri, Ku-Jwa-Myŏn.

191. The tutelary god of Kyo-Nae-Ri, Cho-Ch'ŏn-Myŏn (the god of the fourth ritual song).

192. The main god of T'o-San-Ni, Nam-Wŏn-Myŏn; the youngest daughter of the Dragon Emperor; also, the so-called "Seven Days God" (*Ch'il-Il-Shin*), namely the god who is accorded dominion over all diseases.

193. The original pronunciation of this place-name has been changed to Nam-Wŏn-Myŏn, Nam-Kun.

194. The name of a country.

196. Koe (a cave)-Nae (interior)-Ki-Tto (the honorific suffix of the god's name); presently called the "Kum-Ryŏng Snake Cave," the dwelling place of the ritual god; a famous sightseeing place (see Sect. III, Chapter 5, No. 6, pp. 337-38).

197. The same singer of the fourth ritual song.

198. Improvised words and phrases, almost identical to those found in other ritual songs.

199. As mentioned previously, the name of gods.

200. As mentioned previously, the name of gods.

201. As mentioned previously, the name of gods.

202. A gun that shoots bullets quickly; an improvised word that is commonly used; i.e., "*chil*" in place of "*ch'ŏng.*"

203. Actually "the deer and roe deer pathway."

204. The name of a lake situated at the top of a mountain in a district near Cheju City.

205. The name of a mountain peak in Tae-Ak-Tang, Cho-Ch'ŏn-Myŏn.

206. A mountain range in Cheju City.

207. A place-name.

208. Or "at the same time."

209. *Sa-rak.*

210. The name of a mountain in Cho-Ch'ŏn-Myŏn.

211. A place-name.

212. A place-name.

213. A place-name.

214. A place-name.

215. *O-dŭm.*

216. *Kaja.*

217. Actually "be opposed to," or "dislike to see."

218. The same meaning as 217; an improvised word.

219. The four seas around Cheju Island.

220. *Mu-u namu.*

221. Kŏl-ŏ-ji-ŏ.

222. The middle daughter.

223. The last daughter.

224. *Chŏn-jŏl-lo.*

225. Or "when the eldest daughter was told to open the box."

226. *Ch'ŏng-sŏn.*

227. Or "the surface of the water."

228. A place-name; Hwang-Tong-Ni, Ku-Jwa-Myŏn.

229. The maternal god.

230. The second mother; a concubine.

231. *Sum-ŏ.*

232. The name of a mountain.

233. Or "go and see."

234. *Soe chil-mae.*

235. *Ka-nŭm-ke.*

236. The term by which the wife addresses the husband.

237. Or "calculate."

238. *Se-kyŏng,* an improvised word.

239. *Sang tan-kol-jip.*

240. Actually "600 kilograms."

241. *A-jŏ ka-shi-ni.*

242. *Mŏ-dŭl.*

243. *Ddale.*

244. *Yul-ŏ-sŏ.*

245. *Chuk-yŏ-sŏ.*

246. The husband.

247. *Naeng-k'ŭm.*

248. That is, the lunch which she was carrying.

249. Or "How shall we avoid the responsibility for killing and eating the bull?"

250. *Kal ryŏ a jŏn.*

251. Pat-Sŏng-Sa-Gi; according to the singer, KIM O-saeng, although this is the place of the Snake Cave Shrine above the pathway traversed by the god, a different place, called "An-Sŏng-Sa-Gi," below the pathway traversed by the god, is the location of the shrine where the daughter of the Dragon Emperor is seated. Her shrine is not located in a cave, but rather in a small edifice around which no "spirit trees" are to be found.

252. *Natch'i pu-gŭ-rŏ-wŏ-sŏ.*

253. Women divers.

254. Or "I shall be well-tended."

255. See Ritual Song No. 3, fn. 46, p. 321.

256. According to the singer, KIM, O-saeng, until around the year 1960, aside from the public rituals held at the cave on the first day of the first month and the 14th day of the 7th month, in accordance with the lunar calendar, rituals to the tutelary god of Koe-Nae-Kit-Tto, at which boars, or pigs, were sacrificed, were also held at private homes for the purpose of curing illnesses. The words *yi-re* and *a-gi*, as they appear in the song text, bear a superficial relationship to the god who wards off disease.

257. The shrine where the goddess is seated.

258. The ritual offerings that are sent to Koe-Kit-Tto for the shrine ritual of the daughter of the Dragon Emperor, located at An-Sŏng-Sa-Gi.

259. The shrine where the tutelary god of Kŭm-Ryng-Ni—the so-called Ch'il-Il-Shin—the god who wards off diseases (see Ritual Song No. 3 and Ritual Song No. 5, fn. 192, p. 328).

5. An Explanation of the Shrine Ritual Songs (Mu-ga Pon-P'uri) of Cheju Island

The word *Pon-P'uri is* a combined noun form comprised of the words *Pon* and *P'uri*. *Pon* is translated as "basis" or "foundation," which may be interpreted as the history or the origin of the Mu-ga, and *P'uri* refers to the description, interpretation and analyzation of the ritual songs. Aside from this, the word *Pon-P'uri* also serves to describe or interpret the basic characteristic or the historical origin of the god to whom the ritual is being performed; and, acting upon this god's desire, the myth (describing the basic characteristics or the historical origin of the god) that is sung serves as a source of inspiration to the Mudang in carrying out the ritual. The aforementioned serve as one element upon which the ritual is composed, the singing of the myth, often in nonsense syllables, merely for the purpose of keeping time with the rhythm, being the other.

The course of the ritual is carried out with a pure heart, body and mind, with food offering, with the Pon-P'uri, with supplication for the desires of the devotees, and with prophesies, not to be considered merely for the sake of fortunetelling so much as the revered words of the god.

It is here, then, that the Pon-P'uri functions as the original myth of Korea, brought to life once again in the ritual song.

(1) The Shrine Ritual Song of the Tutelary God of *Mun-Su-Mul-Tang*

This shrine ritual song is dedicated to the tutelary or protector god of the village, Mun-su-Mul-Tang being the place where the shrine is located. According to a survey conducted in 1960, in Cheju Island there are about three-hundred religious shrines, one-hundred fifty of which are village tutelary shrines, that of Mun-Su-Mul-Tang being one of them. Though this Pon-P'uri is the

shortest and most rudimentary of its kind, it serves as one example
of that whose basic compositional element is the origin myth.

The order of the composition is as follows:

1. The presentation of the god's name formed in the likeness
   of mortals.

2. A description of the god's role.

3. The presentation of the names of the villagers who revere
   the god.

4. An explanation of the day chosen for the ritual.

5. The prayer text.

(2) The Shrine Ritual Song of the Tutelary God of *On-P'yŏng-Ni*

This shrine ritual song contains the origin myth of the
Sam-Sŏng god and the entrance motif of the Three-Sister gods of
Cheju Island. In the following ritual, that of the Great Shrine Ritual
of Kŭm-Ryŏng-Ni, though the same motif of the entrance of the
Three-Sister gods appears, the singer, the ritual day, and the tran-
scriber are all different; however, the contents of the myth, passed
on from generation to generation in unwritten form, which tell of
the miracle of the Three Goddesses and how they came to be established, are alike in both rituals.

Though every Mudang can sing the entire shrine ritual song
of the village where they reside from memory, Mudangs famed for
their extraordinary capabilities are familiar with the tutelary gods
of other regions as well, and can thereby also sing the shrine ritual
songs of those areas in addition to their own.

(3) The Great Shrine Ritual Song of the Tutelary God of *Kŭm-Ryŏng-Ni*

Whereas the shrine ritual of On-P'yŏng-Ni is that held to the
youngest of the Three-Sister gods, the ritual of Kŭm-Ryŏng-Ni is
dedicated to the second sister.

The structure of the myth is outlined as follows:

1. The emergence from the country called Kang-Nam-Ch'ŏn-
   Ja-Guk.

2. The lineage of the gods.
3. The role of the gods.
4. An explanation of the ritual day and the ritual's name.

The details on how the gods entered the island and how they were established are contained in the ritual song of On-P'yŏng-Ni. In the case of On-P'yŏng-Ni, the goddesses are dispatched by the divine monarch of Ming (China), whereas in that of Kŭm-Ryŏng-Ni, they appear from Kang-Nam-Ch'ŏn-Ja-Guk. Usually the goddesses enter the island from a place outside, that being, among others, Kang-Nam-Ch'ŏn-Ja-Guk, Seoul, Yong-Wang-Guk (the country ruled over by the Dragon King of the sea), etc. On the other hand, the male gods are always found to appear from a sacred ground within the island; but, here also, the motif of the Sam-Sŏng myth pervades.[1] It is stated in the "History of Koryŏ"(1395) that Japan also has a similiar Sam-Sŏng myth in which the Three Goddesses appear.

(4) The Shrine Ritual Song of the Tutelary God of *Tari-Tang*

This ritual song is composed of the following:

1. The parent Gods.
2. The lineage of the Brother Gods.
3. The myth telling, in detail, how the heroes of the tale, the nine male gods who hunt at the foot of Halla Mountain, came to be established. It should be mentioned here that the myth serves as the kernel of the ritual song, from which it gradually expands by accretion. It should also be mentioned that the element of the male hunter gods hunting at the foot of the mountain bears an even closer resemblance to that the Sam-Sŏng myth.
4. The role of the tutelary god.
5. The names of the gods worshiped in a village other than that of the tutelary god.
6. An explanation of the ritual day and the ritual's name.

From this point onward, the myths gradually become longer.

In Cheju Island, in a group of remote offshore islands located within a radius of four-hundred leagues that contain a total population of 400,000, we can find about six or seven myths in existence similar to that found in the ritual song of the tutelary god of Tari-Tang, but on a more developed level. These three above-mentioned factors thereby provided a specimen-type society that, in turn, offers optimum conditions for the proper study of mythology.

It should be mentioned here in as early a source as the "History of Koryŏ," we find a reference to the origin myth of the Sam-Sŏng under the title *Ko-Gi-Un* ("Ancient Writings"), which is summarized as follows:

> In the beginning of the earth's history, before the advent of humans, the three male gods appeared and engaged in hunting, utilizing the hides of game for clothing and the meat for food; and, from Japan, came the Three Queens (goddesses) who brought the seeds of the Five Grains,[2] and who bred the horse and the cow. Thereafter they bred cattle and conquered the soil by engaging in agriculture; and, by so doing, they did prosper and live well.

These mythological motifs thus form the basic composition of the ritual songs handed down from long ago; and, further, it is believed that, by the Koryŏ period, the descendants of the Sam-Sŏng recorded under the title of *Ko-Gi-Un* mentioned above had grown into very large family clans, who formed the basis of the population later to come.

(5) The Shrine Ritual Song of the Tutelary God of *Song-Tang*

Longer in length than of the previous ritual songs, this song describes in detail throughout the establishment of the Song-Tang god. The paternal god appears at the Song-Tang shrine hunting and eating meat, whereas the maternal god, who enters from Seoul, is a goddess who engages in agriculture. The two become husband and wife. The myth is also similar to that of the Sam-Sŏng. Generally speaking, the male god is aboriginal and falls under the hunting, meat-eating culture, whereas the female god, who falls under the agricultural, grain-eating culture, eventually enters the island from the outside. These aforementioned phenomena are actually reflected in the cultural history of Cheju itself, and also in the economic and dietary habits practiced by the islanders.

Here, in regard to the parental gods of the Song-Tang shrine, the most famous ancestral tutelary god to be found in every region within the island itself, especially that god accorded the most importance and respect, is the goddess called *"Paek-Jo Hal Mang"* (Grandmother Paek-Jo).

The latter part of the narrative poem, in particular the heroic tale of the sea where the youngest son assumes the most important role, as evolved in the Cheju Island version, brings to mind such epics as the *Iliad* and the *Odyssey*; however, because Musok is looked down upon as nothing more than mere superstition, the Mu-ga unfortunately had little chance to develop uninterruptedly as narrative-literary forms in their own right.

Here, in the succeeding last part of the story, the most important roles are assumed by the youngest son and the *Yong-Wang-Nyŏ* ("Dragon Queen") who return to Ch'ang-San-Ni and are established as the "Seven-Day" tutelary gods who exercise power over all forms of disease. The "Seven-Day" shrine ritual is thus added here as a continuance of the Song-Tang ritual at Ch'ang-San-Ni, but the details of it are not elaborated upon.

(6) The Shrine Ritual Song of *Koe-Nae-Kit-Tto*

Koe ("cave") Nae ("in") Kit ("spirit"), the "Spirit Cave" has become well known to sightseers as the "Kŭm-Ryŏng Snake Cave Shrine." The legend of Koe-Nae-Kit and the "Snake Spirit," which was published in the work entitled *T'amna-Ji* ("History of Old Cheju"), is famous. As the legend goes, a virgin was offered as a sacrifice to the "Snake Spirit of the Cave" every year until the reign of King Chung-Jong when a very young judiciary official named Sŏlin intervened in the continuance of the practice.[3] However, upon returning to the palace, he suddenly died. Nevertheless the villagers continued to hold the ritual to the "Snake Spirit" in the great cave until the period of the Japanese annexation (1910). This ceremony, also referred to as the "Ritual of the Swine," due to the fact that one complete body of a pig was offered as a sacrifice, was subject to continual repression by the Japanese so that the ritual place was finally moved to its present location behind the Kŭm-Ryŏng Middle School. At this place, there is also a large cave, the entrance of which is surrounded by huge, densely populated Chinese nettle trees, which are referred to as "spirit trees."

Koe-Nae-Kit-Tto is the son of Paek-Jo Hal-Mang. Most Mudangs say that the number of gods is five in all, while a few claim there are as many as fourteen; however, KIM O-saeng, in his ritual song, states there are seven. The Koe-Nae-Kit, the narrative content of which is similar to the previously mentioned Song-Tang ritual, is also an heroic tale of the sea in which the hero assumes the leading role.

Finally, as has been stated previously, each village's tutelary god shrine ritual, from beginning to end, reflects the very character of Cheju Island itself. In the mountains, the male gods appear hunting, eating meat, and utilizing the hides for clothes, thus being active in nature, whereas the female gods enter the island from the surrounding sea outside, always bringing new things with them. Here, we can find, in the world of mythology, a type of impressionistic myth that reflects not only the character of the land, but one that projects with true preciseness, humanism and reality, the life and cultural history of the island.

Here, only the tutelary god shrine ritual has been discussed. However, there are many more rituals worthy of observation that form an important part of Musok research: the private family ritual, for example, in which gods of fertility, both for agricultural and human propagation, and the *Sa-Ja*[4] are supplicated to, and various other types of ordinary shrine rituals in which long epic-narrative tales consisting of many parts are sung in the ritual songs. In Cheju Island, there are from ten to twelve of these long epic-narrative type Muga, totaling around three-hundred parts in all. Among the three-hundred or so Mudangs on the island,[5] between one- and two-hundred of them can sing all of these parts during the ritual practice.

Though the transmission of the myth depends entirely upon the singer's capability in executing the narrative-epic song, those of the ordinary rite and those of the tutelary god shrine ritual are completely different in dimension. That is, those songs executed in the ordinary rite are similar to those of mainland Korea, whereas those of the tutelary god shrine ritual are indigenous to Cheju Island. Research has proved that proliferation of the songs from the mainland into the ordinary rite came about with the dissemination of Buddhist culture from China to Korea in the Tang Dynasty era (ca. 7-9th century A.D.) during the height of the *Kang-Ch'ang*[6] literary period, and from Japan during the *P'yŏng-An* (Japanese:

Heian) period (ca. 10-12th century A.D.), during the height of the *Chang-U*[7] cultural era, which was accompanied by a strong Buddhist religious movement that was accepted into the Musok society of Korea. It was only in Cheju Island, however, even until the present day, that the purely indigenous elements of the tutelary god shrine ritual songs were retained intact, void of any foreign admixture or influence.

It behooves us here to take particular notice of the fact that the song of the Shrine Ritual of the Poor Emperor and also the Yi Dynasty novel entitled "The Story of Emperor T'ae-Jong" are both similar in content to the biography of the Tang Dynasty emperor T'ae-Jong of China found in the *Ch'ŏn-Bul-Ton-Hwa* cave tombs of China.

It should be mentioned here at the very end, as a sort of post-script, that the method of recording the ritual songs was carried out in the following manner:

1. The sounds of the words sung were first put down in phonetic script.

2. The Chinese letter which is similar in sound and meaning to the phonetic word was substituted.

3. The entire text of the song was then edited into a standard writing system.

Notes

1. "According to the T'amna (old name for Cheju) records, T'amna ancestors Yang, Ko and Pu came out of three holes in Sam-Sŏng-Hyŏl (the "Cave of the Three Surnames") and hunted and fished daily for their food and clothing.

"One day, a stone box which was closed with purple clay, floated to the shore on the east coast, near present-day On-P'yŏng-Ni in Sŏng-San-Myŏn. The three progenitors saw the box and opened it. When they opened it, they saw three princesses in blue clothes, accompanied by live-stock and grains. A messenger said 'I am Pyŏk P'a-Guk, a man from the land of the Blue Waves. Though three sons of God were born on the west coast to found a country in the future, they had no spouse. Our king ordered that the three sons should marry the three princesses and do great work.' The messenger disappeared by riding off on white clouds.

"Concerning Sam-Su-Sŏk, the T'amna records say 'In a fertile place in the spring, the three ancestors of the people of Cheju Island set up the capital. The first men to set up their living places were Yang-Ŭ-la in Il-Do (the First Capital), Ko Ŭl-la in I-Do (the Second Capital) and Pu Ŭl-la in Sam-Do (the Third Capital) by the shots of arrows.'"—from *Echoes of Mt. Halla*, Essays by Yang, Sangick, Cheju Nat'l University, Cheju City.

"Cheju City—Sam-Sŏng-Hyŏl (the "Three Clan Hole"), birthplace of Ko, Yang and Pu families. These three demigods lived on hunting until three princesses came from the kingdom of Pyongnang with seeds of five food grains. The community of these three clans developed into the T'amna Kingdom, which continued to exist until it was conquered by the Koryo Dynasty in 937 A.D. The three ancestors were enshrined in the Sam-Sŏng-Hyŭl by Governor Yi, Su-dong of the Yi Dynasty in 1526, and ritual services were held thereafter every spring and autumn by successive governors. The three clans of Ko, Yang and Pu in Cheju still hold rituals every spring, autumn and winter."—Notes taken from a signboard at the entrance to Sam-Sŏng-Hyŏl, Cheju City.

"Especially noteworthy about this myth is the fact that it alone is closely connected with the earth, while all other myths of Korea are chiefly concerned with heaven."—*The Folk Treasury of Korea*, op. cit., p. 10.

2. Rice, corn, barley, millet and maize.

3. However, "According to the *Samguk Sagi*, King Chijŭng of Shilla officially forbade the practice of human sacrifice in 502 A.D."—Kim, Wŏn-yŏng, *Korean Culture,* op. cit., p. 37.

4. See Sect. I, Chapter 2, p. 94, fn. 19.

5. In his work entitled "Korean Folk-belief" (Tokyo: Kinkasha, 1973), Chang Ju-kŭn put the number at about two-hundred, but Yoon Soon-young, in "Magic, Science and Religion on Cheju Island" (*Korea Journal,* op. cit., p. 10, fn. 6) states the following:

However, in asking the secretary of the shaman's association, she said from 500-600. Of these, over $^2/_3$ are female shamans.

6. A literary genre; literature for the propagation of Buddhism.

7. See no. 6.

Appendix I

The Legend of the Chesŏk Deities

A long time ago there once lived in Old India a king and queen who had no child till they were well advanced in age. They sighed for one, and once offered prayers at a celebrated mountain for a hundred days. Then, in a dream of the queen, a child came before her and said, "I was a fairy in Heaven, but I was driven out because I committed errors. I came down to earth, and I was at a loss where to go. Then the spirit of this mountain led me to you." So saying, the child entered into the queen. When she awoke from her dream, she found signs of conception in her. Both the king and queen were pleased. In due course, the queen gave birth to a boy. The child was named Sŏkkayorae[1] and was raised with affectionate care.

When the boy was ten years old, the king lay ill in bed, and it was not long before he passed away. After a year, the queen fell seriously ill. The young Sŏkkayorae obtained various kinds of medicines and served them to his mother, but to no avail. His mother also departed this life, leaving Sŏkkayorae all alone. While he was in mourning, treacherous ministers plotted together against him to usurp the throne. When he learned of the conspiracy, he made away into a deep mountain. But he was dismayed, not knowing what to do. He fell on his knees and began to pray to God, asking Him what he should do. Then a bean dropped down before him. He thought it might be a gift Heaven had sent him. He sowed it in the ground. It soon put forth shoots and he nurtured it with great care. The plant grew and finally bore abundant fruit. He plucked it and found he had harvested as much as three *toe* three *hop*.[2] Beside the collected beans, he offered a prayer to God. Then there suddenly arose a rainbow and a wind that carried him up to Heaven. The Heavenly Emperor was pleased to see him and gave him a staff, a hat, a wooden bell, and a rosary. Then he told him to descend to

341

the world of human beings again and further perfect himself. Sŏkkayorae came down to the mountain again, taking the gifts with him. Then he collected alms from the people and built a temple to worship Buddha.

By the time Sŏkkayorae was sixteen years old, the temple had grown larger and he had many disciples. He had also acquired the occult art of *P'ungundunkapbŏp*, and thereby could transform himself into anything he wished to be.

One day he turned himself into an old man of about a hundred and eighty years of age, and set out on his way to look into the earthly existence of people, leaving the temple to the care of his disciples. When he came upon good people, he gave them rich blessings, and when he met with wicked people, he punished them severely. In this way, he was gradually proceeding toward the country of Chosŏn (Old Korea).

In the meantime, a courtier of high position was living in Seoul. He had nine sons but no daughter. He was very eager to have a daughter born to him. He talked over his wish with his wife and decided to visit a noted mountain together for a hundred days of prayer. After they had performed the ritual, a small girl appeared in the dream of the wife, and said, "I was formerly a fairy in Heaven but was at a loss where to go. Then the spirit of this mountain led me to you." So saying, the girl approached the wife to be embraced in her arms. After the dream, the woman felt signs of conception and in the course of time gave birth to a girl. The man and wife were overjoyed, and their daughter was named Tanggŭm-agi (Baby Tanggŭm).

She grew up under the tender care of her parents. But when she was thirteen years old, it so happened that her father fell victim to the wiles of villainous retainers of the king and he was sent into exile. Her father and nine brothers took leave of her in tears and went to the place of exile. When they were gone, her mother, too, went away to offer prayers for their early release from exile. Thus, Tanggŭm-agi was left alone with her two maids-in-waiting.

Meanwhile, Sŏkkayorae reached Chosŏn and came into Seoul. While he was looking around the capital, he came across some writing by Tanggŭm-agi, and thought to himself, "Here must be a woman of virtue." Soon he set about finding her. When he got to the gate of her house, he saw another writing by her, and thought, "This must be the house of the virtuous woman." Then he tried to

‑‑‑

enter the gate, but it was barred. He hesitated a moment, and chanting a spell, he hit the door with his staff. With a sound of thunder, the gate opened. At the sound, Tanggŭm-agi was surprised and looked about her, but could find nothing unusual. She therefore thought that it must be a trick of goblins, and began to chant a spell to chase them away. When the gate was opened, Sŏkkayorae found another barred gate. He uttered a spell once again and opened it. Tanggŭm-agi thought it must be more mischief of evil spirits, and began to chant a spell to drive them away. When the second gate was opened, he found a third gate standing in his way. Then he thought that this must be a house with twelve gates. He chanted an incantation once more and thereby opened the rest of the gates all at once.

Finally, Tanggŭm-agi stood up in wonder and came out to see an aged priest chanting prayers, begging for alms. She told one of her maids-in-waiting to ask him where he came from. The monk answered, "I've come from the temple of Kŭmbul-am in Old India. One night, Buddha appeared in my dream and said your father and nine brothers had been sent into exile. Buddha also told me to come and collect alms from you and then offer prayers so that they may return home soon. That's why I've come to visit you."

The young mistress of the house felt grateful toward the monk who was trying to help relieve her father and brothers from their sufferings. She soon had her maid bring some of the rice on which they had fed. The monk, however, refused to accept it, saying that the rice was unclean, since they had been feeding on it. Tanggŭm-agi said, "We have no other rice." Then the monk asked, "Aren't there sealed jars full of rice in your barn within the twelve doors?" She retorted, "But no one can open them. They are all locked." The monk answered, "I have opened the twelve bolted gates. I know how to open the doors of the barn. If you take a bath and stand before the doors, they will open of themselves."

Tanggŭm-agi thought all this was for the good of her family, and did as she was told. To her wonder, the doors opened of themselves. As soon as she brought three *toe* three *hop* of rice from the barn, the doors closed of themselves. She had her maid give the rice to the monk, but he would not accept it from the maid-in-waiting. He said to her, "You were born unclean with the smell of fish." The young mistress sent the other maid-in-waiting, but the monk also refused to take the rice from her hands saying, "You are also by nature unclean with the smell of meat." Then Tanggŭm-agi was compelled to take the rice herself and pour it into the sack of the old monk. The rice, however, all fell to the ground through the sack, since it was ripped open at the bottom. She became angry with him, and snapped, "What a foolish monk you are! You shouldn't carry a torn sack to collect alms." Then he said, "If I carried an unimpaired sack, why should I take the trouble to open the twelve bolted gates and call on you?" Tanggŭm-agi sewed up the rip in the sack for him, and she was about to gather together the rice scattered on the ground with a broom. "No, it won't do," the monk interrupted her, "my Buddha will not accept the unclean rice touched by a broom." "In that case, what do you suggest I do?" she asked. "You are supposed to pick up the grains of rice one by one with a pair of chopsticks made of bush-clover twigs growing on the hill behind your house," the monk said. Only in the hope that it might bring about the release of her father and brothers, she made the chopsticks and picked up the grains of rice into his sack, as she was told. When she finished it, she said to the monk, "Now go away at once." The monk observed, "In my land, people who have left home come back to their houses when the sun sets. But is it the custom here for people to leave their homes in the evening? With your permission, I would like to stay at the doorway for the night." Tanggŭm-agi was so annoyed, but she let him do as he wished. After a while, however, the monk came to her and said, "I can't fall asleep, since I am afraid of the guardian deity of the gate. Let me sleep in your yard." She thought it would not make any difference, and let him use the yard. After a while, the monk called the young mistress of the house again, and said, "I can't fall asleep on the veranda, since I am afraid of the guardian deity of the house."

Finally, after an argument, the monk ended up sleeping in the detached house in the backyard, which Tanggŭm-agi had all to herself. They went to sleep with a screen set between them. About midnight, Tanggŭm-agi had a dream in which a blue dragon and a yellow dragon, entangled together, went through the eastern window up to Heaven. When she woke from the dream, she found her two maids-in-waiting still awake. She told them to sleep, and she herself fell asleep again. At *ho-kyŏng*, the last of the five periods of the night, she had another dream in which a fairy official descended from Heaven and gave her three jewels, and since they were so beautiful, she fondled them, putting them in her mouth, and then on her breast. When she awoke, she was surprised to find herself covered with the tattered black coat worn by the monk. She wondered who should have taken away her brocade quilt. She pushed the screen aside and saw the monk sleeping under it. Boiling with anger, she woke him up and took him to task, saying, "What an impolite monk you are! How dare you take advantage of the quilt of a young lady?" The monk got up with nonchalance, and said, "I might say I coveted this quilt of yours, but how is it that you covered yourself with that ragged coat of mine?" She was abashed and at a loss for words. She could only urge him to leave the house at once. "All right, I'll go," the monk said, "but you must have had dreams last night. Tell me about them and I will give you an interpretation of them before I leave." In anger, she retorted, "It is no business of a monk whether a young lady has a dream or not!" The monk said, "A woman must be bashful to tell a man about her dream. So I will tell you what dream you must have had, and give you an explanation of it." Then the priest proceeded to describe the dream she dreamed around midnight. She was filled with wonder, and asked him, "Then, what is the meaning of it?" He explained, "The blue dragon represents you and the yellow dragon represents me." "Why," she asked, "were they entangled together when they ascended to Heaven?" He said, "I am a man of Old India and you are a woman of Chosŏn. When sleeping in the same room with a screen between us, why should we make an argument over our quilt?" Tanggŭm-agi then asked, "Well, I had another dream later. Tell me what it was." He repeated all the details of the second dream, and said, "It is an indication that you are supposed to give birth to three sons." It was like a bolt from the blue to her. In her irritation, she threw her pillow at the monk, and said, "What on earth do you mean a virgin is supposed to give birth to three sons? Now, begone at once!" So taken to task, he said, "Yes, I will. But in seven years, you are going to visit me, so you may well know who I am. My surname is Wang and my given name Sŏkkayorae. I come from the temple of Kŭmbul-am in Old India. I was born at noon on the eighth of April in the year of *Kap-ja*. Keep it in your memory." With these words, he was gone out of sight.

It was not long before Tanggŭm-agi found herself lying ill in bed for some unknown reason. Somehow she found that boiled rice tasted raw, drinking water smelled fetid, and she wanted to eat sour fruits, such as apricots and peaches.

It was the month of April, the following year, when her father and nine brothers were to return home from their life in exile, and her mother from her three years of prayers. As soon as father entered the village, he began to call her. "Tanggŭm-agi! My dear daughter! Come and greet your father. I am home at last!"

Tanggŭm-agi, however, could not even budge. She had swelled up too much. When her parents found her ill, they tried to cure her with all kinds of medicines, but to little effect. At that time there was living in Seoul a celebrated fortune-teller named Sir Kwakga. Her mother prepared a thousand *ryang* of money and went to consult the fortuneteller. He said, "Your daughter has had nothing happen to her, except that a monk from Old India slept in her room on the sixteenth of October last year." Her parents called the two maids-in-waiting at once and asked them what had happened while they were away, whipping them mercilessly. The maids told them the truth. Her parents thought that since their daughter had brought disgrace upon the family, they should do away with her, but they could not bring themselves to do so. Instead, they dug a small cave in the hill behind their house and kept her in it, and her mother took food to her in the cave in secret. Thus, Tanggŭm-agi came to live in a den.

Time drifted by, and it was the day just ten months after the monk had visited her. It began to rain in the morning and continued to pour down in sheets. Her mother was very much worried about her daughter in the cave. Soon Tanggŭm-agi was going through labor, with two fairies from Heaven waiting upon her. At last, she delivered a boy, and the fairies bathed him in water poured from a jewelled jar and put a blue belt around his waist. When she delivered a second, they bathed him and put a yellow belt on him. And when she delivered a third, they put a white belt on him. Then the fairies gave her some fruit to eat and told her to visit the father of the three children in Old India when they became seven years of age. With these words, the fairies soared up to Heaven. When Tanggŭm-agi ate the fruit the fairies presented to her, she found that the cold she had felt was removed, she was hungry no longer, and that she had recovered her senses. Then the rain stopped and her mother hurried to the cave and found the four of them lying in it. She offered a prayer of thanksgiving to God. Later, she often visited the cave and found that in the cold season it was warm there and in the warm season it was cool.

One day, when the three boys had reached the age of seven, they were playing out in the village and the other boys made fun of them, calling them "homeless and fatherless bastards." When they came back to their mother in the cave, they asked her, "Where is our father?" She answered, "Your father is living in Old India now. He found no favor with my father and went to that country. But I could not go with him because of you, my children." The boys soon called on their grandfather and paid their respects to him, and returned to the cave with the two maids-in-waiting. Then they asked their mother to find their father with them. Soon the boys and their mother set out for Old India together with the two maids.

Day in and day out, they pushed toward their goal. One day, they came to a large river and they were at a loss. Then a monk came up to them and asked them where they were going. Tanggŭm-agi replied, "We are going to Old India to see Wang Sŏkkayorae in the temple of Kŭmbul-am." The monk replied, "Really? He is our honored teacher." So saying, he plucked a willow leaf and dropped it on the water, whereupon it turned into a boat. They got on the boat and the kind monk rowed it. When they had crossed the river and got on shore, Tanggŭm-agi turned around to thank him, but he was nowhere to be found, and the boat was gone as well. She was seized with wonder. They resumed their journey and finally arrived at the temple of Kŭmbul-am. When she asked for Wang Sŏk-kayorae, she was told that he was sleeping in the hall of worship. She went to the hall, but found a very young monk asleep there. Then she came out and asked another monk for a monk who was more than a hundred eighty years old. He said, "It was my honorable teacher in disguise. He knows the occult art of *P'ungun-dunkapbŏp*, and so he transformed himself into an old monk at the time you saw him. The monk in the hall is the one you are looking for." She was very pleased to hear this, and went into the hall and woke him, saying, "Please wake up, my dear monk! Here I am, your Tanggŭm-agi!" Sŏkkayorae got up with his eyes closed, and said to himself, "It seems that the ghost of Tanggŭm-agi has come to me." Then he began to chant a spell to drive the ghost away. She was dumbfounded and burst into tears. But the three boys rushed in and bowed low to Sŏkkayorae, saying, "We are your sons. How have you been, Father?" He opened his eyes and embraced his sons in his arms. Then he held her hand in his, and said, "You must have had a very hard time for the past seven years. It was all my fault. Please forgive me."

Then their happy life began. First of all, the three boys were each given a name. The boy with a blue belt on was called Hyŏng-bul, the boy with a yellow belt Chaebul, and the third with a white belt Magbul.

The years went by and Sŏkkayorae became seventy-three and Tanggŭm-agi seventy. One day, a gust of wind arose and took them on a rainbow to Heaven, as he held her in his arms. The children, left on earth, performed a funeral ceremony. After devoting them-selves to the study of Buddhism, they returned to Chosŏn. They built a temple in Kŭmgang Mountain[3] and lived there until they passed away. After that, people were often visited with famine and epidemics. The reason for the calamities, they found out, was that the bodies of the three brothers were not committed to earth. They therefore soon laid them to rest and performed a ceremony for them. They called them the three Chesŏk Deities and enshrined them in their houses to worship.[4]

—adapted from *The Folk Treasury of Korea*
The Korean Oral Literature Society,
Seoul, 1970, pp. 81-92.

Notes

1. *Sŏk-Ka* Yŏ-Rae—see the Ritual Song of the Bridge, p. 81, no. 10, fn. 51.

2. Units of measure. One *toe* = 10 *hop*.

3. The Diamond Mountains, located in present-day North Korea.

4. In this regard, in his description of the *Chesŏk kut* ("Ritual of the God *Chesŏk*"), which is performed as part of the *Ssikkim kut* ("Soul-Cleansing Ritual") of Chindo Island, Keith Howard states the following:

Chesŏk refers to Sakra devanam Indra (Sŏ Tae-sok 1980: 75), an ancient thunder-god in the Buddhist pantheon, but here we are concerned with *Chesŏk*, incarnate as a monk (the Buddha, according to Alan Covell 1983: 44-45, 47, and 94 *passim*). A myth relates that he met the daughter of heavenly beings and slept with her. She became preg-nant and, after her disillusioned parents had confined her to a stone box, she gave birth to three sons, now known in Kyŏnggi shamanism as the mountain spirit, the dragon king of the sea, and the guardian of the seven stars. Custom had it that a barren woman should consequently pray to *Chesŏk* for sons. His efficacy still enjoyed a broad base, and he was variously described as the bringer of spring, the harvest god, the controller of sun, moon, the four heavenly kings and the 33 heavens, and the provider of good fortune. He is today rarely found in Buddhist temples but in Chindo, unlike most other areas, all shaman death rituals called on him. He represented a union between heaven and earth and was thus a powerful ally in guiding the deceased to the other world. Equally, we might translate his name as 'Emperor Buddha,' and so he had to be approached with care. (Howard, Keith, "Bands, Songs, and Shamanistic Rituals; Folk Music in Korean Society," Royal Asiatic Society, Korea Branch, Seoul, 1989, pp. 181-2.)

Appendix II

Ogu Tae Wang P'uri
("The Legend of King Ogu")

Once, long, long ago, there lived a king ruling in ancient Korea. The king had a son, the prince. When the prince reached the age of fifteen, the king intended to have him married so that the prince could father heirs to the throne.

The king, therefore, had a court lady consult the most celebrated fortuneteller in the kingdom. The divination revealed that if the prince got married in a year of bad omen, he would have seven princesses born to him and if the prince got married in a year of a good omen, he would have seven princes born to him.

The king learned the prediction, but decided to disregard it. The year was a year of bad omen, but the king was very anxious to see his son get married. He could not wait any longer. The king asked the office of astrology to choose a date for the wedding. Soon the office reported to the king that the date of the first choice was the fifth day of the fifth month, and the date of the third choice was the seventh day of the seventh month.

In due time, the prince was married in a royal ceremony and ascended the throne.

Three months later, there were indications of pregnancy in the new queen. The young king again had his fortune told. The fortuneteller told the king, "A princess will be born to you, since your majesty was married in a year of bad omen." But the king would not believe the prophesy, saying "How can a sorcerer tell a person's fortune?"

The fortuneteller, however, was right, for a daughter was born. The king named her Princess Hongdo, and saw to it that she was brought up with tender care.

When the princess was three years old, the queen was found to be with child again. In time, she gave birth to another princess. When the second princess was three years old, the third princess was born. In this way, six princesses were born to the king and queen. Their disappointment was beyond description. When the queen conceived for the seventh time, they eagerly wished that a son would be born to them.

At the time of conception, the queen had a dream in which she saw a blue hawk on her right hand and a white hawk on her left, a gold turtle on her knees, and the sun and moon over her shoulders. The queen also saw in the dream a blue and gold dragon entwining themselves around the beams of the room.

After the dream, the king and queen all rejoiced, since they believed it to be an omen of the birth of a prince. The king sent a maid-in-waiting to the fortuneteller to hear what he would say about the child to be born. But the answer of the fortuneteller was identical to the previous ones: Since the king was married in a year of bad omen, he would have a seventh princess born to him. The king, however, paid no heed to the divination, and looked forward to the birth of a prince. But his expectations were to know disappointment, for it was again that a daughter was born.

The king was terribly dismayed. Heaving a long sigh, he said to himself, "What sins did I commit in the previous life that Heaven wills me to have seven daughters? To whose care can I leave the ancestor shrine?[2] And who is to take care of my subjects?"

In his frustration, the king ordered the baby cast away in the back garden. But the queen said in tears, "The baby is your own flesh and blood. How can you have her thrown away?" Then the king proposed that the child be given away, but the queen felt that it was improper for the royal family to put up their own child for adoption.

So the king had the baby thrown away in the back garden after all. But all of a sudden magpies and crows came flying to the baby and covered her with their wings, as if to protect her, and the atmosphere bore a mysterious sense of awe. The queen was made aware of what happened to the baby. In tears, she brought the baby back and held her in her arms. The king then said, "I think I must send the baby to the Dragon King of the Four Seas as a sacrifice, as I am highly indebted to him." The king ordered that a chest be made and the baby princess sent down a river to the sea in the chest.

Accordingly, a jade chest was made, a jade bottle filled with her mother's milk was put in the baby's mouth, a piece of cloth telling when she was born was attached to a string of the baby's blouse, the lid was placed on the chest, and it was secured with a lock in the shape of a gold turtle. Then the minister of education took the chest away to the sea.

With the chest on his shoulder, the minister left the palace. As he departed, the magpies nodded, pointing the way for him to go. Trees and grass also bent their heads to show him the way. The minister followed the direction they indicated. He walked three thousand *ri* (leagues), crossed the Kalchi and Pulchi Mountains, and finally came to a large river. As he threw the chest in the river, a turtle suddenly appeared from under the water, and, with the sound of a thunderbolt, disappeared from sight with the chest on its back.

At the time, Buddha and his disciples were travelling around the world to bring relief to human beings. When they came to the East Sea, they saw dense clouds and mist over the waters, and flocks of magpies and crows chattering and cawing. In wonder, Buddha approached and found a jade chest. He opened it and found a baby girl lying in it. Buddha thought, "If this girl were a boy, I could make a disciple of him." He took the baby to an old man named Pirigongduk and his wife and asked them to raise her. Then, by magic, Buddha instantly built a thatched hut for them to live in.

The baby princess grew up under the care of the old man and his wife. When she was eight years old, she already knew all the letters of the alphabet without having been taught. Thus she became versed in astronomy and geography.

One day, the girl asked the old man and wife, "Where are my parents? You know, even the birds and animals have their own fathers and mothers!" The old man and his wife answered, "We are your parents!" But the girl did not believe what they said. "How can such old persons as you have given birth to such a young girl as me?" she retorted. Then the old man and his wife told her, "Heaven is your father and earth is your mother." The girl still wouldn't believe, saying, "Heaven and earth have created everything in the universe, but a human being can not be born of them." So the old man and his wife said, "The giant bamboo in Chŏlla Province is your father and the paulownia on the hill in back is your mother." After she heard this, the little girl visited the paulownia three times a day to pay her respects to what she believed to be her mother. She could not visit to what she thought to be her father, since the bamboo thicket was far away in Chŏlla Province.

Years passed and she grew into a maid of fifteen years of age. At this time the king and queen became seriously ill. No medicines could cure them. The fortuneteller consulted ascribed their illness to the sin they committed in throwing away the princess, and predicted that they would both die at the same time and on the same day. One night soon after, the king and queen had a dream in which six cherubs in blue descended from Heaven and told them that they had come to take the souls of the king and queen. Thereupon, the king and queen asked the reason, and the cherubs said that it was because they had cast away a child bestowed upon them by Heaven, and therefore they deserved to die at the same time and on the same day. Then the royal couple begged the cherubs to let them know whatever they could do so as to live. The cherubs answered, "You would live if you could find the ill-treated child again. Then you must find an elixir of life and take it at Sam-Shin ("Three Spirit") Mountain and the medicinal spiritual water of the Mujang-Shinsŏn ("Immortal General").

After the dream, the king called his subordinates together and they discussed the ways and means of finding the princess and the medicine that the cherubs had promised would save the lives of the royal couple. The minister who had cast away the chest containing the baby princess offered to go and seek her. Armed with a missive from the king and letters from the six princesses in the palace, together with some old belongings of the baby princess, the minister set out. But soon after he went out of the gate of the palace, he was at a loss, not knowing which way to go. Just then, magpies and crows came flying toward him and nodded their heads to show him the way. Trees and grass on mountains and plains also bent their heads to guide him in the right direction. Thus he found the house where the old man, Pirigongduk, and his wife were living. He felt sure that the maid whom he found with the old man and wife was the princess. He approached the maid and related the whole story, but she would not believe him. The minister, therefore, brought forth a tray on which was the blood drawn from the hands of the king and queen. He had some blood drawn from the ring finger of the maid, and dropped it on the blood on the tray. Then, behold! There arose a cloud, the two bloods blending themselves into one. At the sight, the maid decided that she would go to see the king and queen. The princess declined to ride in a palanquin and soon started for the palace on horseback by herself.

From then on she became known as Princess Pari.

The king and queen greeted their seventh princess in delighted tears, but the medicinal spiritual water was yet to be found. The problem was who should be sent to get it. The king asked the first princess if she would go for him. The first princess answered, "How do you think a little girl could do that when even three thousand court ladies refuse?" The second princess replied, "How do you think I can do that when my elder sister refuses?" In this way, all the six princesses refused to go and seek the medicine for their father. But Princess Pari said, "I owe no gratitude to the king, but I will go and find it in order to repay my debt to my mother who gave birth to me."

Thus Princess Pari, in man's attire, left the palace for Old India, all by herself. When she waved her staff once, she was one thousand leagues away. When she waved it once again, she was two thousand leagues away, and found herself in Old India.

It so happened that Buddha was preaching to his disciples at the moment Princess Pari in man's attire came up to him and gave him nine courteous bows. When asked why she had come to the land, she said she was the crown prince of Korea and was seeking the medicine that would cure her parents of disease. When he heard this, Buddha said, "I have heard that the king has seven princesses, but no prince. It was I who saved your life when you were deserted. I cannot but help you, now that you have come to find the medicine." Then he added, "You have crossed over three thousand leagues of plain, but now that you are to travel another three thousand leagues over rough and rugged country, you will need this." So saying, Buddha gave her a Lahwa. Princess Pari took leave of him and proceeded on her way. It was not long before she came to a sea. She was at a loss as how to cross it. Then she shook the Lahwa, and, in a instant, the sea was gone and dry land lay before her. The princess travelled her way for a while when she was halted by a thorn castle and an iron castle. The castles towered so high they seemed to reach the sky. Once again, the princess shook the Lahwa. The door of the castle opened and the Supreme Spirit stood before her.

He was so tall, he seemed to reach the sky, his face as large as a salver, his eyes like lamps, and his nose like a bottle. But she rose above her fear, stepped forward, made a bow, and told him the story of her journey in search of the medicine. Then the Supreme Spirit asked her, "Have you brought with you the money to pay for the firewood and the water?" Princess Pari answered, "No, I haven't. I've forgotten to bring it with me, since I was in such a hurry." The Supreme Spirit said, "In that case, you will have to bring water for me for three years, provide me with firewood for three years, and build a fire for me for three years." There was no choice for the princess but to comply with his request. Thus, she worked for him for nine full years.

At the end of that period, the Supreme Spirit asked Princess Pari to marry him and give birth to seven sons. She could not refuse. She married the Supreme Spirit and bore seven sons by him. One night, she saw in a dream a broken silver bowl and a pair of broken chopsticks. She interpreted the dream as an omen of death for her parents. The princess, therefore urged the Supreme Spirit to give her the medicine. Then he said, "The water you brought for me is the medicinal spiritual water, the wood you chopped for me is the medicine that revives flesh and bones. You may take them with you." At once, she made preparations for departure. But the Supreme Spirit heaved a deep sigh and said, "Before you came, there was only one who had to live alone; but now there are eight of us. So take the seven children with you."

She obeyed and was about to take leave with her sons when the Supreme Spirit asked her if he might not go with her as well. She gratified his wish, and Princess Pari, with the Supreme Spirit and their seven sons, left for her home country, ancient Korea.

When she arrived home, the king and queen were already dead, and it was the day of their funeral. There were many people in the palace. Princess Pari had no time to lose. She hid her seven sons under a bush and the Supreme Spirit in a forest. Then she went to the bier and removed the bodies of her parents. She put the spiritual water into their eyes, mouths and nostrils, and the wood medicine into their flesh and bones. In a moment, the king and queen began to breathe again and finally they were revived. Then the king said, "How fast we must have slept! But what are so many people here for? Are they here for a view of water or for a view of blossoms?" The ministers who were present gave the king a detailed account of Princess Pari and the medicines she had brought back. The king at once called Princess Pari to him and sent for the

Supreme Spirit and his seven grandsons. They all rejoiced at the family reunion.

Later, Princess Pari became the queen who ruled over all the gods.

> —adapted from "Princess Pari," *The Folk Treasury of Korea,*
> op. cit., pp. 64-73.

Notes

1. Also known as The Legend of *Pari Kongju* ("Princess Pari"), *Pari-Degi* ("The Outcast or Deserted One," or "The Outcast or Deserted Princess"), *Puri-Degi,* or *Pŏri-Degi.* Lee, Jung-young (op. cit., p. 31, fn. 5) lists four additional names: *Malmi, Pulin Gongju* (Kongju), *Awong Gongju,* and *Chil Gongju* ("The Seventh Princess"). In regard to the variety of names used, Lee (ibid., p. 31, fn. 9) states the following:

> It seems reasonable to believe that the use of "Degi" was the deterio-ration of "Gongju" ("Kongju") as shamanism became more and more deteriorated and spread to the lower classes and illiterate people in the south. Except for Cheju Island, Pari-congju (Pari Kongju) is regarded as the ancestor of modern shamans in Korea, even though she has been known by many different names.

Lee also gives a brief synopsis (ibid., pp. 20-1) of two somewhat dif-fering versions of the myth: one ". . . as told in the central portion of Korea, especially in the Seoul area . . . ," and the other in the southern seacoast region. He further surmises (p. 31) that the myth must have ". . . originated sometime after Buddhism was introduced into Korea (4th century A.D., in early Silla)," and that "It is difficult to date the origin of this myth. It is commonly believed that the myth had its origin in the later period of the Silla dynasty." He takes as the basis for his reasoning the version of the myth as told in the central region of Korea in which medicinal water from the western sky is said to be the only cure for the ailing King Ogu (p. 20), the idea of the western sky ("Western Paradise") having been borrowed from Amita Buddhism (p. 31) (see also The Ritual Song of the Bridge, p. 35). The appearance of the Buddha in the version given here in Appendix II might also substantiate Lee's hypothesis, but, here again, this is mere conjecture.

2. The duty of the first son.

Appendix III

The Legend of the Guardian Deities of *Sŏ-Gwi-P'o*

A long time ago there arose from the ground an imposing god named Il-Mun-Gwan-Param-Un, in the country of Sŏlmae-Guk. He had the eyes of a phoenix and a tapering beard. He knew the arts of astronomy and geography. Once he shot an arrow, there arose at once an army of three thousand, and when he shot another, they disappeared instantly.

He heard that a beauty, called Ko-San-Guk, lived in the country of Hong-Do, which lay far away beyond mountains and seas. Immediately he mounted a blue cloud and reached the country in an instant. Sure enough, he found a beautiful goddess living in the land. He said to her, "I've come all the way here since I've so longed to see you." In reply, the goddess said, "I dreamed a strange dream last night. Now I see it meant I would have this pleasure of seeing you." In this way, they became husband and wife, and began to live together.

But it was only three days before another beauty appeared before the god Il-Mun-Gwan. She was his wife's younger sister, the most beautiful woman to be found under the sun. He fell in love with her and she was also in love with him. One evening they met stealthily and confessed their love to each other. It did not take long for them to decide to elope. That night, when Ko-San-Guk was fast asleep, they rode a blue cloud and stole away to Halla Mountain on the island Cheju.

The next morning, when Ko awoke from sleep, her husband was not there beside her. She looked about for him, but he was nowhere to be found. Finally, she noticed that his clothing had also disappeared. She went to her sister to see if she knew anything about his disappearance. But her beautiful sister was gone as well.

357

Now she realized what had become of them, and at once set about discovering their whereabouts. Ko was also versed in the arts of astronomy and geography, and could perform magic feats as well. After offering a prayer to Heaven, she put up a holy flag which fluttered vigorously in the wind toward Halla Mountain. When she arrived there, she found Il-Mun-Gwan and her sister in their hide-out, deeply immersed in love. At the sight, she was thrown into a fury and wished to see both of them die there and then. At once, she let loose a sharp arrow at them. But her sister did not sit idle. She produced a dense fog all around, suddenly turning the earth and heaven dark. Ko could hardly keep her senses. She repeated prayers to Heaven to lift the suffocating fog. But her sister's magic prevailed, and Ko was finally compelled to yield.

Ko said to her sister, "Through I shot an arrow at you, how could I have intended to kill you? And even if I wished to see you die, how could you, who have committed a mortal sin, entrap me in such a suffocating fog? Let us promise not to hurt each other here-after. Now, remove the fog!"

When he heard this, Il-Mun-Gwan broke off a branch of Chi-nese juniper and stuck it on the side of a precipice. The branch turned into a large cock which crowed. Then the fog lifted. When night fell, a beautiful moon rose over the peaks in the east, shed-ding a mellow light on the earth.

Now Ko could see their faces clearly in the moonlight. She said in an angry voice, "At first, I thought nothing could allay my mortification. Then, I could have butchered you both, you wench who deserves to be cut up on a chopping block, and you, Il-Mun-Gwan, who are no better than an animal. But I couldn't bear to do so. Shameless hussy, you are no longer my sister. So change your surname to Chi. Now, I'll go my way." With these words, Ko left them.

Il-Mun-Gwan and Chi-San-Guk wandered about Halla Moun-tain for a while. Then they wanted to decide on their residence, but they could not find any suitable place. They were taking a rest under a white sunshade put up on the mountain side, when a man, out hunting, saw the sunshade. He knew that it was a sign of sacred beings. He came up to the gods, bowed low to them, and asked them who they were. Il-Mun-Gwan answered, "I am Il-Mun-Gwan Param-Un, who arose from the ground in the country of Sŏlmae-Guk. This goddess, Chi-San-Guk, comes from the country of Hong-

Do. At the order of the Heavenly Emperor, we have come to rule over human beings. Lead us to your world now."

The hunter led them to his house, and built a small house for them in the vicinity. They began to live there, but men on horseback and dogs were so loathsome for them to see. They left the house in three months. When they called on Ko-San-Guk and asked her about a proper place to settle down, she said, still in anger, "I am going to rule in the village of Sŏhung-ri. You can go to Sŏ-Gwi-P'o if you like. But your people shall never marry my people, nor shall your Mudangs ever cross the boundaries of my land." So saying, Ko departed from them.

Eventually, Il-Mun-Gwan and Chi-San-Guk went to Sŏ-Gwi-P'o. But the villagers there took no notice of them. One day, a grandson of the O family fell ill, and talked about the god and the goddess. He said it was because the villagers neglected to worship them that he was ill in bed. Soon the villagers built a sacred house to enshrine them.

Hitherto, the village had been ruled over by a goddess, the Heavenly Empress. One day, she called on Il-Mun-Gwan and said, "Now I've grown so weak. I'd like to entrust this place to your care. I am intending to go to the Dragon Palace to take care of the ships and the women drivers."

Thus Il-Mun-Gwan and Chi-San-Guk became the guardian deities of Sŏ-Gwi-P'o.

—adapted from *The Folk Treasury of Korea*,
op. cit., pp. 93-6.

Bibliography

Akamatsu Chijo and Akiba Takashi, *Chōsen Fuzoku no Kenkyŭ* ("A Study of Korean *Musok*"), Keijŏ (Seoul): Ōsaka Yagŏ Shoten, 1938, transl. by Shim U-sŏng, 1991.

Canda, Edw. R., "The Korean Mountain Spirit," *Korea Journal,* Vol. 20:9, pp. 11-16, Seoul, 1980.

Chang Chu-kŭn, "Korean Folk-belief," Tokyo: Kinkasha, 1973.

———, "*Musok*—The Shaman Culture of Korea," *Folk Culture in Korea,* Korean Culture Series No. 4, Int'l Cult. Found., pp. 58-88, Seoul: Si-Sa-Yŏng-Ŏ-Sa Publ., Inc., 1982, transl. by Alan C. Heyman, 1974.

Clark, Charles A., *Religions of Old Korea,* 1930.

Covell, Alan C., *Ecstasy: Shamanism in Korea,* Seoul: Hollym Int'l Corp., 1983.

Dimcock, Edw. C. Jr. and Denise Leverton, "In Praise of Krishna," *Songs from the Bengali,* New York: Doubleday, 1967.

Eliade, Mircea, *Shamanism: Archaic Techniques of Ecstasy,* Princeton: Princeton University Press, 1964.

Evans-Wentz, W.Y., *The Tibetan Book of the Dead,* London: Oxford University Press, 1971.

Heyman, Alan C. "*Mu-ga*: The Shaman Song of Korea," *Korean Culture,* Vol. l:l, New York, 1980.

———, "*P'an-sori*: The Dramatic-Epic-Narrative Song of Korea," *Essays in Asian Music and Theater,* New York: Pratt Institute Press, 1972.

———, "Folk Music and Dance," *Folk Culture in Korea,* Korean Culture Series No. 4, Int'l Cult. Found., pp. 91-110, Seoul: Si-Sa-Yŏng-Ŏ-Sa Publications, Inc., 1982.

Hogarth, Hyun-key Kim, "Reciprocity, Status, and the Korean Shamanistic Ritual," Ph.D. Thesis, 1995.

————, *Kut: Happiness Through Reciprocity*, Budapest: Akademiai Kiado, 1998.

Howard, Keith, "Bands, Songs, and Shamanistic Rituals; Folk Music in Korean Society," Seoul: Royal Asiatic Society, Korea Branch, 1989.

————(ed.), "Korean Shamanism: Revivals, Survivals, and Change," Seoul: Royal Asiatic Society, Korea Branch, 1998.

Huhm, Halla Pai, *Kut: Korean Shamanist Rituals*, Seoul: Hollym, 1980.

Im, Sŏkjae, *Hanguk Musok Yŏngu Sŏsŏl* ("An Introduction to the Study of Korean *Musok*"), *Asia Yŏsong Yŏngu* ("The Journal of Asian Women's Studies"), Vols. 9-10, Seoul: Sukmyong Women's University, 1970.

Janelli, Roger L. and Dawnhee Yim, *Ancestor Worship and Korean Society*, Stanford: Stanford University Press, 1982.

Kendall, Laurel, "*Mugam*: The Dance in Shaman's Clothing," *Korea Journal*, Vol. 17:12, pp. 38-44, Seoul, 1977.

————, *Shamans, Housewives, and Other Restless Spirits*, Honolulu: University of Hawaii Press, 1985.

————, *The Life and Hard Times of a Korean Shaman*, Honolulu: University of Hawaii Press, 1988.

————, and Dix, Griffin, "Religion and Ritual in Korean Society," *Korea Research Monograph* No. 12, Center for Korean Studies, Institute of East Asian Studies, University of California, Berkeley, 1987.

Kim T'ae-gon, "The Idea of Soul in Korean Shamanism," *The Idea of Soul in Asia*, Seoul: Association of Asian Folklore, 1979.

Kim, Won-yong, "Three Royal Tombs," *Korean Culture*, Vol. 1:1, New York, 1980.

Kim Yol-kyu, "Concepts of the Soul in Korean Myths," *The Idea of Soul in Asia*, Seoul: Association of Asian Folklore, 1979.

Kinsler, Arthur, "A Study of the Fertility Cult for Children in Korean Shamanism," Ph.D. Thesis, Yonsei University, Seoul; abstract reprinted in *The Idea of Soul in Asia*, Seoul: Association of Asian Folklore, 1979.

Kister, Daniel A., *Korean Shamanist Ritual: Symbols and Dramas of Transformation*, Budapest: Akademiai Kiado, 1997.

Lee, Du-hyun, "Korean Mask Drama," transl. by Alan C. Heyman, *Traditional Performing Arts of Korea*, Seoul: Korean Nat'l Comm. for UNESCO, 1975.

Lee, Jung-young, "Korean Shamanism and Sexual Repression," *Asian and Pacific Quarterly*, Vol. XII, No. 1, Seoul, 1980.

Lee, Kwang-kyu, "Folk Beliefs and Shamanism," *An Introduction to Korean Culture*, Seoul: Hollym Int'l Corp., 1997.

Lee, Sherman E., "5,000 Years of Korean Art," *Korean Culture*, Vol. 1:1, New York, 1980.

Mason, David A., "A Study of Korea's Mountain Spirit (*San-sin*) and Its Relationship With Korean Buddhism," Yonsei University, M.A. Thesis, Seoul, 1997.

Owens, Donald D., "Korean Shamanism: Its Components, Context, and Functions," Ph.D. Dissert., University of Oklahoma, Norman, 1975.

Park, Sun-hee, "An Empirical Study of the Physical Changes Exhibited in Korean Shamans during Spirit-possession," transl. by Alan C. Heyman, *Korea Journal*, Vol. 37:1, pp. 5-34, Seoul, 1997.

Pihl, Marshall R., "Korea in the Bardic Tradition: *P'an-sori* as an Oral Art," *Korean Studies Forum*, No. 2, Seoul, 1977.

Pratt, Keith, "Politics and Culture Within the Sinic Zone: Chinese Influences on Medieval Korea," *Korea Journal*, Vol. 20:6, pp. 15-29, Seoul, 1980.

"Religious Culture in Korea," Ministry of Culture and Sports, Republic of Korea, pp. 8-10, Seoul, 1996.

"Shamanism," "Village Rites," *Thought and Religion*, Korean Cultural Heritage, Vol. II, Seoul: The Korea Foundation, 1995.

Sŏng, Kyŏng-rin, "Korean Classic Dance," *Korea Journal*, Vol. 3:2, pp. 6-10, Seoul, 1963.

The Folk Treasury of Korea, compiled by The Korean Oral Lit. Soc., Seoul, 1970.

Walraven, Boudewijn, *Songs of the Shaman: The Ritual Chants of the Korean Mudang*, London: KPI, 1994.

Wilson, Brian, "*Kut*: Catharsis, Ritual Healing, or Redressive Strategy?" *Conference on Korean Religion and Society*, Macinac Island, 1980.

Yang, Sang-ick, *Echoes of Mt. Halla*, Cheju Nat'l University, Cheju City.

Yi Nŭng-hwa, *Chosŏn Musok-ko* ("A Study of Korean *Musok*"), Seoul: Tongmunsŏn, 1991.

Yi, Po-hyŏng, "The Performing Style of Korean Traditional Music," *Korea Journal*, Vol. 20:11, pp. 27-31, Seoul, 1980.

Yoon, Soon-yong, "Magic, Science, and Religion on Cheju Island," *Korea Journal*, Vol. 16:3, pp. 4-11, Seoul, 1976.

Yu, Chai-shin and Guisso, R. (eds.), *Shamanism: The Spirit World of Korea*, Studies in Korean Religion and Culture, Vol. I, Berkeley, Calif.: Asian Humanities Press, 1988.

About the Authors

Im Sŏk-jae was Professor Emeritus of Seoul National University, College of Education, and Chungang University, both located in Seoul, Korea. He was formerly chairman of the Korean Cultural Anthropology Society, a position he held for ten years, and conducted study and research on Korean folk religion, folklore, folktales and mythology for over fifty years. In addition to being the author of innumerable articles and several books on these subjects, he was also a former adviser to the Cultural Properties Bureau, Ministry of Culture & Information, Republic of Korea.

Alan C. Heyman has conducted study and research on Korean folk, court and religious music, dance and drama in Korea for many years. In 1964, he was the recipient of a John D. Rockefeller IIIrd (JDR IIIrd) Fund grant. He is the author of several publications and innumerable articles on these subjects, and has lectured at various universities throughout the United States. In 1980, he was the recipient of a scholarship at the School of Graduate Studies of Dharma Realm Buddhist University in California. He has translated works on Korean folk, court, and religious music, dance and drama for such organizations as the National Academy of Arts of Korea, the International Cultural Foundation of Korea, the Korean National Commission for UNESCO, the Academy of Korean Studies, the Nat'l Ctr for Korean Traditional Performing Arts, and the Nat'l Research Institute of Cultural Properties.

He is also the recipient of the Cultural Award of both the President and Prime Minister of the Republic of Korea, and the Cultural Award of the Korean National Commission for UNESCO.